To Betty,

Best wishes!
 Franke Reuba

Enjoy reading this in
retirement —
 Ellen Miller

"All This Reading"

"All This Reading"

The Literary World of Barbara Pym

Edited by
Frauke Elisabeth Lenckos
and Ellen J. Miller

Madison • Teaneck
Fairleigh Dickinson University Press
London: Associated University Presses

Associated University Presses
2010 Eastpark Boulevard
Cranbury, NJ 08512

Associated University Presses
16 Barter Street
London WC1A 2AH, England

Associated University Presses
P.O. Box 338, Port Credit
Mississauga, Ontario
Canada L5G 4L8

The paper used in this publication meets the requirements of the American National Standard for Permanence of Paper for Printed Library Materials Z39.48-1984.

Library of Congress Cataloging-in-Publication Data

"All this reading" : the literary world of Barbara Pym / edited by Frauke Elisabeth Lenckos and Ellen J. Miller.
    p. cm.
Includes bibliographical references and index.
ISBN 0-8386-3956-9
    1. Pym, Barbara—Criticism and interpretation. 2. Women and literature—England—History—20th century. 3. Pym, Barbara—Views on books and reading. 4. Pym, Barbara—Knowledge—Literature. 5. Books and reading in literature. I. Lenckos, Frauke Elisabeth, 1960– II. Miller, Ellen J.
PR6066.Y58 Z538   2003
823'.914—dc21

2002071285

This book is dedicated to our husbands, John and Bill,
and to Leia and Kira, our sources of inspiration.

Contents

Part I: Reading in Barbara Pym's Novels

Foreword

I AM REMINDED OF AN INCIDENT FROM THE DISTANT PAST WHEN someone, on meeting Barbara and me with our mother, asked, "And which is the clever one?" I am afraid that she was referring to me, as I had drawn a picture of a horse at an early age and had received some sort of certificate. I am very glad that the passing of time has revealed the truth: it was Barbara, the writer.

Her first complete novel, handwritten in a hard-backed notebook, was a seventeen-year-old's tribute to Aldous Huxley called "Young Men in Fancy Dress." Some time after that, she invented (verbally) an elderly character called Miss Emily Moberly, who was always ready with unwelcome advice and criticism. I am sure it was this rather unexpected projection into middle and old age that led her to write *Some Tame Gazelle*, which began its life as a series of short pieces typed on an old machine our father had given her from his office. Barbara sent them to me (I was then staying in London with our cousins) and her friends, Henry Harvey and Robert Liddell.

I am glad, too, that she lived long enough to see recognition in the 1950s develop into something like fame in the late '70s. Perhaps it isn't too fantastic to feel that each of the pieces in this loving collection makes up for at least one of the years when she was, as it were, "in the wilderness." I know how much they would have pleased her.

Hilary Pym Walton

Acknowledgments

WE THANK OUR FELLOW MEMBERS OF THE BARBARA PYM SOCIETY, whose heartfelt enthusiasm and interest in our project have encouraged and sustained us through the challenging process of bringing this book to completion. Special thanks go to Hilary Pym Walton, Hazel Holt, and Eileen Roberts for their generous and unwavering support of our endeavor, to Hazel Bell for compiling the index, and to Beverly Bell for helping us to ready the manuscript for publication. We are also grateful to Kate Charles, Father Gabriel Myers, Catherine Wallace, Anne Marie Owens, Nancy Talburt and Lesley Grant-Adamson for their assistance with our book. Above all, we are indebted to our distinguished contributors for their splendid work.

Finally, we pay tribute to Barbara Pym herself. Her steady spirit has inspired and guided the making of this book, and she continues to enrich our lives immeasurably.

List of Abbreviations

FOR THE CONVENIENCE OF OUR READERS, WE HAVE ABBREVIATED the titles of all works by and major works about Barbara Pym that are referred to throughout this book. In the text, the relevant page numbers follow the abbreviation.

AQ   *An Academic Question*
CS   *Civil to Strangers and Other Writings*
CH   *Crampton Hodnet*
EW   *Excellent Women*
FGL   *A Few Green Leaves*
GB   *A Glass of Blessings*
JP   *Jane and Prudence*
LTA   *Less than Angels*
ALTA   *A Lot to Ask*
NFRL   *No Fond Return of Love*
QIA   *Quartet in Autumn*
STG   *Some Tame Gazelle*
SDD   *The Sweet Dove Died*
UA   *An Unsuitable Attachment*
VPE   *A Very Private Eye: An Autobiography in Diaries and Letters*

"All This Reading"

Introduction

FRAUKE ELISABETH LENCKOS

The creative act is only an incomplete and abstract moment in the production of a work. . . . It is the joint effort of author and reader that brings upon the scene that concrete and imaginary object which is the work of the mind. There is no art except for and by others.
　　　　　　　　　　　—Jean Paul Sartre, *What Is Literature?*

At the end of *A Few Green Leaves*, Barbara Pym's last novel and written when she was dying of cancer, the author makes her readers a generous and comforting bequest: the promise of another novel, the prospect of continued creativity. When the story closes, Emma Howick, a hitherto detached observer of society, summons up enough courage to act upon her vision—that is, to move to the center of activity and, by virtue of her commitment to the life around her, transform herself into a writer. Emma knows that these two activities are intricately linked: she must become an agent of social change if she is to find the inspiration her novel will require.

It is no coincidence that *A Few Green Leaves* contrasts the limitations inherent in the cool, scientific methods of analyzing society with the unending possibilities that open up to the novelist as she becomes passionately involved in the world of her characters. Pym's final narrative therefore reflects the connection that she perceived between human engagement and the artistic imagination—the profundity of compassion and the depth of an author's insight. Conceived when Pym was terminally ill, *A Few Green Leaves* captures the essence of her life's oeuvre. At its center is her awareness of the moral responsibility of the writer toward her readers.

Concern for one's fellow beings is the most sacred duty set forth in Pym's novels. When Mildred Lathbury, the protagonist of Pym's early work *Excellent Women* and perhaps Pym's most popular heroine, surveys the vast sea of human beings that floods a dark, dingy self-service cafeteria in 1950s London, she remarks only half-jokingly that "one wouldn't believe that there could be so many people . . . and

17

one must love them all."[1] Mildred has a penetrating eye for human eccentricity, and her compassionate nature plays a key role in bringing solace to the strange personalities that inhabit her world. In her role as charity worker, Mildred must identify the lonely and the aged in order to determine who is in need of aid; in private, she is an avid observer of her friends and acquaintances so she can be on hand when they need her. Like her most popular heroine, Pym also observes, records, and renders remarkable lives that would otherwise go unnoticed, unread, and unloved. Not only does she render visible certain personalities that in most works of mid-twentieth-century fiction remain on the margins—the aging, the lonely, the odd—but by the power of her pen, she makes them lovable, deserving of our care and interest as readers. For Pym, reading means forging relationships: her books give us "something to love," the possibility to take note of other people's humanity, and our own, through reading, and to allow us to reciprocate with the gift of attentiveness.[2]

Following Pym's example, many distinguished writers have described the loneliness of middle-aged, middle-class, unattached, biologically unproductive women and men in modern times. But unlike John Updike, Anne Tyler, and Anita Brookner,[3] Pym wrote about excellent women and peevish bachelors of advanced years during the much less sympathetic, more youth-obsessed decades of the 1950s and 1960s. Although portrayals of spinsters and their world led publishers to shun her books after 1961, she continued to document their lives as if they were part of mainstream society and thereby kept them in the literary canon. In doing so, Pym became the only link in the chain that reaches from the earlier portrayers of the unattached—Elizabeth von Arnim, Katherine Mansfield, Rebecca West, Vera Brittain, Ivy Compton-Burnett, Elizabeth Bowen, Muriel Spark, and the now less-well-known Elizabeth Taylor—to the late-twentieth-century chroniclers of solitary lives and fates.[4] Pym's work also establishes a bridge in literary history between the early modernists' depiction of single womanhood and similar depictions in our times. As a result, we find many references to Barbara Pym in volumes on twentieth-century literature, critical books about women's writing, and contemporary reviews of women's novels.[5] Although popular fame still eludes Barbara Pym, she has gained status in many literary circles and is considered one of the most distinguished women of letters of the twentieth century.[6]

"All This Reading": The Literary World of Barbara Pym, a collection of original essays by scholars and writers, focuses on the role of reading and the reader. It demonstrates that Barbara Pym emphasizes the discursive over the solely expressive model of literature. In examining Pym's novels from the viewpoint of reading, we recognize that our undertaking is both timely and problematic because of recent discussions among literary critics concerning the future of reading itself. Wayne C. Booth, a proponent of an ethics of reading, argues that "ethical criticism is relevant to all literature, no matter how broadly or narrowly we define that controversial term."[7] By contrast, Harold Bloom notes that the "pleasures of reading indeed are selfish rather than social" and that he remains "skeptical of the traditional social hope that care for others may be stimulated by the growth of the individual imagination." In fact, Bloom is "wary of any arguments whatsoever that connect the pleasures of solitary reading to the public good."[8]

Our approach draws on both of these divergent viewpoints. In the essays that follow, it is clear that Barbara Pym viewed reading as an activity that centers on the individual, broadening his or her personal perspective on the universal human experience. Our contributors show that she bestows her stories upon her audience as though they were precious gifts of sustenance. In turn, her readers react to her generosity with their own wish for a continued communion—which is the reason Pym's fans read and reread her novels year after year. Since Pym portrays her excellent heroines as readers, she presents them as implicated in, not superior to, the destinies and lives they describe. In this way, her heroines and her reading audience are put on somewhat equal footing. As the excellent women who recount their fates abdicate their positions of privilege, readers are encouraged to take control of the text and to discover for themselves the meaning of a situation and the secret that lies at the heart of their stories. What follows is a process of interaction between reader and text, an invitation to participate in the creation of the literary work of art. Therefore, perhaps surprisingly, the statement of Jean Paul Sartre quoted at the outset explains why Barbara Pym and her novels seem to have a renewed appeal today. More than any other twentieth-century writer, she invites us to share her world—not the make-believe world of her characters, but the imaginary sphere of the author as she builds a text that initiates a continuing discourse with her readers.[9] As a result, the aesthetic and moral validity of Pym's novels, more than that of other writers, depends on the quality, intensity, and durability of the relationship they set up with their audiences.

"All This Reading": The Literary World of Barbara Pym is born out of the desire to pay tribute to this possibility for readerly identification inherent in Pym's books. Our collection of essays defines and conceptualizes the importance of this writer and her acclaimed works for our modern world. Barbara Pym died two decades ago, yet her books are being read, ritually reread, studied, and discussed by a growing, devoted, and knowledgeable circle of interested men and women. Those of her readers whom we have gathered together for the purpose of our book show how this modern-day Jane Austen has transformed their lives and minds in such a way as to turn them into writers in their own right. Their literary endeavors put into practice Sartre's postulate that the narrative endows us with the knowledge that the artistic process is in its essence discursive, and transforms us from passive receivers into productive interlocutors. As a result of this "joint effort," a new and compellingly progressive image of Barbara Pym emerges: that of an author whose works establish an ongoing dialogue with those who consider reading a reciprocal act between reader and writer.

In the essays that follow, it is clear that Pym uses her art to keep alive the pleasure of human intercourse and to preserve its integrity; in so doing, she lightens the heavier burdens of everyday life. Readers bear witness to the realization, shared by many, that Pym's books provide them with spiritual and emotional solace in times of extreme hardship; she is a writer whose books create the possibility of a mutual understanding. But Pym offers readers yet another, immeasurable gift. She evokes in us a deeply reflective response to the world and imbues us with enough confidence to improve it, and to make complete our less-than-perfect selves. Virginia Woolf, a writer Pym admired, tells us in her essay "How Should One Read a Book?" that the best reader is one who simply "loves reading" and considers it one of the "pleasures that are final."[10] With these concluding words of *The Second Common Reader*, Woolf reminds us of the ancient affinity between reading and romance. Pym, too, celebrates the intense kinship, experienced through the ages by poets and writers, between the pleasure we take in studying the words on the page and the joy of discussing them with a beloved person. Although reading is often deemed a solitary activity, most famously by Ralph Waldo Emerson and most recently by Harold Bloom,[11] Pym reminds us that the language most intimately associated with reading refers not to isolationist practices, but to making connections as humans—including, of course, making love. The possibility of our rapport with her is the lasting legacy that Pym has bestowed upon her readers. *"All This Reading": The Literary World of Barbara Pym* intends to live up to this inheritance.

The first group of essays examines the significance of reading, and the places, personalities, and objects that make up the world of Pym's literature-loving characters. In her essay "'All This Reading': The Importance of Literature in the Novels of Barbara Pym," Katherine Anne Ackley shows that Pym's heroines draw personal and spiritual succor from the works of fiction they peruse. Frauke Elisabeth Len-ckos suggests in "'A Life Ruined by Literature'?: Barbara Pym's Excellent Women Readers" that Pym's approach to the theme of reading in her late works permanently changes the position of the female reader in British literary history. Barbara Everett in *"Excellent Women* and After: The Art of Popularity" examines Pym's own position as a reader of classical and modern works. Turning to the settings of literary perusal, Helen Clare Taylor argues in "A Suitable Detachment: Barbara Pym and the Romance of the Library" that the library provides a catalogue of options for Pym's heroines to secure their intellectual independence. Orphia Jane Allen and Anthony Kaufman turn their attention to Pym as reader and interpreter of her own life. Kaufman's "'Love Like Bedsocks': Barbara Pym's *Some Tame Gazelle"* reflects upon Pym's early love for pretense, playacting, and keeping a journal, as well as her skillful exploitation and organization of autobiographical material in the harmonious literary product that is her first published novel. Allen's "Reading Barbara Pym Autobiographically: Metaphors of Aging and Death in *The Sweet Dove Died, Quartet in Autumn,* and *A Few Green Leaves"* traces Pym's autobiographical writing as a transformational process that organizes the self into a new and richer entity that accepts aging and death. Ellie Wymard in "The Quest for Ritual and Celebration in the Comedic World of Barbara Pym" extends the discussion of Pym's scenarios to the significance that private and communal ceremonies have in her world, and asserts that reading and writing are ceremonial acts for Pym. Anne Pilgrim's contribution, "Full of Quotations, Like *Hamlet*: Literary Quotations and Allusions in *Some Tame Gazelle,"* shows that the study of literature and the awareness of shared knowledge establishes a feeling of kinship between otherwise disconnected individuals.

The idea of kinship leads the way to the second part of the book, which concentrates on literary encounters and collaborations in Pym's life and works. Here we begin with an essay by a writer who was close to Barbara Pym. In "My First Reader," Hazel Holt recalls her thirty years of friendship with Pym and describes her work as Pym's literary executor. This is followed by "Autumn Leaves: Publishing Barbara Pym," in which Paul De Angelis, former editor with E. P. Dutton and the person responsible for bringing Pym's work to North America, tells how his reading of *Quartet in Autumn* coincided with his coming to terms with his father's death. Similarly, John Bayley contemplates the personal implication of Matthew Arnold's thesis that art has the capacity to provide spiritual sustenance in his essay "Barbara Pym as Comforter," and recounts the consoling effects of reading Pym while his wife, Iris Murdoch, was dying of Alzheimer's disease. Janice Rossen's "Philip Larkin: Barbara Pym's Ideal Reader" honors an important epistolary relationship and shows that the encounter between one of England's greatest poets and the woman he called "the most underrated writer of the twentieth century" exerted a beneficial influence upon her work. Similarly, Barbara J. Dunlap's essay "Reading Charlotte M. Yonge into the Novels of Barbara Pym" illuminates a significant literary influence upon Pym, whose ideas about female decorum were shaped by her study of Victorian women's fiction. Looking to the future, Jan Fergus examines Pym's appeal to young people in "Reading Barbara Pym with College Students." Jane Nardin's "A Critic's Confession" succinctly analyzes the postmodern implications of Pym's irony, discovering in the author's novels a humorous hierarchy of readers that undermines the literary specialist's status.

Appropriately, *"All This Reading": The Literary World of Barbara Pym* concludes with another parting gift from the author to her readers. This is Pym's autobiographical account of a year late in her life in the Oxfordshire village of Finstock. This work, the result of her last literary collaboration, was originally written on a set of postcards from her hospital bed in an Oxford infirmary during her final illness. It is here reprinted with the permission of Ronald Blythe, a formidable writer and editor in his own right, who had asked Barbara Pym for a contribution to his book, *Places.*[12] Although she was gravely ill, she acquiesced, and as editors of a book on Barbara Pym and her readers, we find it telling that one of the last acts she performed before her demise was her gracious fulfillment of a request from a reader. Thus, in our last vision of the author, Barbara Pym again gives of herself unsparingly, an excellent woman who dispenses generosity liberally and with great courtesy. *"All This Reading": The Literary World of Barbara Pym* at long last endeavors to return the long-owed favor.

Finally, the epilogue by Dale Salwak assesses the legacy of the author and her place in twentieth-century literature. Salwak also updates his annotated 1987 bibliography to include works written about Pym during the past decade.

NOTES

1. Barbara Pym, *Excellent Women* (New York: E. P. Dutton, 1978), 78.
2. On this point, see also Diana Benet, *Something to Love: Barbara Pym's Novels* (Columbia: University of Missouri Press, 1986), 1–15. Our thesis is also indebted to Edward Hirsch, *How to Read a Poem* (New York: Harcourt Brace, 1999).
3. Brookner's heroines are often compared to Pym's excellent women. See, for example, Judy Little, *The Experimental Self: Dialogic Subjectivity in Woolf, Pym, and*

Brooke-Rose (Carbondale: Southern Illinois University Press, 1996). Although Brookner has written several fair and mostly sympathetic reviews of Pym's works, the connection is perhaps hard to make in respect to these two authors, who both display an elegant sense of humor, but differ so decidedly in other ways. Brookner's Jewish heritage, her distinguished professional career in art history, and her affinity for French literature and culture mark her as a more cosmopolitan writer than Pym, although many of their novels share the literary territory of the City of London. However, Brookner's popular novel *Hotel du Lac* may contain a clue that she is influenced by Pym. At one point, Mr. Neville, a man who proposes marriage to the heroine Edith Hope during their stay at the hotel, tells her, "You are an excellent woman, and I have offended you." See Anita Brookner, *Hotel du Lac* (New York: Random House, 1984), 101.

4. This is a line of (mostly) women who have in common that they write about the fate of unmarried, middle-aged, or aging females. To this tradition also belong the Victorian author Charlotte M. Yonge, the Edwardian writer Flora M. Mayor, E. H. Young, Vera Brittain, Margery Sharp, and Laura Talbot, some of whose books have been reissued by the Virago Press in England in recent years. Pym, of course, read the books of Austen, Yonge, von Arnim, Bowen, Taylor, Compton-Burnett, and Murdoch. John Bayley remarks upon the affinity between Pym and Young in his introduction to Young's *William* (London: Virago, 1987). Frauke Elisabeth Lenckos has examined the influence of Elizabeth von Arnim and Bowen on Pym in "The Passionate Language of Geography: Journeys in Barbara Pym's Novels," *Green Leaves* 6, no. 1 (2000): 3–6. Janice Rossen also compares the heroines of Bowen's novels with Pym's; see *The World of Barbara Pym* (New York: St. Martin's Press, 1987), passim. Several books, articles, dissertations, and reviews have made associations between Pym and writers of her generation or with her literary ancestors. For an overview, see Dale Salwak, *Barbara Pym: A Reference Guide* (Boston: G. K. Hall, 1991) and Salwak's annotated bibliography at the end of this book.

5. Recent reviewers and critics have mentioned Barbara Pym in their discussion of the work of Julian Barnes (John Bayley), Clare Hanson (Kate Fulbrook), Elizabeth Taylor (Margaret Drabble), A. S. Byatt (Olga Kenyon), Ben Elton (Christina Konig), Salley Vickers (Jessica Mann), Anita Brookner (Angela Huth), Nancy Mitford (Hannah Betts), Joanna Trollope (interview in *The Guardian*), and Dodie Smith (Valerie Grove). See *Green Leaves* 7, no. 1 (2001): 11–12.

6. See, for example, the *Bloomsbury Guide to English Literature*, ed. Marion Wynne-Davies (London: Bloomsbury, 1995), 309. In the introductory essay, "Culture and Consciousness: The Twentieth Century Novel in English," Andrew Michael Roberts pays tribute to Barbara Pym as the twentieth century's most important representative of "realism, satire, [and] social comedy." The online *Encyclopedia Britannica*'s "Overview of English Literature" describes Barbara Pym as "an English novelist . . . whose elegant and satiric comedies of manners are marked by poignant observation and psychological insight." *The Columbia Electronic Encyclopedia*, 6th ed. [database online at www.bartleby.com] (New York: Columbia University Press, 2000) makes mention of Pym, as does *The New Grolier Multimedia Encyclopedia* [database online at gi.grolier.com]. See also the annotated bibliography prepared by Dale Salwak at the end of this book, which lists the many books, articles, and dissertations that have been written about Pym in the past two decades.

7. On reader-response criticism, see also Louise Rosenblatt, *The Reader, the Text, and the Poem: The Transactional Theory of the Literary Work* (Carbondale: Southern Illinois University Press, 1978). She defines literature as a coming together, a compenetration of a reader and a text. While Rosenblatt's critique centers on the

pure aesthetics of the process, a new school of reading has evolved that promotes the ethics of reading. Its most respected proponent is Wayne C. Booth, "Why Ethical Criticism Can Never Be Simple," in *Style* (Summer 1998), 1–14. See also *The Company We Keep: An Ethics of Fiction* (Berkeley: University of California Press, 1988).

8. Harold Bloom, *How to Read and Why* (New York: Scribner, 2000), 22.

9. As the title implies, the essays gathered in this book concentrate on Pym and *reading*. The importance of writing in her life has been discussed in many books about Pym's oeuvre, including Rossen, *The World of Barbara Pym*, 7–20, and Anne M. Wyatt-Brown, *Barbara Pym: A Critical Biography* (Columbia: University of Missouri Press, 1992), 11–22.

10. Virginia Woolf, "How Should One Read a Book?" in *The Second Common Reader*, ed. Andrew McNeillie (London: Harcourt Brace, 1986), 269–70.

11. Bloom, *How to Read and Why*, 19–29.

12. *Places: An Anthology of Britain*, ed. Ronald Blythe (Oxford: Oxford University Press, 1981).

Barbara Pym (1913–1980)

ELLEN J. MILLER

MORE THAN TWENTY YEARS AFTER HER DEATH, THE LITERARY world still equates the name of Barbara Pym with a certain kind of writing. "A droll, Barbara Pymish debut novel" describes a new book by a cloistered monk in the *New Yorker*'s 2001 summer fiction issue,[1] and a review of Anita Brookner's *The Bay of Angels* in *The Spectator* refers to the main characters' contentment with their "low-key lives, rather in the manner of Barbara Pym's quiet and uncomplaining women."[2] In our book Katherine Anne Ackley writes, "Barbara Pym . . . had the creative writer's talent not only to turn life's seemingly insignificant events and people into highly readable and immensely pleasurable material but also to make of them meaningful observations on the human condition."

These tributes represent the latest in an ongoing parade of references in the scholarly and general press comparing Pym to a great diversity of writers.[3] Moreover, Pym continues to be the subject of new books and dissertations, and she is the eponym of a flourishing literary society in England and the United States. Three international literary conferences are held each year to study her works and explore their meaning for a new generation of readers. Her books are being republished in England and the United States and her novels are taught at a growing number of American colleges and universities.[4] Pym has her own page in the New York Public Library's 2001 calendar of celebrated women writers, she is the subject of two major Web sites, and an Internet discussion group connects her readers around the world.[5] The acclaim Pym was accorded late in her lifetime gathers force, ensuring a lasting place for her in English literary studies.

Barbara Mary Crampton Pym was destined to become a writer. She was born to Frederic and Irena Pym on June 2, 1913, in the town of Oswestry, Shropshire, on the Welsh border. Barbara's sister Hilary was born there in 1916. Since Irena Pym was assistant organist at the parish church of St. Oswald, entertaining vicars and curates became part of Pym family life—and would later provide Barbara with some of her most enduring and endearing characters.

At the age of sixteen, inspired by Aldous Huxley's *Crome Yellow*, Barbara attempted her first novel, "Young Men in Fancy Dress," a work that remains in the Pym Archives at the Bodleian Library at Oxford University but that holds the seeds of her singular talent. Her dedication in the manuscript reads: "To H. D. M. G., who kindly informed me that I had the makings of a style of my own."[6] In 1931, Barbara entered St. Hilda's College at Oxford. Her notebooks and diaries, also archived at the Bodleian but with excerpts published as *A Very Private Eye*,[7] document her Oxford years. It was here that Barbara read English literature, fell in love, and made lifelong friends who would later influence her literary career.

After earning her second-class honors degree in English Literature, Barbara returned to Oswestry, where she began writing *Some Tame Gazelle*, about two fiftyish spinsters. Remarkably, she projected herself and Hilary thirty years into the future, wove her Oxford friends into the story, and further refined the Pym style, marked by wit, humor, and delightful details of her characters' everyday life. She completed this novel in 1935 when she was only twenty-two, and periodically submitted it to publishers, but without initial success. Barbara started other stories and novels in the 1930s, notably *Crampton Hodnet*, which was published posthumously.

When war overtook Europe in 1940, Barbara was assigned to the censorship office at Bristol and after a painful romance she decided to join the Wrens (Women's Royal Naval Service). From 1944 until the end of the war she was posted to Naples. There she continued writing her diaries and notebooks, gathering material for the stuff of her novels. One of the naval officers she knew in Naples became the inspiration for Rocky Napier in *Excellent Women*.

After the war, Barbara took a job at the International African Institute in London, and soon became the assistant editor for the journal *Africa*. Here the world of anthropologists provided rich and amusing fodder for Barbara's comedic pen. During this time Barbara lived with her sister Hilary, then with the BBC, in a Pimlico flat where she wrote stories for women's magazines, but without success. More significantly, she revised *Some Tame Gazelle* and submitted it to the publisher Jonathan Cape in 1949. To her delight it was accepted and published in 1950, to favorable reviews. Her career as a published writer was launched.

From then on every few years Pym produced a new novel. *Excellent Women* was published by Cape in 1952, followed the next year by *Jane and Prudence*. *Less than Angels* appeared in 1955, *A Glass of Blessings* in 1958, and *No Fond Return of Love* in 1961. To scholars and critics, these six early novels form the Barbara Pym canon, a body of work that establishes her unique style and presages her lasting importance. In them she probes the human condition, seen through the prism of such quotidian events as jumble sales and walks in the woods. Her characters are unassuming people leading unremarkable lives; Pym became the chronicler of quiet lives.

In 1963, Barbara submitted *An Unsuitable Attachment* to Jonathan Cape; to her dismay, it was rejected as being out of step with the times. She tried sending *An Unsuitable Attachment* to other publishers, only to have it rejected. She revised it, but still the rejection letters came. In all, twenty publishers refused to publish the novel.

This devastating experience plunged Barbara Pym into what she and her friends would ruefully term "the wilderness," a literary limbo from which it appeared she would never emerge. "I get moments of gloom and pessimism when it seems as if nobody could ever like my kind of writing again," she wrote in 1970.[8] Yet she continued to write. Drawing on her relationship, at the age of forty-nine, with a thirty-two-year-old antiques dealer, Barbara started writing *The Sweet Dove Died*. A darker novel than her previous works, it brings to life the self-absorbed Leonora Eyre, who seeks to possess a younger man. It, too, was rejected by several publishers in the late sixties and early seventies.

Misfortune of another kind struck Barbara in 1971—she was diagnosed with breast cancer and underwent a mastectomy; in 1974 she suffered a minor stroke. She then retired from the International African Institute and went to live with Hilary at her cottage in Finstock, Oxfordshire. Still writing, Barbara turned her energies toward a new novel inspired by her recent retirement. The story of four office workers, two on the verge of retirement, became *Quartet in Autumn*, darker still than *The Sweet Dove Died* but unmistakably Pym. Jonathan Cape rejected this book too in 1976, as did another publisher.

A few months later her fortunes changed with startling suddenness. In the January 21, 1977, issue of the *Times Literary Supplement*, Barbara Pym was twice named (by Philip Larkin and Lord David Cecil) as "the most underrated novelist of the century." She emerged from sixteen years in "the wilderness" to almost instant fame and recognition. Macmillan accepted *Quartet in Autumn* for publication in 1977, and it was short-listed that year for the Booker Prize. In 1978 Macmillan published *The Sweet Dove Died*. Both new novels drew critical acclaim in the United Kingdom and Macmillan hastened to reprint all the novels. American audiences were quickly introduced to Barbara by E. P. Dutton, which in 1978 began publishing all of her novels. Furthermore, the books were translated into many foreign languages and Pym enjoyed international acclaim.[9]

But fate intervened once again, dealing Barbara its final blow. Only two years after her literary rediscovery, her cancer returned, and this time treatments were unsuccessful. She rushed to finish her new novel, *A Few Green Leaves*; she died at the Michael Sobell House, a hospice in Oxford, on January 11, 1980. She is buried in the church-yard at Finstock.

Hazel Holt, Barbara's close friend, Institute colleague, and literary executor, in 1982 prepared *An Unsuitable Attachment* for publication, followed by *Crampton Hodnet* in 1985. In 1987 *Civil to Strangers* was published, together with several short stories selected by Holt.

Barbara Pym novels still sparkle as brightly as jewels on the literary landscape. The real world has changed enormously in the years since she wrote her last story, but the "entirely recognizable world"[10] she created remains forever intact, beckoning readers to return time and again. They are rewarded anew by the richness of Pym's unique gifts. It appears that Barbara Pym has achieved the "immortality that most authors would want—to feel that their work would be immediately recognized as having been written by them and nobody else."[11]

NOTES

1. Brief review of *All We Know of Heaven*, by Remy Rougeau, *New Yorker*, 19 and 25 June 2001, 164.

2. Angela Huth review of *The Bay of Angels*, by Anita Brookner, *Spectator*, 20 January 2001, 7.

3. Among the writers most often compared to Pym are Salley Vickers, Anita Brookner, Nancy Mitford, Joanna Trollope, Elizabeth Taylor, A. S. Byatt, Penelope Fitzgerald, Sylvia Townsend Warner, and Elizabeth Bowen. See *Green Leaves* 7, no. 1 (2001): 11–12.

4. Pym has been taught in classes and seminars at, for example, the University of Iowa, Vanderbilt University, Temple University, the University of Wisconsin, the University of Virginia, Harvard College, the University of Chicago, York University (Canada), and the Newberry Library, Chicago. Pym's novel *Excellent Women* was also chosen for the National Endowment for the Humanities Reading Program in the state of South Dakota.

5. The Web sites are www.spore.it/pym/home_english.htm and www.barbara-pym.org. The discussion group is pym-l@yahoogroups.com.

6. Hazel Holt, *A Lot to Ask: A Life of Barbara Pym* (New York: E. P. Dutton, 1991), 16. In correspondence with Ellen Miller, Hazel Holt writes, "H. D. M. G. was Dewi Griffith, a young man (son of a Welsh Methodist Minister) whom Barbara and Hilary met and became friends with when they went with their parents on holiday every year to Pwellhi (North Wales). Barbara dedicated 'Young Men in Fancy Dress' to him. I don't think they ever met again after the last holiday in the 1930s."

7. Barbara Pym, *A Very Private Eye: An Autobiography in Diaries and Letters*, ed. Hazel Holt and Hilary Pym (New York: E. P. Dutton, 1984).

8. Holt, *A Lot to Ask*, 217.

9. Pym novels have been translated into French, Italian, German, Dutch, Portuguese, Hungarian, and Russian. See Holt, *A Lot to Ask,* 279.

10. Hazel Holt in the videocassette *Barbara Pym: Out of the Wilderness* (Belmont, Mass.: Greybirch Productions, 1984).

11. Barbara Pym, "Finding a Voice," a talk broadcast on BBC Radio 3, 4 April 1978, printed in *Civil to Strangers,* ed. Hazel Holt (New York: E. P. Dutton, 1987), 282–83.

Part I
Reading in Barbara Pym's Novels

"All This Reading":
The Importance of Literature in the
Novels of Barbara Pym

KATHERINE ANNE ACKLEY

LITERATURE WAS A DELIGHT AND A COMFORT TO BARBARA PYM, WHO once told an interviewer that "the Anglican Church and English literature [were] the two most important things" in her life.[1] The frequency with which her characters turn to literature for pleasure or consolation and the many references to the imaginative talents of poets and novelists attest to Pym's firm belief in the power of literature to speak to one's own experience, especially in matters of the heart. She is, as Janice Rossen notes in *The World of Barbara Pym*, "an intensely literary author."[2] Her books are filled with allusions to poems, novels, plays, and hymns—a device that, as Robert J. Graham observes, "every Pym reader associates with her work."[3] Her characters read widely, if indiscriminately; they are just as likely to allude to half-remembered lines from a poet now forgotten as they are to recall passages from an Austen novel or a Donne poem. Furthermore, Pym frequently contrasts the fiction writer and the social scientist, making a compelling argument for the liberating power of the imagination over the almost dehumanizing force of science. She is an excellent spokesperson for the value of liberal arts in a world committed to scientific inquiry and hard-nosed practicality. Barbara Pym may never have had to defend herself as Dulcie does when challenged by her housekeeper, Miss Lord: "All this reading. . . . But what does it lead to, Miss Mainwaring?"[4] Nevertheless, her novels can be seen as an extended answer to that question.

Perhaps most importantly, literature is a rich source of comfort in both emotionally troubled and happy times. Pym's lifelong practice of filling notebooks with quotations from her favorite poets and novelists is reflected in her creation of characters who take the same pleasure as she in recalling familiar passages from poetry or fiction, particularly when those passages speak to their own lives. Pym deliberately searched for quotations that expressed her own feelings, especially in her painful relationship with Henry Harvey, as recorded in this 1933 diary entry: "I ordered a copy of Ernest Dowson's poems in Bodleiana and spent some time in finding appropriate lines and poems. I'm beginning to enjoy my pose of romantically unrequited love."[5] This passage not only points to the practical application of literature but also articulates a coping strategy Pym often used. Many of her diary entries express genuine anguish over Harvey's cold treatment of her, but if she could see herself as striking a "pose," as she does here, then she could put some distance between herself and those feelings. Similarly, her fictional heroines look with detachment at their own silliness for loving men who are not worthy of them or do not return their affection. We see the sentiment of this early diary entry in *Some Tame Gazelle*, for instance, when Belinda Bede, having quoted lines of poetry to express her undying love for Henry Hoccleve, reflects: "How much more one appreciated our great literature if one loved, . . . especially if the love were unrequited!"[7] It is not surprising that Pym created fictional characters who, like herself, find consolation in literature. Life, she learned early, is difficult and often disappointing, but literature could provide some relief from real emotional trauma.

Pym's early works are more heavily filled with literary references than her later ones, perhaps because she was so close to her years at Oxford, where she had read English, and was still very much influenced by her studies. In "Finding a Voice," a 1978 BBC radio talk in which she discussed the influence of other writers on her work, Pym said of her first novel, written at 16, that "all the 'best' or at least the most fashionable names are dropped, from Swinburne and Rupert Brooke to D. H. Lawrence and Beverley Nichols."[6] That novel, "Young Men in Fancy Dress," was never published, but *Some Tame Gazelle* came into print in 1950. It was her first published novel, begun when she was an undergraduate and polished and refined over the next fifteen years. Its central character, Belinda Bede, is patterned after Pym herself and is therefore inordinately fond of literature. Indeed, on the opening page of the novel, we are told that Belinda still "retained some smattering of the culture acquired in her college days. Even now a light would shine in her mild greenish eyes . . . at the mention of Young's *Night Thoughts* or the dear Earl of Rochester's *Poems on Several Occasions*" (7). Belinda's horrified response to seeing a dead caterpillar in the cauliflower cheese she has served her sewing woman—"It needed a modern poet to put this into words. Eliot perhaps" (51)—suggests the degree of confidence Belinda places in the imaginative power of poets.

In addition to her overt fondness for literature, Belinda has harbored a quiet, abiding love for Henry Hoccleve, a self-centered, pompous curate whose own love for obscure literary references is a bore to everyone in his congregation except the faithful Belinda. Both the Archdeacon and she like the sound of his voice. But while Belinda finds comfort and reassurance from her favorite poets, Henry uses literature primarily to display his erudition. Members of his congregation grumble about his penchant for reading lengthy passages from difficult writers. His famous Judgment Day sermon, largely a string of obscure quotations with very little explanation from the Archdeacon, loses everyone almost immediately, and finally even Belinda cannot follow his point. The Archdeacon's preference for literary sermons reveals a lack of originality, for, as Belinda notes, he is not particularly clever theologically. This observation is borne out in *Excellent Women* when the Archdeacon, as a guest speaker during a Lenten service attended by Mildred Lathbury, delivers that same Judgment Day sermon to an equally disgusted and unimpressed congregation.

Belinda's adoration of Henry and her willingness to listen to his literary self-indulgence are not only indications of how modest her needs and unassuming her expectations in love are, but they are also measures of her high regard for literature. When the two pleasures merge, she is serenely content. One of the happiest times in her life is the hour Henry spends reading to her aloud from *The Faerie Queene* and *The Prelude*: "Just one evening like that every thirty years or so. It might not seem much to other people, but it was really all one needed to be happy" (*STG*, 158). It is the combination of the pleasure of Henry's company and his reading poetry to her that provides the magic for Belinda.

Pym capitalizes on Belinda's love of a good quotation by making it the source of humor in a very comic scene. When he proposes to Belinda, Bishop Grote first mistakenly attributes a line about beauty not being everything to the wrong poet and then unwittingly insults her when he refers to *Paradise Lost*: "Belinda interrupted him with a startled exclamation. 'Paradise Lost!' she echoed in horror. 'Milton . . .'" (224). Pym's female characters do not think much of Milton and his treatment of women, so this ill-timed allusion puts an end to Grote's proposal. When Belinda admits that she cannot marry him because she loves another, Grote assumes this beloved has died and hints that Lord Byron had said something particularly appropriate. Belinda wonders, "Could Lord Byron have said anything at all suitable?" (224). When she cannot imagine what it could be, she is more interested in the literary point than in the actual matter at hand, but the bishop leaves without enlightening her. At the end of the novel, the offensive intruders on her quiet life having gone away, Belinda is greatly comforted by the prospect of life going on as it always has done, taking pleasure and consolation in her passions for the great English poets and Henry Hoccleve.

Throughout her novels Pym affirms that a life without literature is an impoverished life. From *Some Tame Gazelle* to *A Few Green Leaves*, she makes clear her belief that literature comments eloquently and poignantly on the range of emotions from anguish to joy in a way that speaks directly to its readers. Finding one's feelings well expressed can be bittersweet, but it gives comfort nonetheless. The narrator of *Less than Angels* describes it well in remarking on "the consolation and pain of coming upon [one's] feelings expressed for [one]" in literature.[8] Almost all of Pym's central character heroines and many of her minor characters turn to literature for meaningful observations on their own experiences. Indeed, as Charles Burkhart has remarked, "her characters drop a quotation as readily as they drink a cup of tea."[9] Burkhart calls this aspect of Pym's novels "odd" and even says that it "might be considered a defect. . . . [Her characters'] 'literariness' is rather endearing, but it is limiting and to a degree unlikely." Nevertheless, he admits that "these penchants have their value in that they establish a recognizable world, one we come to feel at home in."[10] Diana Benet sees much more to their value than that: she quite rightly believes that the frequent literary allusions and Pym's characters' familiarity with literature add irony and comedy to the novels.[11] Whom Pym's characters read and whom they quote are reflections of their personalities and provide an extra dimension to our understanding of them.

Dulcie Mainwaring, Belinda Bede, and both Jane Cleveland and Prudence Bates of *Jane and Prudence* have university degrees in English literature and are avid novel readers. Emma Howick, though her degree is in anthropology, was named for a Jane Austen heroine, prefers to identify herself with Thomas Hardy's wife, and contemplates writing her own novel by the end of *A Few Green Leaves*. Characters without university degrees also delight in remembering passages of poems, novels, or hymns. Ianthe Broome of *An Unsuitable Attachment*, for instance, is a librarian who sees herself as an Elizabeth Bowen heroine, and Letty Crowe of *Quartet in Autumn* spends her lunch hours in the library searching for contemporary romances or biographies. Catherine Oliphant in *Less than Angels* makes her living as a fiction writer and thinks of herself as looking like Jane Eyre. Even those who are not otherwise noted as "great readers" demonstrate familiarity with works of literature: Mildred Lathbury assures readers of *Excellent Women* that she is not at all like Jane Eyre, and reads

Christina Rossetti's poetry; Leonora Eyre in *The Sweet Dove Died* reads Elizabeth Bowen and keeps the poetry of Browning and Arnold on her bedside table, drawing comfort from the beauty of their images; and Wilmet Forsyth in *A Glass of Blessings*, herself possessor of a vivid imagination, has an idea of what Virginia Woolf might make of a scene she witnesses.

Numerous other characters quote lines of poetry and allude to works of both great and obscure writers, and people are always reading fiction by their favorite female author. Even the most unlikely characters have a supply of apt (or not-so-apt) quotations. In *Jane and Prudence*, for instance, Geoffrey Manifold startles Prudence Bates by quoting lines from Coventry Patmore, while John Challow of *An Unsuitable Attachment* reads Tennyson at tea. In *A Few Green Leaves* Tom Dagnall, on the other hand, feels he has made a fool of himself when he impulsively quotes some lines to Emma: "'Leigh Hunt,' said Tom quickly, attempting to cover his foolishness. 'Not a good poem.'"[12] Perhaps most surprising of all, Marcia Ivory of *Quartet in Autumn* keeps an anthology of poetry on her bedside table and has been known to allude to a poem, prompting Letty Crowe to consider buying her a book when she is in the hospital. Intriguingly, like Miss Lord in *No Fond Return of Love*, Letty's landlady also challenges her: "'A *book*?' Mrs. Pope's tone rang out scornfully. 'What would she want with a book?'"[13] Mrs. Pope's attitude simply irritates Letty, who finally chooses lavender water. But Miss Lord's remark unsettles Dulcie, who can only reply weakly that she may not know exactly what reading leads to, but she does know that it gives her pleasure. If reading literature needs any justification, then Dulcie's response is perhaps the best reason of all. Pym herself explained in her BBC radio talk that she wrote for her own pleasure and amusement, though always with the hope that people who read her work might like it as well.[14]

One of Pym's favorite characters, Prudence Bates of *Jane and Prudence*, is very much a creation of the Barbara Pym we know from her diaries, with her fondness for reading, her predilection for romance, and her vision of herself as acting a role. Although Prudence reads Coventry Patmore, she enjoys novels that are "not very nice," the kind that "described a love affair in the fullest sense of the word and sparing no detail, but all in a very intellectual sort of way."[15] The books that Prudence reads are the books that she lives, for Prudence seems quite content with her own "inevitable but satisfying unhappy endings" to relationships (47). For instance, she is not genuinely upset by the news that Fabian Driver will marry Jessie Morrow, but she acts out the role of jilted lover for all of a weekend, writing a "sad, re-

signed letter, a little masterpiece in its way" that brings tears to the
eyes of the guilty Fabian (199). Prudence's relationship with Geoffrey
Manifold is an indication of the way she seems destined always to repeat her past, following the literary tradition of the romance novel.
She has become so much like the characters she reads about that she
anticipates the inevitable ending of her own "plot." As she tells Jane,
"We shall probably hurt each other very much before it's finished,
but we're doomed really" (217). Reminded of a Marvell passage in
response to Prudence, Jane observes, "How much easier it was when
one could find a quotation to light up the way" (217). It is a feeling
shared by many of Pym's characters.[16]

Pym often blurs the distinction between literature and life. She implies that her characters have a life of their own outside the realm of
her fictional world and sometimes suggests that those in the "real
world" are more like fictional characters. A case in point is the scene
in which Dulcie Mainwaring in *No Fond Return of Love* has a conversation with Wilmet Forsyth from *A Glass of Blessings*. Here, Keith
and Piers, still together, are on holiday with Wilmet and Rodney, all
four perfectly in character and exactly as we remember them from the
earlier book. In a brilliant, ironic stroke, Viola Dace says of them:
"What odd people they were! Like characters in a novel!" (193). That
Pym felt the line between fiction and reality was a thin one is illustrated by a journal entry she made on December 28, 1945: "Your spinster in two ages—first as a governess in a large family house, perhaps
in Warwick Square. Then later in a modern reincarnation about which
you know quite a lot. Is this book to be a novel or a clever sort of
commonplace book—fiction—autobiography . . .?"[17] This comment
clearly suggests Pym's view that fiction and real life are firmly interrelated.

Perhaps because it is about academics rather than anthropologists
or village inhabitants, *No Fond Return of Love* is one of Pym's fullest
explorations of the uses of literature and the subtle interconnected-
ness of fiction and reality. Viola Dace, Dulcie Mainwaring, and Aylwin Forbes have all read extensively, are influenced by what they have
read, and often see themselves or others as if they were fictional. Thus
Aylwin, who takes James's *Portrait of a Lady* with him to Italy and
comes back talking like a James character, can justify turning his attention to Dulcie because that very thing happens in an Austen novel.
Dulcie is especially inclined to see fiction as in some ways more appealing than reality. For instance, when she indignantly berates
Alywin for entertaining the hope that her niece Laurel might return
his affection, she thinks, "She was by no means at her best this morning, though if it had been a romantic novel . . . he would have been

struck by how handsome she looked when she was angry" (229). This wistful thinking is echoed in *An Academic Question*, when Caroline Grimstone, married to someone else but lunching with the man she first loved, tells us, "I wished I were in a novel or even some other person's life where we could have gone back to his flat or to a hotel, sleazily romantic with heavy dingy lace curtains."[18] In contrast to what happens in fiction, however, Caroline does not act out her fantasy, nor does Aylwin notice how anger enhances Dulcie's looks.

Dulcie tends to see her habit of prying into people's lives as if it were no different from viewing a film or play: "It seemed . . . so much safer and more comfortable to live in the lives of other people—to observe their joys and sorrows with detachment" (*NFRL*, 108). The emotional danger lies in becoming too involved with other people, as Dulcie finds out. But by the time she has traveled to Taviscombe to spy on Aylwin's mother, her position has shifted from that of the detached observer to that of an actor in a drama: events, she feels, will unfold with the "inevitability of a Greek tragedy" (178). Not only can she imagine herself as a character in a novel or an actor in a play, but she also sees herself in the role of creator, expressing her disappointment in Viola in terms of that role: "In a sense, Dulcie felt as if she had created her and that she had not come up to expectations, like a character in a book who had failed to come alive, and how many people in life, if one transferred them to fiction just as they were, would fail to do that!" (167–68). Well-read and educated, Dulcie is sensitive to what makes characters and real people "come alive."

Like Barbara Pym the novelist, jotting down overheard bits of conversation or noting observations that might work well in a novel, her characters sometimes view the world as if they, too, were writers. A chance phrase might become a book title; an unusual situation might turn into the plot of a novel. Pym characters everywhere seem to have this imaginative turn of mind. For instance, Mark Ainger in *An Unsuitable Attachment*, amused by Father Anstruther's reminiscence about the delicious fairies someone used to make for bazaars, says to Sophia: "'A bond of fairies. . . .' Obviously a title for something."[19] *Excellent Women*'s Mildred Lathbury, referring to Everard Bone's mother's eccentric interests, thinks, "Birds, worms, and Jesuits. . . . It might almost have been a poem, but I could not remember that anybody had ever written it."[20] Elsewhere, dining at Mrs. Forbes's hotel, Dulcie Mainwaring and Viola Dace overhear a clergyman remark to a companion that the place must be "a change from Uganda." Dulcie whispers to Viola: "What a lovely title for a novel that would be . . . and one can see that it would be almost easy to write. The plot is beginning to take shape already" (*NFRL*, 175). It is no accident that

Pym chooses this moment to bring onto the scene a woman who can be none other than Barbara Pym herself: "she was a woman of about forty, ordinary-looking and unaccompanied, nobody took much notice of her. As it happened, she was a novelist; indeed, some of the occupants of the tables had read and enjoyed her books" (176). Besides the delight of dropping into her own novel, Pym must also have taken great pleasure in including among the books on the shelf in Dulcie's bathroom a copy of *Some Tame Gazelle* (73). Examples of this type abound through the novels.

Pym's toying with what is real and what is fiction is an intriguing device that seldom seems forced. Like so much in Pym's works, its cumulative effect over all the novels is to imply a basic truth about the complicated mystery of life. We are all actors, she suggests, and the plot possibilities are endless. Just months before she died, Pym wrote in her diary that she had found herself "reflecting on the mystery of life and death and the way we all pass through this world in a kind of procession. The whole business as inexplicable and mysterious as the John Le Carré TV serial, *Tinker, Tailor, Soldier, Spy*, which we are all finding so baffling" (*VPE,* 331). How absolutely appropriate for her to compare the deep mystery of life with the complicated plot of a spy novel. Fascinated by the potential for any real-life situation to be turned into fiction, Pym herself had been a kind of spy, always looking for raw material that she could use in her novels, skillfully transforming this material in ways that help shed light on the "inexplicable and mysterious" meaning of life. Good writers of fiction and poetry, she always intimated, have the power to distill the significant meaning from ordinary reality.

Catherine Oliphant of *Less than Angels,* herself a fiction writer, is an ingenious representation of Pym's belief in the power of art to make meaning of life, and in the close connection between reality and fiction. Catherine struggles with how to write a convincing short story, thinking rather skeptically that it is difficult to get women to read beyond the first page and imagining them sitting under a hair dryer, flipping through pages of a magazine. Then she has the bad luck to witness her lover Tom holding hands with another woman at the table where she and Tom always sit at their favorite Greek restaurant. We learn in *A Glass of Blessings* that Catherine turns this incident into a short story, for that novel finds Wilmet and Rowena sitting under hair dryers and discussing the fiction in the magazines they are reading. Commenting on a story by Catherine Oliphant, Rowena says it begins with a man's former mistress watching a man and a young woman hold hands in a Greek restaurant. Wilmet protests, "But what a far-fetched situation. . . . As if it would happen like that!

Still, it must be dreadful to have to write fiction. Do you suppose Catherine Oliphant drew it from her own experience of life?" Laughing, Rowena replies, "I should hardly think so!"[21] This dismissal of her story as improbable is exactly the reaction that Catherine had expected. Thus Pym not only legitimizes the use of even the most unlikely coincidence in fiction but also suggests the therapeutic power of writing about one's own experiences. She might very well have seen herself in the character of Catherine, trying to write a convincing story based on her own painful personal experience. Literature, she implies, can be cathartic for both writer and reader.

It seems a logical step for Pym to write the kind of fiction that her characters themselves would turn to. Her extended treatment of the unmarried woman provides a literary model that is largely missing in fiction before hers. In *Quartet in Autumn*, Pym directly addresses this neglect of spinsters in literature when she describes Letty's reading habits: "She had always been an unashamed reader of novels, but if she hoped to find one which reflected her own sort of life she had come to realize that the position of an unmarried, unattached, ageing woman is of no interest whatever to the writer of modern fiction" (3). But Pym not only writes the novel that Letty wants to read, she also makes Letty its central character. Interestingly, when Letty abandons "romantic novels" because she cannot find what she needs in them, she turns to biographies. "And because they were 'true' they were really better than fiction," Pym writes. "Not perhaps better than Jane Austen or Tolstoy . . . but certainly more 'worth while' than the works of any modern novelist" (3–4). Pym cannot resist championing the great writers of fiction, whose "worth" transcends even that of "reality." It is fitting, then, that Letty returns in her retirement to reading novels, which are so much more satisfying.

Letty actually plans to read some "serious" works in her retirement, and on her very first day of retirement she goes to the sociology shelves of her library, having been attracted by "the idea and the name 'social studies'" (114). What a disappointment the books turn out to be. Within a week she comes to the conclusion that "sociology was not quite all that she had hoped for. . . . She had imagined herself revelling and wallowing—perhaps those words were too violent to describe what she had imagined—in her chosen subject, not frozen with boredom, baffled and bogged down by incomprehensible jargon" (117). When she returns the books to the library, feeling guilty and inadequate, she alleviates that guilt somewhat by reminding herself that, as a retired person, she has earned the right to read whatever she likes. Elsewhere, in *Less than Angels*, Rhoda Wellcome and Mabel Swann, vaguely conscious that they should be worried about the larger problems of the world, sometimes write down titles of books they feel they ought to read but are "secretly relieved when each time they went to get a book the librarian handed out yet another novel" (40–41). Pym would no doubt be the first to say that the "greater English poets" and novelists are the most astute at seeing the larger truths and grander meanings of life, but she would never deny the sheer pleasure of reading for its own sake or writing as a form of imaginative expression. She has no pretensions in this regard, celebrating the cozy delights of elderly women reading popular novels any day over the baffling coldness of social science, political science, or any other science.

The argument in favor of literature over science is made nowhere as forcefully as in Pym's treatment of anthropologists. Her observations are often amusing, as in *Excellent Women*, when Mildred Lathbury attends a meeting of the Learned Society at which Helena Napier and Everard Bone give their paper on the results of their anthropological study. Finding herself completely incapable of following Helena's lecture, Mildred lets her eye wander to the open window, noting the lovely details of garden squares on this fine spring day. The passage makes a wry comment on the stuffiness of such meetings, with the Americans taking notes furiously while Mildred rebukes herself mildly for not having prepared better for this meeting by reading up on the subject instead of buying a new hat.

Anthropologists themselves are aware of the potentially stifling nature of their written reports on their fieldwork. This self-awareness is humorously illustrated in *An Unsuitable Attachment*, when Rupert Stonebird, working up courage to make a romantic overture to Ianthe Broome, blurts out the title of his latest article:

> 'The implication of jural processes among the Ngumu: a structural dichotomy'. . . . 'Oh . . .' [Ianthe] turned her head away as if she were in pain or distress. At least she had not been facetious or made some cheaply witty rejoinder, he thought. 'It's quite simple, really,' he began, but he knew that it was not. It was the kind of thing that could be, and so often was, the stumbling block between men and women, or, if a relationship had progressed through several stages, the last straw. 'Let's have some more tea,' he said. (213)

Unlike science, literature is an inquiry that makes no claims to objectivity; indeed, the real power of literature is the imaginative freedom it gives both readers and writers. Its only claims to validity are personal. It is a subjective interpretation of human experience that, if well done, strikes a chord of recognition and touches the heart.

In her essay "The Novelist as Anthropologist," Muriel Schulz makes the point that Pym implies throughout her novels: it is "not the anthropologist, [but] the novelist" who will "preserve the memory of England's institutions and customs. . . . Pym was exploring in her works the possibility that the novelist is a kind of anthropologist of her own culture."[22] The anthropologist and the novelist may have superficially similar goals, as Catherine Oliphant recognizes when, entering a large restaurant and noting that the people seem without direction, in need of someone to guide them not only in their choice of food but also "to the deeper or higher things of life." Who would supply this need, Catherine wonders—"the anthropologist, laying bare the structure of society, or the writer of romantic fiction, covering it up?" (*LTA*, 194–95). Both may observe behavior with detachment; the crucial difference is that the writer is ultimately more emotional, more interested in those "deeper or higher things of life"—the heart, the soul, the intensely felt experience of human relationships—than the anthropologist. Catherine "not only sees more details than others: she can also see into the heart of people."[23] The contrast between science and literature, particularly between anthropologists and fiction writers, is a subject that Pym returns to again and again.

In *A Few Green Leaves*, for instance, the anthropologist Emma Howick takes notes on the village and its inhabitants in just the way a novelist might, listing characters and behavioral traits and describing situations, but she finds herself thinking more and more as a novelist than as a social scientist. Everard Bone, the anthropologist, would see the writer and the social scientist as doing the same thing. "After all," he says in *An Unsuitable Attachment*, "both study life in communities" (127). But Emma notices important differences between the two. She prefers the cozy term "village" over the more scientific "jargon word 'community'" (*FGL*, 38), and at the end of *A Few Green Leaves* she may very well be planning to write a novel, not an anthropological tract, on her observations. Ianthe's defense of novelists in *An Unsuitable Attachment* is particularly apt, for she points out to a party of anthropologists that because life can be interpreted in so many ways, the novelist has the advantage, letting her imagination roam where it will (127). While both the writer and the social scientist record human behavior and attempt to explain its larger implications, the writer of fiction has almost unlimited freedom in the way she represents that behavior. Furthermore, she is more interested in the emotional ramifications of human interaction. Literature has a liberating, humanizing component missing in science, with its mission to classify and codify.

Perhaps Pym's sharpest insight on this subject occurs in *Less than Angels*. Alaric Lydgate, plagued for eleven years by a trunk full of field notes he is unable to write up, regards himself as a failure and sits alone in his room at night wearing an African mask. How much easier life would be if one could hide behind a mask and not have to actually look people in the eye, he thinks. This scientific observer of human behavior wishes to cut himself off from social intercourse and its attendant difficulties. It is the fiction writer Catherine who liberates him from his crippling inability to make human contact by suggesting that he might not have to write up his notes after all. At first visibly shaken by the idea, he later jubilantly burns his notes. It is a wonderful scene—Alaric now free of his burden, confronted by the outraged anthropologists Esther Clovis and Gertrude Lydgate. When Miss Clovis snatches burning pages of kinship tables from the fire, Alaric pokes them back in with his stick. The anthropologists are horrified at the loss to the scientific world as he throws bundles of papers into the fire, but Catherine responds to the aesthetic quality of the scene: "Oh, *pretty*," she cries, as "some of it, eaten by white ants, fell away like a shower of confetti" (228). When Alaric's sister demands to know what he will do now, he tells her that not only will he go on reviewing scholarly books but he may also very well write a novel. Catherine's remark that he has wonderful material refers not to his anthropological observations but to his subjective experiences in Africa. It is a powerful affirmation of the potential for imaginative fiction to free the spirit.

Pym illustrates over and over this power of literature to speak to the human experience and to make its readers more sensitive human beings. Early in *No Fond Return of Love*, Dulcie Mainwaring gives money to

> a new and particularly upsetting beggar selling matches; both legs were in irons and he was hugging himself as if in pain. She had given him sixpence and walked quickly on, telling herself there was no need for this sort of thing now, with the Welfare State. But she still felt disturbed, even at the idea that he might be sitting by his television set later that evening, no longer hugging himself as if in pain. (39–40)

Near the end of the novel she sees this very "beggar," walking briskly down the street, wearing a good suit. Far from being upset, she thinks it must be an omen of something, though she cannot articulate what it is at the moment. Aware of life's inconsistencies and unfairness, Dulcie accepts with equanimity this confirmation of her earlier suspicion. An avid reader, she recognizes the possibility of its having a higher meaning.

Though the meaning of this particular incident escapes her, often Dulcie *is* able to draw connections between seemingly trivial things and their larger implications: she compares having one's choice of cakes at tea with Life, for example, pointing out the distinct difference that one does not have the same freedom in Life as at tea. Or, feeling sympathy for Miss Lord's upsetting experience at a cafeteria, where she did not get baked beans but the man behind her did, Dulcie remarks,

'Yes, I know, that's what life is like. And it *is* humiliating. One feels a sense of one's own inadequacy, somehow, almost unworthiness. . . . But then life is cruel in small ways, isn't it. Not exactly nature red in tooth and claw, though one does sometimes feel. . . . And what will you have for pudding today?' she asked, jerking herself back to reality by a sudden awareness of Miss Lord's pitying look at her vague philosophizings. If this is what education does for you . . . she seemed to imply. Well might one ask, 'But what will it lead to?' (88)

The implication is that "all this reading" has led Dulcie Mainwaring to a sensitivity to the plight of others and to a greater understanding of her position in the grand scheme of things. It has made her more attuned to the "higher meaning" of, for instance, a choice of cakes or the availability of baked beans.

"All this reading" has also made Dulcie in some small way like Barbara Pym herself, who had the creative writer's talent not only to turn life's seemingly insignificant events and people into highly readable and immensely pleasurable material but also to make meaningful observations on the human condition. Pym's novels and her personal diaries demonstrate that literature has enormous power. Imaginative fiction and poetry can give comfort, provide consolation through the pain of recognition, help people connect with one another, liberate the spirit, and ultimately make readers more compassionate human beings.

NOTES

1. Carolyn Moorhead. "How Barbara Pym Was Rediscovered after Sixteen Years Out in the Cold," *Times* (London), 14 September 1977, 11.

2. Janice Rossen, *The World of Barbara Pym* (New York: St. Martin's Press, 1987), 7.

3. Robert J. Graham, "The Narrative Sense of Barbara Pym," in *The Life and Work of Barbara Pym*, ed. Dale Salwak (Iowa City: University of Iowa Press, 1987), 151.

4. Barbara Pym, *No Fond Return of Love* (New York: E. P. Dutton, 1982), 34.

5. Pym, *A Very Private Eye: An Autobiography in Diaries and Letters,* ed. Hazel Holt and Hilary Pym (New York: E. P. Dutton, 1984), 27.

6. Pym, "Finding a Voice: A Radio Talk," in *Civil to Strangers,* ed. Hazel Holt (New York: E. P. Dutton, 1987), 382.

7. Pym, *Some Tame Gazelle* (New York: E. P. Dutton, 1983), 7.

8. Pym, *Less than Angels* (New York: E. P. Dutton, 1980), 186.

9. Charles Burkhart, *The Pleasure of Miss Pym* (Austin: University of Texas Press, 1987), 25.

10. Ibid., 25, 26.

11. Diana Benet, *Something to Love: Barbara Pym's Novels* (Columbia: University of Missouri Press, 1986), 5.

12. Pym, *A Few Green Leaves* (New York: E. P. Dutton, 1980), 76.

13. Pym, *Quartet in Autumn* (New York: E. P. Dutton, 1978), 178.

14. Pym, "Finding a Voice," 386.

15. Pym, *Jane and Prudence* (New York: E. P. Dutton, 1981), 47.

16. Lotus Snow has identified many of the allusions in Pym's novels in her article "Literary Allusions in the Novels," in Salwak. Cataloguing the many references throughout the novels, she says, shows Pym's "range of knowledge and her preferences among the English poets and novelists" (121). She concludes that

> A survey of Miss Pym's allusions to the English poets reveals not only her devotion to and remarkable familiarity with them, but also her especial kinship with Matthew Arnold and her preference for the Metaphysicals, particularly Donne. Among the older novelists, she read and reread Jane Austen and Trollope, the lives of whose characters resemble those of her own, and vividly remembered the more dramatic characters in the novels of Charlotte Brontë and Charlotte M. Yonge. Among the moderns, she said in her talk for the BBC, she was most influenced by Aldous Huxley in *Crome Yellow,* and, later, by Ivy Compton-Burnett (MS Pym, 96). (141)

17. MS Pym 84, fol. 4, Bodleian Library, Oxford.

18. Pym, *An Academic Question* (New York: E. P. Dutton, 1986), 96.

19. Pym, *An Unsuitable Attachment* (New York: E. P. Dutton, 1982), 66.

20. Pym, *Excellent Women* (New York: E. P. Dutton, 1978), 151.

21. Pym, *A Glass of Blessings* (New York: E. P. Dutton, 1980), 152.

22. Schulz, "The Novelist as Anthropologist," in Salwak, 108.

23. Ibid., 111.

"A Life Ruined by Literature"?:
Barbara Pym's Excellent Women Readers

FRAUKE ELISABETH LENCKOS

A FEW GREEN LEAVES IS NOT THE ONLY LATE WORK BY BARBARA PYM to titillate our imaginations with the possibilities of an open ending.[1] From *The Sweet Dove Died* to *Quartet in Autumn*, Pym's finales sound the tantalizing note of uncertainty, an appeal to the speculative resources of her readers.[2] Will Leonora Eyre, the heroine of *The Sweet Dove Died*, finally develop the generosity of heart to conquer the feeling of superiority she harbors over those who love her not wisely, but well? Will Letty Crowe, the protagonist of Pym's penultimate story, succeed in fighting the isolation of old age by bringing together the lonely retirees of her acquaintance? The mood of Pym's endings is ruminative, and in these last instances she generously leaves it to her audiences to supply the conclusions to her stories. Nor is Pym's gesture to her reading public to complete her narratives her only attempt at empowering us as critics and writers. Her journals and letters show that she herself was a born reader and observer who knew intimately not only the joys and frustrations that characterize great lovers of literature but also the need to make a study of her fellow human beings.[3] Pym portrays her heroines as both avid consumers of books and perspicacious recorders of human eccentricity—as readers, therefore, with whom we are invited to identify.

Also, reading emerges as a central theme in the oeuvre of Barbara Pym.[4] Her novels exhibit the author's rich literary erudition, demonstrating that she read her way keenly through some of the most important writers and poets of the British canon.[5] Pym especially appreciated Jane Austen, the great Victorian women novelists, Henry James, Elizabeth von Arnim, Elizabeth Bowen, and Ivy Compton-Burnett, and references to the works of these authors surface in her novels.[6] As a good author, however, Pym not merely absorbed the influences of these writers, but appropriated, updated, and translated their aesthetic example for the benefit of her own characteristic world.

Readers can enjoy *The Sweet Dove Died, Quartet in Autumn*, or

A Few Green Leaves without following up their allusions to *Emma*, *Portrait of a Lady*, or *To the North* (to name but a few examples). However, an investigation into these sources lays bare unexpected levels of profundity in Pym's texts, revealing the sophistication of a writer whose plots seem at first surprisingly simple, but whose character studies, because of their intricate relationship with their literary role models, as well as the history of the intellect and the sensibility these represent, bear rereading. Like the best mysteries, Pym's novels reward the effort of closer study by standing up to the test of literary sleuthing. The intertextual references she works into her novels disclose to us that despite the light tone of voice Pym favors, her subject matter is nothing less serious than the examination of the position of the female reader in literature.

Observing, detecting, and investigating: the pastimes of the reader and writer are also the favorite occupations of Pym's excellent women. Mildred Lathbury, the heroine of Pym's second published book, begins her first day in the novel that tells her story by spying on her neighbors and ends it by reading a book (although she selects *Chinese Cookery* instead of *Religio Medici*).[7] Similarly, Leonora Eyre in *The Sweet Dove Died* encounters the men who will be, respectively, the agents of her nemesis and her salvation, James and Humphrey Boyce, when she faints from the excitement of bidding for a Victorian flower-book at an auction. *Quartet in Autumn*, too, starts with an excursion to a library. Letty Crowe desperately searches for books to help her cope with the onset of old age. When she is unable to find such works, she engages in an astute critique of modern fiction and its lack of interest in the older generation, especially in single, childless women of advanced years. Finally, Emma Howick of *A Few Green Leaves* has moved to the community where her mother owns a cottage to undertake an anthropological study of village life, but abandons the role of researcher in order to become a writer of novels.

Although these women appear otherwise to have little in common, they share one crucial characteristic: their view of the world is informed (or perhaps *deformed*) by their readings of literature. Leonora has modeled her looks, poise, and style after the elegant heroines of Elizabeth Bowen's novels, without perceiving the sense of frigidity and repression that chills the air around women like Cecilia Summers in *To the North*. Letty has subsisted on a rich diet of romantic novels and biographies, and her tendency to seek consolation in fiction, rather than in human intercourse, has made her a lonely, saddened woman. Emma of *A Few Green Leaves* is likewise burdened by her literary heritage, although it is her mother's ambitions that have adversely influenced her view of the arts. Fearful of sharing the sad fate of Thomas Hardy's wife, Emma is instead doomed to repeat the mistakes of Austen's heroine, after whom her mother named her.

The question that arises in discussing the fates of Emma, Leonora, and Letty is that of the role of reading in the *sentimental education* of Pym's excellent women. Is reading good for women, Pym asks in these novels, or does literature instead deplete their ambitions, instilling in them expectations of bright happiness that are of necessity dashed by the dire facts of experience? And, even more importantly, is reading an act that connects self and world for the woman reader? Or does it instead cause a disjunction between the mind and reality, trapping the faculties of reason in a harmful, parallel sphere of romantic fantasy?

It can be argued that the problem of reading preoccupied Pym during her entire writing career. She considered its implications in each of her books, beginning with *Excellent Women*, whose heroine protests that she "is not at all like Jane Eyre" (7), and concluding with *A Few Green Leaves*, whose protagonist rebels against the complex literary associations of the name Emma. To judge from Leonora Eyre in *The Sweet Dove Died* and Letty Crowe in *Quartet in Autumn*, however, Pym's answer seems abundantly clear. Their reading has served them ill, since as a result they expect reality to conform to their desires, and they romanticize rather than rationalize their predicament. However, in the case of Emma Howick the situation is rather more confusing. She has chosen science instead of literature, and she lacks neither critical discernment nor common sense. Thus, the obvious gap in her reading causes her to behave like Austen's Emma, and she commits similar acts of superciliousness. It seems that Emma Howick could have used a session with an improving book, which would have disclosed to her eloquently the dangers of looking down on others as if from a great height and remaining aloof from her community. As it is, she has to become the protagonist in her own drama of misplaced affection, rejection, humiliation, and reconciliation in order to share the insights of her namesake.

A Few Green Leaves demonstrates that the interrelated topics of reading, romance, and redemption are for Pym in turn tied to the notion of the writer's responsibility towards her readers. Her task consists not only in representing the complexities and subtleties of reading, but in revealing the many ways in which readers misinterpret the relationship between life and literature. Thus, Emma's story shows that although the contemplation of literature refines and intensifies our response to the world, it cannot serve as a stand-in for experience, but only as an aid to character formation (*Bildung*). Thus, the question of whether Emma Howick's having studied *Emma* would have helped her to avoid the pitfalls of her behavior, must in the end be answered in the negative. Irrespective of her erudition, Emma must undergo her own education of the heart, a process through which literature can assist her, but from which it cannot save her.

The reason why reading cannot replace experience can be found in any number of Pym's novels. For while her excellent women often make reference to works of literature that might tell them the truth about their situation, they either unintentionally or deliberately misread these texts.[8] As a result, they remain unaware of their predicament until it is nearly too late. However, Pym often shows her heroines to be poor readers not to poke fun at their limitations, but to remind us that while reading is necessary to our survival, misreading is a fact of existence, too, conditioned as our infinite varieties of interpretation are by our individual yearnings for wish-fulfillment.

In addition, the writer's role, as Pym conceives it, is to outline the possibility of transcending the disjunction between expectation and disillusion. As mentioned before, Pym's last stories conclude on a note of optimism, offering a silver lining of dignity recovered and paradise regained, after the cloud of misguided confidence in the powers of literature has been lifted. However, the reader can almost miss the faint-sounding bell of hope in the first of these final works, *The Sweet Dove Died*, whose ending shows the heroine, reduced in stature, forced to rely on the company of others to divert her from her lost sense of identity. But it is there, in the very last sentence of the book, when Leonora Eyre suddenly realizes that the flowers her suitor Humphrey brings her are to be appreciated not for their beauty, but for the devotion that prompts his offering. Her insight that aesthetic representation has meaning only when it issues from the springs of affection helps her to restore her impaired self. For the first in her life, Leonora understands that she will find self-affirmation not as she has before, in the tributes exacted from others as a matter of course by the sheer force of her character and good looks. In the future, she will rely on the liberal gesture of generosity bestowed on her by others out of the kindness of their hearts. It is at this moment that she surmounts the sterile isolationism of her former existence, leaving behind the cold realm of aesthetic *Ersatz* (symbolized by the flower book she purchases at the beginning of the story) and heading for life in all its full richness (the flowers).

Leonora, despite her lack of affinity with Letty and Emma, who seem altogether more human, thus represents another take on the problem of the woman reader. She is the purest aesthete of all of Pym's misguided readers, not so much a Cecilia Summers in Bowen's *To the North*, but a modern-day Isabel Archer of James's *Portrait of a*

Lady, who equates beauty with morality and pleasing appearances with profundity of character.[9] It is no coincidence that the American Ned, Leonora's rival for the affection of her young friend James, informs Leonora that she should have read Henry James because "he is so very much *your* kind of novelist."[10] James's novels point to the tragic fallacy of Leonora's reading, which, like Isabel Archer's in *Portrait of Lady* and Catherine Sloper's in *Washington Square*, mistakes aesthetic pose for true worth. In this way Pym indicates that Leonora's greatest weakness, akin to that of James's Isabel, is her condescension, which prompts her to appraise others mercilessly while failing to look at herself honestly. Leonora's inability to see that her relationship with James resembles the bind that ties her friend Meg to young, gay Colin proves to be her downfall, and she never truly recovers her former self-sufficiency after James leaves her for Ned. Only later does Leonora realize that beauty in the abstract signifies nothing and that objects matter not in themselves, but only when they are given as the result of love and cherishing. It is at this moment that she finally begins to perceive the true, quiet meaning of things hidden behind the signs.

It has been noted that *The Sweet Dove Died* is Pym's most disconsolate novel, lacking even the warm glow of sympathy that tempers the cold process of growing old in *Quartet in Autumn*,[11] and that Ned is a true villain, while Pym's other leading men are only helpless and pitiful. However, there is a reason for this sudden extremism on the part of the author. For in *The Sweet Dove Died*, Pym finally spells out what she had only playfully alluded to in her former novels, *Jane and Prudence*, *A Glass of Blessings*, and *An Unsuitable Attachment*. This is the dark side of misreading in the case of a woman who has succeeded in making her life comply almost perfectly with her limited grasp of romance, and whose disillusionment must therefore equal the full, cruel extent of her self-deception before she can be allowed to find peace. The moment of disillusionment, always a focal point in Pym's novels, here forms the absolute, raw climax of the story, whose intensity is foreshadowed in the vaguely violent title of the novel.

The Sweet Dove Died, an obvious counterpart to *Some Tame Gazelle*, as both titles are taken from poems describing the *Ersatz* love of pets, explodes in the wild flow of tears Leonora sheds in front of her friend Meg, to whom she has hitherto condescended. Leonora's outburst is completely out of character, not only because of the pride she has invested in her customary composure, but because Pym's heroines as a rule do not break down in front of others. There is no other scene in Pym's oeuvre as embarrassing (without being funny) as Leonora's collapse, just as there is none as tense as the one that precedes her crisis of nerves, her last encounter with Ned.

Ned's ruthless destruction of Leonora's carefully constructed self-image is the most uncharitable act committed by a human being upon another in Pym's novels, unless one counts Leonora's own cold-hearted expulsion of Miss Foxe. Lenora gets rid of the elderly gentle-woman when she decides in James's absence that she would prefer to have the young man with her always. Thus, she asks Miss Foxe to leave even before her lease on the little apartment she rents on the top of Leonora's building expires. For such a refined person, Leonora's instincts are remarkably barbarian and unscrupulous. She does not like Miss Foxe, so out she goes; she likes James, so in he moves. Leonora fails to take into account that such behavior will not remain without its dire consequences and that she will in the end have to pay a price for her cruelty towards the many people she has hurt in the pursuit of self-gratification.

Leonora's failure here is double. She not only forgets conveniently to examine her own feelings, she dismisses the needs and motivations of her fellow human beings as well. Since Leonora has lived for a long time on the verisimilitude of emotions, she is unable to tell the difference between real and imagined love not only in herself, but also in others. The aesthetic posturing she has copied from her literary hero-ines has served her well in establishing a distance between herself and the people around her, but also prevents her from realizing that her superiority is not her own creation entirely; she needs the complicity of others in order to play her chosen role as an object of adoration. Only when that complicity is taken from her does she see that her independence has been an illusion all along.

Leonora's admission of her hubris and fall comes in the form of the unromantic, unattractive, wracking sobs she cries in the presence of Meg, although she soon pulls herself together and takes up her cus-tomary habit of observing and judging others: "Leonora, now recov-ering her composure, was beginning to be conscious of how ridiculous Meg looked, kneeling there on the floor, even when she was voicing such noble and unselfish sentiments as the need to accept people as they are and to love them whatever they did" (*SDD*, 202). However, the balance of power has been upset, as becomes obvious at the end of the scene, when Meg, for the first time in her life, rebukes Leonora for her conceit "with a faint air of superiority" (203).

More than Meg's well-intentioned but confused message of human forgiveness and tolerance, though, it is Ned's casuistic, even insensi-tive allusion to the tragic ending of Henry James's novel of growth *Washington Square* that exerts a bracing, beneficial effect on Leonora.

Ironically, the very inappropriateness of Ned's reference to a story that features two people whose hope for marriage is thwarted and who meet again in middle age startles Leonora into a new awareness of the ludicrous nature of her situation. For there can be no question that the mature, educated Leonora ever loved James Boyce the way that young, innocent Catherine Sloper loved Morris Townsend, nor that she will dedicate the rest of her life to the memory of his betrayal as does James's heroine. In contrast to Catherine, who suffers penance in self-imposed isolation, Leonora realizes that her salvation lies in companionship, and instead of mourning in seclusion, she begins to look more kindly upon Humphrey's attempts to court her.

Leonora's new self-understanding also allows her to read more successfully the truth of the emotions directed at her. Her simple statement that "the only flowers that were really perfect were those . . . that had the added grace of being presented to oneself" (208) reflects the monumental change that has taken place in Leonora's understanding of her image as perceived by others. The implicit reference to Humphrey as a worshipper at a shrine is mitigated here by the fact that Leonora no longer considers herself an icon in that shrine, as she did before, but reduces herself to—just herself. No longer wishing to style herself as an object of male adoration but to be seen as a subject in her own right, Leonora puts an end to her former processes of self-mystification. Her intention to stop her aesthetic self-celebration signals her transition from the smooth realm of fantasy to the rougher, more honest territory of reality-testing.

Pym's sophistication as a novelist is evident in her depiction of Leonora's belated apprenticeship in the art of self-appraisal. Unlike her predecessors, Prudence Bates (*Jane and Prudence*) and Ianthe Broome (*An Unsuitable Attachment*), who are doomed to repeat their mistakes or to live with them indefinitely, she is permitted to discover her failures of perception and achieve a sort of redemption. In the end, Leonora's experiencing and coming to terms with her newfound sympathy for human frailty allows her to cut the chains of literature—"the thread of [her] own hand's weaving"—that once bound her to a preconceived notion of her life. And in a final contrast to her literary peer Catherine Sloper, whom James at the conclusion of *Washington Square* shows trapped in a web of self-defeat, symbolized by the "fancywork" to which she devotes her life,[12] Leonora's roaming reader's eye embraces the fullness of existence. Flowers, the symbols of love and nature's continuation, surround her in her last glorious vision of herself, and signal the warm dawn of rebirth from the cold ashes of grieving.

The exuberance of a beautiful woman surrounded by radiant, fecund creation remains unmatched in Pym's late opus. Life unfurls once more in her work, but this time only as a "few green leaves," a handful of muted autumn gleanings from Leonora's once iridescent summer garden. Consequently, the two novels that follow *The Sweet Dove Died* are more moderate in tone and intensity, though *Quartet in Autumn* has been hailed as Pym's masterpiece and is certainly superior to *The Sweet Dove Died* in many respects. However, the Booker Prize–nominated story of four people coping with retirement, infirmity, and death could not have been written were it not for *The Sweet Dove Died*, finished some four years before Pym began work on *Quartet in Autumn*, allowing her to achieve a sense of closure. Leonora's story, more tragic than those of Pym's previous heroines, obviously provided the author with a kind of catharsis and enabled her finally to kill off the sweet bird of her youthful infatuation with literature that had been the focus of her writing career to that point. The dove that dies is, of course, an image of lost innocence, the alienation of a reader from the naïve belief in the fairy tale–like spells woven by literary fantasy. Whereas Pym's earlier novels depict her excellent women as persisting in their attempts to reconcile the pet love of their romantic dreams with the sad realities of life, the women of *Quartet in Autumn* and *A Few Green Leaves* have surrendered these objects of their affection. Letty Crowe, Marcia Ivory, and Emma Howick are women after the fall, and they have left behind the world of magic wish-fulfillment to fight the very real battle of survival.

Seen within a continuum, *The Sweet Dove Died* is a novel about a woman reader who experiences the end of her incongruous love for literature, while *Quartet in Autumn* is the story of a woman trying to survive this loss.[13] In this novel, Letty Crowe, the central protagonist in the group of four, notes that representations of single, elderly women like herself are conspicuously absent from contemporary narratives. As a result, she decides to abstain from the consumption of fiction, as others would from an addiction, displaying all the classical symptoms of disorientation and withdrawal that a person who has sworn off drugs would.

Although Letty's discovery is touched on lightly in regard to her reading habits, the ironic tone with which her insight is delivered paradoxically hints at the terrible implications of her realization. The ambiguous statement that "the position of the unattached, unmarried ageing woman is of no interest whatsoever to the writer of modern fiction"[14] implies that art masks the indifference of society. Moreover, it suggests that the blame for the neglect of spinsters past their middle years must be laid at the door of fiction itself, since this genre, in contrast to biography, has chosen to ignore old age and chronology in favor of youth. Letty, who seeks "pleasure and possible edification" (*QIA*, 3) from books, is portrayed as the sad victim of the single-minded celebration of immaturity in literature, a casualty of the romantic novel that no longer provides her with the possibility of a positive and uplifting identification. As a result, she is lost to reading, turning instead to television and shopping.

Pym's own changing opinion about the significance of reading in female lives surfaces in the finely voiced moral criticism inherent in the portrait of Letty, who once "hopefully filled her Boots Book Lovers library list from novels reviewed in the Sunday papers," but has since turned to true stories (3). Whereas Pym's earlier excellent women appear content with the solitary and often purely aesthetic enjoyment of *belles lettres*, this later protagonist seeks in reading a shared and ethically meaningful experience. Letty has not read Tolstoy or, like her colleague Marcia Ivory, has consigned the great writers to oblivion. Marcia too looks not for pleasure but for advice and identification in literature, and when she cannot find either, begins to collect informative pamphlets for senior citizens instead.[15]

The sense of literature's betrayal is even clearer in the story of Letty's colleague and double, Marcia Ivory. This poor emaciated woman dies "unreachable inside a room," and although she has kept an anthology of poetry on her bedside table, "there [is] no sense of that little room becoming an everywhere, in the fantasy of an earlier poet" (172). This sad statement of affairs seems to indicate that Marcia, and with her, the author, has closed the door on literature and abandoned her implicit trust in the house of fiction as a place to contemplate eternity. The open-eyed rejection of one of the most precious tropes of poetry—the poet's ability to create a private sphere of bliss to the exclusion of reality and death—seems a reassessment of Pym's earlier conception of the literary imagination that erects a lasting refuge against unhappiness and mortality. Pym here shows that despite the comfort that poetry and prose may offer, many die unconsoled, and the tragedy of their lives remains unrelieved by the uplifting effect of fiction: "No fragment of poetry from long ago lingered in Marcia's mind" (172).

Marcia's death is rendered even more tragically absurd because her progressive (and possibly mental) illness leads her to amass consumer products in a strange parody of a serious literary collector. Marcia orders and classifies her food supplies and plastic bags as others treat books on their library shelves. Thus, she has not really given up reading, although her choice of literature has taken an odd turn. She takes home pamphlets, and looks to consumer products and their messages for spiritual sustenance. So important is the reassuring influence they exert over Marcia that she abstains from eating into her store of goods. She hoards the items she has purchased as would a bookworm with rare and precious editions, refusing to touch them for fear of spoiling the beauty of her arrangement. Marcia's other colleagues share similar, consumer-style habits. Edwin browses through the list of church festivals, as if he were bargain-hunting for the one that offers him the best client "service" (92). Meanwhile, Norman treats the British Museum library as he would a department store, taking advantage of its free warmth and comfort. Letty, it is explicitly stated, brightens at the thought of going shopping, and regards the sale on the day after Boxing Day as the highlight of her Christmas (90).

Marcia's behavior indicates that she and Letty have more in common than one might at first assume, given the contrast in their respective personalities, and Pym reiterates their affinities in the similar résumés she created for her protagonists in her notes for *Quartet in Autumn*.[16] Both women were born shortly before World War I to middle-class parents. Neither has friends or marries, although Letty has lived a more interesting life, working in a ministry and suffering through an affair with a married man. Letty expects only to have to take care of her aging relatives whereas Marcia, abandoned by the young man she loved as a girl and finding only menial employment, lives with her mother until the latter dies. The difference between Marcia and Letty, as Pym notes in her outline, is that Letty has a clear recollection of the past while Marcia's is confused. Along with Letty's capacity to remember goes a love for literature, nurtured in public school. She has enjoyed reading most of her life and still knows quotations.

However, Letty's recollections are mostly of a sentimental and literary nature, and she shuns contact with others because she prefers the pleasures of solitary reading and remembering to the present actuality of human companionship. By contrast, the recalled past of Marcia, who has suffered an early disappointment, had "an experience" on Clapham Common, and must cope with the after-effects of an invasive operation, is deeply traumatic. The fact that Marcia's mind is beleaguered by the horrors of actual experiences rather than the recall of aesthetic titillation points to Pym's mature insight that pain and suffering might in certain cases render a person momentarily or even lastingly unreceptive to the edification and enjoyment of literature.[17] Thus, Marcia has no recourse to the consolations that literature might proffer, and her death is more desperate than any other moment in Pym's novels. What Marcia lacks is the sense of self-awareness that can only be learned from literature, and she dies unenlightened about the meaning of her existence.

By contrast, Letty's unhappiness stems from her heightened sensitivity as a reader of literature, since her perusals have led her to agonize over whether hers is a life misspent. Her keen sense of missed chances, intensified by the study of books, causes Letty deep suffering. Because of her upbringing on the class-conscious romances of the twentieth century, Letty judges life and people in terms of suitability and affinity of race and class, a tendency of character that has often led to her exclusion from society. When the friendly African owner of her house, Mr. Olatunde, and his family invite her to supper, Letty instinctively withdraws into her shell, thinking "hopelessly" but emphatically that she cannot accept because "we are *not* the same" (67). Always hesitant to take chances, she remains "on the outside," seeking refuge in the well-ordered, cold security of Mrs. Pope's dwelling.

Only when Letty realizes that she has made a poor choice in exchanging the "vitality and warmth of Mr. Olatunde's house" for the "bleak and silent" unfriendliness of Mrs. Pope's residence (77) does she begin to feel more acutely the need for change. Having taken leave from work, she is free to consider the past developments that have brought her to her present state of "useless retirement" (124). Unable to concentrate on the "serious reading" she intended to do (113), Letty has ample time to contemplate the many ways in which she thinks she has "failed." At the same time, other people begin to fail her; her colleagues neglect to contact her, and her friend Marjorie reneges on their plans for a shared retirement when she falls in love with the vicar in her home village. In Letty's state of bereavement, the news that Marcia has died and that Marjorie's clergyman has left her for another woman represent welcome opportunities to make herself useful and to renew the bonds of friendship. Letty generously forgives the people who have hurt her and begins life anew. She insists on seeing life as an opening of doors to other and more exciting rooms than the one she formerly occupied.

Thus, the education that Letty has received from reading novels does not seriously betray her. Although she has misused literature in the past as a means of emotional escape, it has nonetheless trained her in the capacity to probe and test her resources of reason and sensibility. For example, Letty's abilities of perception, honed by fiction, enable her to doubt the wisdom of the union between her friend Marjorie and David Lydell, since he is several decades Marjorie's junior and a man for whose favor another, more determined woman fiercely competes. When Marjorie calls Letty telling her of his treachery and inviting her once more to come live at her cottage, Letty reacts in characteristic Pym fashion. She sees herself, in a sudden burst of humor, as another, perhaps more "ludicrous" Emma, who gladly indulges Marjorie's "romantic speculation" and advances her friend's need for amorous dalliances (218).

Letty's literary training in the school of literary decorum puts her in good stead in this respect. It aids her in weathering periods of personal loneliness and prevents her from feeling resentment at others' lack of generosity. This is why, at the end of her life, she is able to choose among several different options. Nonetheless, her assertion "that life still holds infinite possibilities for change" (219) is a brave one, made by a woman whose horizons of confidence are far wider than one would expect the limitations of her life to allow.

Letty's literary fantasy in *Quartet in Autumn* wherein she conceives herself as the facilitator of new and fortunate alliances thus represents an ending just as upbeat as Leonora's burst of confidence in *The Sweet Dove Died*. However, given Letty's advanced age and limited means, her heroic transformation is even more touching to observe than that of Leonora, who is, after all, wealthy and still in her prime of life. In addition, the decline that Letty suffers before her triumph is not so much conditioned by a misreading of literature (as it was for Leonora) as by literature misrepresenting (or not representing) her. Although Letty has in the past been guilty of treating literature as a refuge from the unpleasantness of her existence, she realizes in the end that (modern) literature can provide no substitute for the reality of human experience and the forging of relationships—in particular because it fails to speak to the problem of how to overcome the isolation of unattached old age. After Letty understands that she has to seek counsel outside the realm of contemporary romantic fiction, she looks for it in her own resources of good sense and understanding, which have been honed by years of reading a literature that has since gone out of fashion. To her surprise, Letty finds that these resources give her the fortitude to face the facts of her existence. Thus Letty's ability as a reader inclines her in the course of time to a tough practice of self-examination. Because of the absence of appropriate reading matter to aid her in her quest for self-improvement, Letty, in contrast to Leonora, appears more sinned against than a sinner.

Unlike Leonora, who reads novels that could reveal her moral disability to her if only she read them properly, Letty seeks but is unable to find literature that enlightens her about the nature of her late crisis of conscience. However, as she learns to draw wisdom not only from texts, but from the rich *context* that is human life, she finds greater contentment as a reader. Her parting vision of herself as a modern-day Emma, all the more startling since Letty has perhaps not read

Austen in a while, turns a book that at first seemed about the death of reading into a tribute to the unimpaired powers of the literary imagination. Also, Letty's gallant determination to see limitless scope where others would only find constriction anticipates the leap of faith about to be taken by another Emma. Her trust in the future bodes well for the heroine of *A Few Green Leaves*, who will also end her story with the promise of a fresh start, envisioning a self-expansion that transposes her from the realm of reading to that of writing.

If reading is indeed the activity that conditions women into colluding with the male establishment that represses them, as some writers have disconcertingly proposed,[18] then Emma's graduation from reading to writing represents an important step towards personal and artistic independence. As such, it signifies Barbara Pym's own newfound confidence as an author: her heroines no longer rely solely on the support of literature produced by others. It at first appears that Emma of *A Few Green Leaves* will join the ranks of women whose hopes for happiness are dashed by literature. Named after the Jane Austen heroine who suffers from misapprehensions about her seemingly invincible powers of perception, she inadvertently copies the latter's behavior. Disregarding the kind attentions of the neighboring vicar Tom Dagnall, Emma instead pursues Graham Pettifer, a man she once loved but has only reencountered as an image on television. Like her namesake, whose pretense prompts her to look for a suitor outside of her immediate circle, Pym's Emma, on account of her anthropological studies that demand she remain impartial, refuses to participate in the life of the village where she has recently settled. However, in the course of her story Pym's latter-day heroine is prompted to abandon her reserve, deciding in the end to be friendly to the kindly man who courts her and to write a novel rather than a scientific treatise. Suspending the activity that has kept her from becoming intimate with the inhabitants of the rural community, Emma, thanks to Tom, contemplates creating a work of fiction that will bring together his interest in the past, hers in the future, and the two of them as lovers.[19]

Thus, *A Few Green Leaves* is, despite its sad undertone, Pym's most utopian novel. Abandoning the severity that in other stories had caused her to represent the carving out of a free space as a flight from social responsibility, Pym here grants women their own sphere of artistic and individual activity. Remembering perhaps Virginia Woolf's famous plea for the necessity of a haven for the creative woman, Pym allows Emma a room of her own, where preoccupation with literature neither destroys nor mars her chances of contentment. Instead, Pym predicts that writing will complete Emma's fulfillment as a human being, forming the foundation of her relationship with Tom as well as fortifying her position in society. This move is, of course, highly symbolic, signifying Pym's own rebirth in literature as her life was in actuality waning. Pym wrote *A Few Green Leaves* while she was dying from cancer, but the sad elegiac quality of the work is relieved by the many references in the novel to life and work continuing. It seems as if, having come to terms with loss and death in *The Sweet Dove Died* and *Quartet in Autumn*, the author was now free to turn her attention to thoughts of continued fame and her afterlife in the minds and memories of readers to come.

Quartet in Autumn in particular lays out the reason why the incitement to writing in *A Few Green Leaves* is not only an idle trope, but provides a valuable hint as to what kind of novels Emma will be writing. In the experience of her protagonist Letty, Pym points to real, acute lack: the absence of any kind of depiction of the unattached, biologically unproductive, aging females of the middle classes, as Anita Brookner describes them, in the contemporary literature Pym perused. Knowing full well the terrible causes and effects of erasure, which she herself suffered as a rejected writer between 1961 and 1977, and as an unmarried, older woman, Pym changed her line of attack. Instead of merely testing the moral capacity of her protagonists to resist the seductions of romantic make-believe, as she had done in her earlier works, Pym in *The Sweet Dove Died*, *Quartet in Autumn*, and *A Few Green Leaves* also examines the ethics of contemporary literature. When she finds in particular its treatment of middle-aged and senior women readers wanting, she bears powerful testimony to the feelings of disillusionment plaguing a neglected stratum of society. It is gratifying to think that Pym's legacy is indeed being honored even today, and that her late novels are still lauded as compelling portrayals of old age for contemporary writers to emulate in the twenty-first century.[20]

The line of writing readers that Pym establishes by means of her allusions and associations thus does not end with the works she cites in her late novels. It continues on with the writers who still read Pym and hitch their star to the rich literary heritage she brings to bear in her fiction. The genealogy of readers/writers shows that the "scene of reading,"[21] an intensely debated issue in feminist theory, comprises one of Pym's central interests, and that the place of the (aging) woman reader in English literary history represents the underlying concern of the author in many of her works. Pym does not merely identify herself as a student of English literature, designating many of her heroines as college graduates in the humanities and sprinkling her works with references to the greatest works of the British canon. She also examines the position of women *in* and their attitude *towards* these socially, morally, and philosophically important works. For this reason, she serves as an inspiration to her own readers as to how to experience and enjoy literature as a woman.

Pym thus intuits the crucial role literature plays in the forming of a feminine ideology. As a result, her protagonists are shown in turns to be debating and combating its diverse tenets. It is in the execution of this task that Pym's importance for audiences of the twenty-first century lies. She outlines a compromise in the fight, still ongoing, about how to create a literature that serves the cause of female reading while remaining true to the values of aesthetic quality and authenticity that are the highest aspiration of the novelist. The novels of Barbara Pym treat the idealism of their protagonists' passion for letters—shared by and thus directed at their creator—with gentle irony. Therefore, even as Pym's humor reminds us that reading, or misreading, is one of life's necessities, it celebrates that very ambiguity as potential material to be exploited for the benefit of producing novels of the highest comic caliber. These are indeed the "infinite possibilities" of the text that illuminate the many subtleties of signification associated with the act of reading. They alert us to the fact that as lovers of literature we remain suspended between our ardent wish for security and the risky world outside, where antagonisms between desire and reality continue unresolved. Let us hope that we share Letty's courage in facing up to the uncertainty that is a life lived on the luminous promises of literature.

NOTES

1. The quotation used in the title is taken from the opening sentence of the novel by Anita Brookner, *A Start in Life* (London: Jonathan Cape, 1981). The novel appeared under the title *The Debut* in the United States.

2. Earlier novels by Pym also have open endings, in particular where her unmarried protagonists are concerned. Thus, we do not know that Mildred Lathbury (*Excellent Women*) marries Everard Bone until we read about it in the later work *Jane and Prudence*. Prudence's fate, too, is disclosed only later in *A Glass of Blessings*, where she has an affair with the heroine's husband, Rodney Forsyth, a misalliance that proves she persists falling in love with the wrong man. Likewise, *Less than Angels* ends with a mere musing by one of the characters, Rhoda Wellcome, about the possibility of a marriage between Catherine Oliphant and the mysterious Alaric Lydgate, but there is no indication that such a match will take place. Again, *No Fond Return of Love* concludes with Aylwin Forbes setting out to propose to Dulcie Mainwaring, whose infatuation with him leads us to assume that he will be accepted, though this remains a matter of speculation. Similarly, the doubts and criticisms of the guests at the wedding of Ianthe Broome and John Challow in *An Unsuitable Attachment* make one wonder about the future of their union. Even Wilmet Forsyth's

realization at the end of *A Glass of Blessings* that she has more reason to be contented than not seems conditional, depending as it does on her determination to remain vigilant in examining her faults and failures. It thus appears that Pym's novels on the whole resist traditional endings.

3. See Barbara Pym, *A Very Private Eye: An Autobiography in Diaries and Letters*, ed. Hazel Holt and Hilary Pym (New York: E. P. Dutton, 1984).

4. See also Deborah Ann Interdonato, "Reading Barbara Pym" (Ph.D. diss., City University of New York, 1996).

5. Since it would take up too much space in an essay to list all the writers and poets Pym perused and enjoyed, I refer the reader to the excerpted journals and correspondence of the author. Pym, *VPE*, shows that the author read and made ample reference to an impressive array of literature.

6. Barbara Pym listed these writers in a radio interview that was aired by the BBC in 1978. See "Finding a Voice: A Radio Talk," in *Civil to Strangers*, ed. Hazel Holt (London: Macmillan, 1987), 381–88.

7. Pym, *Excellent Women* (New York: E. P. Dutton, 1978), 20.

8. As mentioned before, Leonora Eyre is the most obvious poor reader in Pym's late works, but there are others to be found in earlier works. Jane Cleveland (*Jane and Prudence*) remembers incorrectly the novels of Charlotte Yonge and as a result finds life in a rural parish and her role as wife of a clergyman wanting. Similarly, Ianthe Broome (*An Unsuitable Attachment*) has only the haziest recollection of *The Enchanted April* and its warning of incongruous marriages and winds up marrying an unsuitable younger man.

9. Leonora Eyre, though not an excellent woman, has several predecessors in Pym's fiction who share her main characteristics, *e.g.*, her inability to see what lies beneath the surface of beauty, as well as her aestheticism and talent for home decoration and stylish housekeeping. She could be Prudence (*Jane and Prudence*) in middle age, since both women have many admirers, or Ianthe Broome in *An Unsuitable Attachment*, who prefers the devotion of a younger man to a relationship with a more suitable partner. Finally, Wilmet Forsyth in *A Glass of Blessings* anticipates Leonora's old-fashioned elegance and fecklessness, and her involvement with homosexual men.

10. Pym, *The Sweet Dove Died* (New York: E. P. Dutton, 1979), 200.

11. Diana Benet, *Something to Love: Barbara Pym's Novels* (Columbia: University of Missouri Press, 1986), 118.

12. Henry James, *Washington Square* (1881; New York: Modern Library, 1997), 248.

13. *A Few Green Leaves*, finally, is the tale of a woman reader's renascence as writer, created by an author who has, at the end of her life, come to terms with a new ethics of reading and tackles, in the last work she would complete, the question of the significance of female rereading and rewriting.

14. Pym, *Quartet in Autumn* (New York: E. P. Dutton, 1978), 3.

15. There are many ways in which Pym anticipates postmodern ideas about reading to include the perusal of all kinds of texts. Pym's protagonists "read" directories (Dulcie Mainwaring, *No Fond Return of Love*), pamphlets and labels (Mrs. Bone, *Excellent Women*), magazines (Catherine Oliphant, *Less than Angels*; Wilmet Forsyth, *A Glass of Blessings*), catalogues (Harriet Bede, *Some Tame Gazelle*), listings of church services (Dulcie), recipes (Mildred Lathbury, *Excellent Women*), and wine lists (Catherine and Alaric Lydgate, *Less than Angels*).

16. See MS Pym 33, Bodleian Library, Oxford (1973). In her notes for the novel Pym develops complete curricula vitae for Marcia Ivory and Letty Crowe. I am obliged to Anne Pilgrim for this information.

17. Letty also has trouble reading; see *QIA*, 116.

18. The novels of Anita Brookner contain many references to the culpability of romantic literature in conditioning women into passivity and submission. Apart from the opening of her first novel, *A Start in Life*, her very recent work, *The Bay of Angels* (New York: Random House, 2001) begins with an indictment of the persuasive powers of the literary romance and the fairy tale. However, Brookner blames not only fiction, but also the female consumer, who all too readily assents to the possibilities of self-deception.

19. Emma's story resembles that of Catherine Oliphant, the heroine of *Less than Angels*, who is also given the chance to alter the story that she had originally conceived for herself. However, in one important respect Emma differs from Catherine. Instead of winning a man's love because of her selfless devotion to him, as does Catherine, Emma falls in love with Tom because he has helped her to design a new life. Theirs, finally, is a union of true minds, based on a mutual give-and-take.

20. *Green Leaves* 7, no. 1 (2001) makes mention of contemporary authors inspired by Pym: Salley Vickers, Anita Brookner, Nancy Mitford, and Joanna Trollope. She is also compared to Elizabeth Bowen, Elizabeth Taylor, Penelope Fitzgerald, and Sylvia Townsend Warner, while Anne Tyler, Shirley Hazzard, Angela Huth, Jill Cooper, John Bayley, and many other modern writers have praised her in reviews and essays. See the introduction to this book for further discussion.

21. See, for example, Judith Fetterly, *The Resisting Reader: A Feminist Approach to American Fiction* (Bloomington: Indiana University Press, 1979).

Excellent Women and After:
The Art of Popularity
BARBARA EVERETT

BARBARA PYM'S SPECIAL QUALITIES AS A WRITER—HER IMMEDIACY, her social presence—conceivably attach themselves to the simple fact that she was a woman writer, that she wrote from the strengths and weaknesses deriving from the female place in society, especially (though not only) that of forty or fifty years ago. Holden Caulfield, the hero of *The Catcher in the Rye*, says somewhere that a book is good if you want to write a letter to the author after reading it. Of course, you can be quite a good, competent novelist, especially if you are male, without having this sense of social presence, of warmth and humor and amiability, coming through in your work at all.

But Barbara Pym had it. Her novels have such social grace—the freshness and modesty of good company, the sharp humor of the best gossip—that they can sometimes seem more wholly personal, even more directly from her own life, than perhaps they precisely were. She had this sociality as a writer, an acceptance of certain social ends of good behavior, of demure decorum and a reticent popularity, to such a degree that sometimes the apparent lack of impersonality perhaps made her vulnerable.

It is worth recalling that the whole great Modernism movement in literature, from *The Waste Land* onwards to the end of World War II (to date it loosely), was a defensive art movement. It grew out of mid- and late-nineteenth-century Symbolism, which in its turn had moved, in France especially, towards an elitist obscurity to defend the menaced arts from the great dominance in society of an industrial civilization that was essentially philistine. Similarly, it is instructive to remember a smaller and more local fact: Pym, in her heart of hearts, seems to have loved, let us say, John Betjeman's work more than Eliot's, and probably even more than Larkin's. She also clearly adored, and knew extremely well and with the original taste of an almost scholarly artist, the whole world of the minor Victorian poet. Her literary stance delicately and nostalgically harks back to the sheer unguardedness of Victorian or neo-Victorian poetry.

To all appearance, there is no nonsense of the Modernist mask in Pym. These are the fictions—so the books smilingly present themselves—of the unpretentious writing woman, whose vein flows just as charmingly as she talks. Her ambition in these simple stories is merely to please, to pass the time, to be popular. The tutelary spirits standing behind the first-published *Some Tame Gazelle* are those professionals of the 1930s, E. M. Delafield and Angela Thirkell, the first of whom has, in her modest way, retained the power to entertain. The smallness of existence in Delafield's very "Provincial Lady" (both place and class are significant) is matched, even if not reflected, in the dotty, timeless, unlocalizable distance of Pym's English village. But the very modesty of this approach possibly worked to Pym's disadvantage during the period when her manuscripts were being rejected. It also makes her too easy to dismiss now, even by those writers and critics who have no very marked or super-subtle literary sense.

Barbara Pym herself clearly valued and pursued the art that conceals art (the ancient tag is, of course, Horace on poetry). She achieved it, moreover, to the degree that a greatly gifted as well as sympathetic critic such as John Bayley can suggest that she is a writer impossible to criticize; we can only like or love her. (Milton, of course, described Shakespeare as warbling his native woodnotes wild.) Even Barbara Pym herself once remarked that when people asked her what her friend Philip Larkin was like, she could only reply, "like his poems." If we ask whether Pym was like her novels, I think the answer is, "Well, yes and no." Based on conversations and things he said in print, I suspect that Larkin himself was just a little shaken—not disappointed, just somewhat shaken in confidence—when Pym's journals came out as *A Very Private Eye*, to find that he hadn't known the whole person, that even his affectionate and admiring social sense of her had been dependent on the fictions, works that should perhaps themselves not be taken as completely artless. He met in the journals a complexity of messy experience, and later especially, a maturity of female tone: sophisticated, inward, dry, ironical, defeated, exasperated, independent, and professional. This voice wasn't quite identical with the voice of one of those "sweet girl-graduates" that she perhaps started out as, or pretended to be, and with whom she, up to a point, peopled her novels.

Similarly, Philip Larkin was indeed "like his poems." But he himself said in print that they were far from the whole of himself, as his later published letters and biography startled some of the unwary into discovering.[1] Pym's phrase doesn't quite meet the fact that it was only after fourteen years of friendly and loyal letter-writing that the poet could bring himself to meet her in person, this woman who was so obviously unassuming and agreeable.

Both Larkin and Pym took the Holden Caulfield approach and wrote a letter to the author. But the person each met was in some sense not the author. Shocks and mild astonishment awaited both, and awaited their readers, however constant and sustained the appreciative goodwill of all concerned. This is because the public is not the private, and an art is not a life. A writer who, accepting the female manners and social morals of her time, sets out to entertain, to be popular, may find herself tragically out of print for sixteen years, or (more comically) a cult.

In the same way, readers drawn together, perhaps in part by the curious likability of the writer they enjoy, reach a point at which they must dehumanize. That is, within the twentieth century, Modernism was largely right in its literary assumptions. I admire Eliot and Auden and Larkin (who was never as antimodernist as he seemed) more than I do, let us say, Betjeman—a gifted talent, but not a major figure like the others. Consonantly, I want to try to speak critically about Pym's books. By critically I don't mean adversely: I like and admire them all. I mean rather that I want to sidestep that affectionate reaction which points out, perfectly justly, that there is a Pym world that unites all the novels, and our primary job is to relish it and live in it. There is indeed a Pym world. Nobody saw and imagined and felt quite as she did, and it can be genuinely difficult to remember in exactly which novel this or that minor character or joke or meal occurs, they are all so good and so recognizably Pym. Clearly, the writer jotted down in her notebook vivid fragments of experience, each of which would revive as one of the hundreds of delightful mosaic-pieces in her work. The value of her fictions is this "very private eye," rather than their powerful mastery of narrative or giant range of lives.

All the same, the books differ. Robert Liddell, one of the very best of her critics as well as a lifelong friend, chooses to call the six earlier books, written before the rejection of the later-published *An Unsuitable Attachment*, "the canon." It is a useful and adoptable phrase. Of this canon, *Excellent Women* has always, I think, been the most popular book, outselling all the others in the 1960s. Pym's biographer and good friend, Hazel Holt, recommends that new Pym readers begin with this novel.

These various judgments are all worthy of real respect. But honesty makes me add that the popular *Excellent Women* has always been the Pym novel that I happen to like least, though I can reread it with unvarying admiration. The reason is not the relativism or meaninglessness of all critical judgments. It is that writing and thinking about writing are hard exercises because they reckon with those enormous and themselves respect-worthy values, Life and Art: things that must be brought together, but that resist fusion endlessly. I suggested earlier that even writers as gifted as Larkin and Pym may not have quite "known" each other by knowing each other's work. Put another way, the fact that they are professionals who keep diaries and write letters allows us to watch them recognize that there is always, in their calling and their living, a gulf to be crossed.

The Pym novels are always aesthetic constructs, not social events or talk; in other words, "the world of Barbara Pym" is always a series of interdependent but by no means identical worlds, as in a science-fiction theory. Moreover, in writing as in life, to be liked and likable, to be popular in fact, is not necessarily to be good—although a book, like a person, must be good enough to survive at all. Nor is the converse much safer, since boringness is unlikely to guarantee literary virtue. Conventions are useful but not necessarily wholly trustworthy. Mildred in *Excellent Women* is, along with the much trickier Wilmet in *A Glass of Blessings,* one of only two first-person narrators in Pym's novels. Likable and decent as Mildred is, these qualities do not necessarily endow her with a superior resemblance to the novelist herself, or make the book more *echt* Barbara Pym.

Excellent Women strikes me as the most accomplished of these earlier novels, the most admirably competent. But interestingly, it lacks certain qualities that are more wayward, more resistant to that splendid professional efficiency, yet are also more creative and idiosyncratic—a lack that gives us some sense of Pym's problems in attempting an art of popularity. The novel's predecessor, *Some Tame Gazelle,* is more brilliantly and dottily entertaining, and has a more intense and a more characteristically nostalgic charm. *Jane and Prudence* has solider, richer, and more lovable characters (more hateful ones, too). *Less than Angels* is funnier and cleverer. *A Glass of Blessings* has more complexity of vision and a darker, sharper edge. Even *No Fond Return of Love,* a plainly imperfect work, has a remarkable imaginative embodiment of the London suburban scene, while *An Unsuitable Attachment* has a first-rate cat and a wholly believable public library.

I am confining myself here to the earlier writing. The six earliest books of the canon are all individual and enjoyable works of art and of entertainment, and *Excellent Women* seemingly remains the most popular of them. But this popularity does not prevent it from having to be considered, like the rest of the canon, as probably minor art. It must strike a reader as minor in comparison with *Quartet in Autumn,* which claims consideration as a major work of art. It is not my wish to play from mere pretension with these terms "minor" and "major," but they seem necessary if we are to make serious distinctions.

Major novels are rare in any period. There are excellent and prolific talents of the last fifty or sixty years who have left behind bodies of successful work that are respect-worthy, yet that may not contain genuinely major fiction. A major novel, if lost, deprives its period of a work that speaks for its age, that translates the events and questions of its time into what Donald Davie calls in a poem the "terms of art"—a kind of rock-crystal formula that toughens with time instead of wearing away. *Quartet in Autumn* seems to me to solidify and clarify with every year that passes. Its successor, *The Sweet Dove Died*, is recognizable as work by a major novelist, but its artistic fineness is flawed by mood. It is too thinly social, too emotional, even (with all its coolness) too much a personal work, not largely humane enough. Yet it is brilliant, too. *A Few Green Leaves* is the ghost of a major novel, hauntingly achieved but faint in its effect. But this final phase of Pym's work, taken together, has a solidity and depth that go startlingly further than the delightful early fictions in the canon. In it, Barbara Pym has become a different kind of writer; within the conventions of popularity, she has achieved a toughness that could not have been easily predicted from the pleasures of the canon.

If one wanted to be severely, almost Leavisitely critical, one could see the whole of Pym's career as existing to produce the one major novel, *Quartet in Autumn*. In it, everything falls into place. It is extraordinary evidence of the writer's true and serious calling that she could produce this book when prevented from publishing not only it but indeed *any* of her books. In a sense it includes the earlier books in its perspectives. It is as though Pym had to write *Excellent Women*, enjoy its success, and see it diminish in the void of publication in order to write *Quartet in Autumn*, a fiction that captures its characters' small but intense sufferings and successes as in a ball of crystal. I mean that although no reader really wants to praise a book by making it supersede another, and although there is a charm and precision and sweetness and lightness in *Excellent Women* that *Quartet in Autumn* has lost, the greater depth and scale of the latter work does nonetheless make us perhaps question the popularity of the former— popularity taken not as a fact but as a standard.

These perspectives help us to see how the earlier book works. *Excellent Women* is good because it lightly establishes for itself a social ideal and lives up to it. It is popular in its well-mannered affability and charming willingness to meet its given audience half-way— perhaps even more than half. In this it contrasts markedly and self-correctively with the dreamy (though extremely funny) nostalgia, the poetic fantasy-past of *Some Tame Gazelle*. *A Very Private Eye* makes it clear that, though intelligent, shrewd, and observant, Pym was always an artist in the sense of reserving her attention for the subjects that really interested her. About the world in general and people in general, she could be strikingly innocent, sometimes even ignorant. All of her writing before *Excellent Women* gives some sign of her difficulties with the real, simply-not-comic political truths of the period. Even as late as *No Fond Return of Love*, she uses a pair of ex-refugees, the two Sedges—both presumably Jewish Austrians—as examples of the alienly vulgar and sham in a manner that can only be viewed as regrettable. This "little England" xenophobia makes a reader restively aware that Pym is approaching certain social borderlines. The area where Pym is safe and indeed wonderful as a writer is always socially somewhat restricted; in fact, it depends on its own restriction for its virtue. Hence the marvelous comic coziness of *Some Tame Gazelle* and the humor that derives from the clarity of its boundaries. The novel that followed it is territorially bounded, too.

Excellent Women was written nearly twenty years after its predecessor in publication was first begun. The novel's village, a form of what Auden called in a poem "the village of the heart," is now a fragment of a great metropolis, a part of Pimlico, a mile or so southwest of Mayfair. The novel maps out this gathering of streets and squares—the poor end, so to speak, of Belgravia—with considerable topographical alertness and fidelity. This is a London I still remember and recognize with real gratitude for its scenic truth. Even the Coventry Street Corner House, location of my childhood post-theater celebrations, is there. The sense of time is strong, too. These are the years immediately following the end of World War II, a period of thinness, of deprivation and shortages almost worse than those of the war itself. There is a meagerness here, a poverty of experience, that is finely used to act as context for the "excellent woman" herself (Mildred at one time forbears to remark that women like her "really expected very little—nothing, almost."[2] The sweet and zany, though far from witless, Belinda of *Some Tame Gazelle* has evolved into a heroine halfway opposite, who has never been in love, and who is engaged in coming to terms with a world whose naked edges (as Matthew Arnold reflects in *Dover Beach*) are always perceptible. Mildred is one of those wholly decent women whose role in life is, seemingly, to be made use of by people less principled and whose only freedom therefore is to be consciously an observer, one who lives and survives by biding her time. She is perhaps Pym's most Henry Jamesian character.

The world Mildred observes is made up of a clear system of interlocking circles. Nearest and most important to her is her church, St.

Mary's, where the Mallorys, brother and sister, are her friends. Neither is satirized. Julian is a good and upright man, even if Winifred is maddeningly, gauchely charmless and unworldly. But both are certainly characteristic of those "worthy but uninteresting people" with whom Mildred feels most at home. The novel starts at the moment, classic in fiction, at which newcomers and outsiders arrive to excite, disturb, and break up this little group. The Napiers, who move into the flat beneath Mildred's, are the Mallorys' antithesis, not uninteresting and perhaps not worthy. They are charm, they are glamor, they are the World and the Flesh, if probably not the Devil. They are presumably "the World" in a simple sense: Pimlico is to them a Belgravia manqué (and Belgravia was once and is still the preserve of the grandest English houses, perhaps even more so than the merely smart Mayfair). The Napiers belong to a world that seems as well-born as it is furiously, fluidly, and faithlessly sociable, whereas Julian and Winifred are merely domesticated gentlefolk, liable to be fooled by that merry widow, the false Allegra.

Uncomfortably though perhaps excitingly married, the Napiers span two worlds in themselves. Rockingham has spent the war as liaison officer to an admiral in Italy, a status recalled to our attention several times in the novel. In a gesture possibly learned from Frederick Wentworth in *Persuasion*, he brings into the story the exhilarating and liberating romance of the sea, of the Mediterranean. Mildred's narrow imagination is excited by new perspectives, just as she and Rocky, at one point, amiably share a branch of mimosa that rapidly withers. Helena in her turn is a New Woman, even an early feminist. She needs and wants a profession, detests housework and refuses to do it. Mildred dislikes her from the start and, up to a point, is frightened of her; nevertheless, Helena affects her just as much as Rocky does.

Helena introduces into the book, and into Mildred's life, the world of the intellect and of the professions. Rocky Napier awakens Mildred to the simple fact that the opposite sex can be the greatest possible fun. She may not be, strictly speaking, in love with him, but she is brought alive to the possibility of being in love with somebody. It is Helena who provides her with that somebody, that "Not Impossible He" (to misquote Crashaw): enter, as the unwilling object of Helena's animated pursuit, the severe Everard Bone. His name and his apparent nature are as bleak as the whole of postwar London existence is. But Everard is a churchgoer, even if his church is not St. Mary's, Mildred's home church. And as the novel gets under way, he humanizes steadily. Everard's intellectual male dignity and austerity soften considerably when he reveals an obvious gratitude to Mildred, whose churchy background has taught her how to take on elderly ladies as mad, even if as vaguely grand, as his own peculiarly difficult mother. "I could make it a Lent resolution to try to like him" (56), Mildred says, with her own impassive and serious humor.

Excellent Women handles with a beautiful deftness its own structuring, the steady *Bildungsroman* expansion of poor quiet Mildred's small experience. The book develops through London rooms and houses, which multiply outwards like the city itself. Mildred's modest top-floor flat, over another flat and then ground-floor offices, is at first only paralleled by the vicarage and the church. But in succession, the story moves through jumble sales in the church hall, through interestingly various eating places, through meetings of the anthropologists in Bloomsbury. Julian and Rockingham are joined in the novel by William Caldecote, a man whose companionably clearheaded sterility enhances by contrast their and Everard's masculinity. William takes Mildred back to what is presumably his Whitehall office, just as she herself accompanies his sister, her old friend Dora, back to the rustic suburban school where the two women first met.

A memorial service at their school leads the always delicately reflective heroine to meditate on the relationship between maturity and childhood. "In a sense we all go far, don't we? I mean far from those days when we were considered brilliant or otherwise" (109). She adds a thought about the religiosity of the adolescent, sweetly "expecting something that never quite came" (111). Neither thought is irrelevant to the subtle ways in which the book works: the going far, the not arriving. Really, *Excellent Women* has a direct if ironic relation to the traditions of 1930s romance writing. Though she tersely denies being even remotely like Jane Eyre, Mildred probably is, all the same, a Cinderella, whom we, like the loyal Mrs. Morris, defensively wish well. We want to see her in a happy ending.

The book does travel towards just such an ending. It begins with the male churchwarden's genuinely impertinent categorization of the innocently enquiring woman as one of those nosy little females with time on their hands, and it ends with the three equally egoistic men— Rocky, Julian, and Everard—all lining up for some useful share of her company. However shallowly flirtatious, Rocky has made his preference plain for Mildred's calm kindness. Julian can now see "what flowers" are at his feet (212), and Everard has plenty of work to offer "a sensible person, with no axe to grind" (151). Even if we guess that, as a future novel will indicate, she will end as wife of the most honorably acceptable of the three, Mildred does not need to do so. She achieves what her three descendants in *Quartet in Autumn* much later also achieve—immediate freedom to be and to choose, thereby presenting a more realistic and feminist version of the Cinderella ending, which entails merely being chosen. No wonder the novel has always been relatively popular: it offers the sweet 1930s happiness of romance, of cozy fiction and of screwball comedy, set into circumstances of considerable originality and realism.

In *Jane and Prudence,* Jane nods off to Sunday afternoon sleep just as a reviewer in the newspaper she is clutching is describing this or that character in a novel as "emerging triumphantly in the round."[3] And it is a fact that the characters in *Excellent Women* are in their decorous way beyond the newspaper cliché. It is their being beyond cliché, their being the work of an individual artist, that gives the book its precise aesthetic value, and also perhaps its problems.

I have suggested that the novel has an open ending, which is unexpected for a romance so theoretically conventional. I suspect that Pym's habit of allowing characters to haunt future novels is another aspect of that heroic openness, that desire to inhabit cozy romance but to make it true, to open it up to the longer perspectives of real existence. There are secure social worlds on which Barbara Pym's novels plainly depend. These are without doubt touched with romantic snobberies, but the writer is regularly able to unmask them. The feeling of these worlds, but the ability to see through them, is surely at the heart of Barbara Pym's fiction, a position remarkable in itself and always nervous or fragile. Mildred's alternative church, St. Ermin's, is partly in ruins, a reflection of scenes that were familiar after World War II. Helena snorts, "Fancy having services in a ruin!" (*EW,* 87) and the reader may be tempted to echo Helena when shown in the churchyard "a little grey woman heating a saucepan of coffee on a Primus stove" (50). A little later, when fewer churches were still in ruins, *A Glass of Blessings* opens with a telephone shrilling in a church. Though the sound is perfectly ordinary, it perhaps haunted the writer (who had heard it herself) because it gave a comparable, though even more elusive, sense of her world's securities as fragile, as all too easily penetrable or dissolvable.

The "Barbara Pym world" takes its character from its obstinate prepossession for old securities that offer themselves in this world— the established Church, the class system, the professional honor of work, and, above all, love and marriage. All are vulnerable, surprisingly and comically prone to lapse, tending to confuse themselves and interpenetrate farcically and rather disturbingly: "Some of our jumble sale crowd would make splendid Commandos" (*EW,* 60); William Caldecote hates his change of office because "different pigeons come to the windows" (71); Julian receives his dismissal from a demonic Allegra Gray while holding a pair of ping-pong paddles in his hand;

when the visiting Archdeacon comes to preach, he says things that are "really quite abusive" according to Mrs. Bonner, who complains that the *Dies Irae* "ought not to be allowed here" (78–79). What sets these fictions far above the intransigently reactionary, women's-magazine, self-pleasing "popularity" of an Angela Thirkell (to be cruel and to keep away from the present), is the high originality in them of a creative imagination. Up to a point, Pym's books share this imagination, within a tacit political and national context of acceptances. Nonetheless, in these works, it shimmers and enriches and disturbs everywhere. *Excellent Women* looks from the outside like a love story and certainly gives the pleasure of romance. But the male characters are in a way as undesirable as the writer's men are always said to be, and their unsatisfactoriness is not just a matter of some writerly lack of skill. After all, Pym's women, her excellent women, are faulty in the same ways.

If these fictions beautifully balance romance and non-illusion, their temper is also poised in much the same way between kind attentiveness and the coolest of wit. Although Everard Bone may be the most marriageable, he is the book's hero rather in the sense that he is the shortest straw to be drawn. This is the reason, I suspect, that Pym has the habit—for which the always-to-be-attended-to Robert Liddell several times rebukes her—of telling us firmly that all the men in these stories conceived of as marriageable are "handsome," "good-looking." Their unimaginable male beauty is really a datum, a donnée, for what must be accepted as a given law of life here: specifically, the human propensity to think a mere gender or Other is beautiful, to need to believe that this one or that one is marvelous. It is an objectification of what are named "all the romantic ideals of the unmarried" in *Excellent Women*. Nor is this simply a detail from a prefeminist society, expendable when the state has withered away. Because she is a narrator, the "excellent woman" herself moves beyond spinsterhood to become the thinking and feeling individual. Her little romance reticently, even at moments helplessly, addresses itself to the question of what is to be done about indestructible yet inutile emotion and imagination. And yet the fiction never cheats, never symbolizes, never abandons the medium. It handles with real subtlety and tact the manner in which Mildred, like other characters through these comedies, comes to change her sharp mind about Everard and to breed a reciprocal warmth within him. She is like Letty, her less heroic, less definitive descendant in *Quartet in Autumn*, in that she clearly does see love as a necessary ingredient for marriage. Though Mildred really does not love anyone in this book, we can suppose that when she turns up married later in *A Few Green Leaves*, that grace will have mysteriously come to her.

Both Robert Liddell and Philip Larkin gently criticized Pym for letting characters turn up in later novels. It is true that this device seems related to the cozy and social side of the work, a side that might stay dangerously close to the pleasures of gossip, which is not quite art. I suspect that when characters had ceased to inhabit the center of a story, the writer allowed them that strong kindness, that social reassurance (even that "popularity") that she herself needed in the background of her novels. Elsewhere and later, characters are given those happy endings which the truth of her fictions could not allow *in situ*. Her role in this is not unlike that of the always-watchful Señor Macbride-Pereira, one of Pym's Borges-like stand-ins for herself as narrator, in the wonderfully oblique close of *No Fond Return of Love*, who "takes a mauve sugared almond out of a bag" and sucks it "thoughtfully, wondering what, if anything, he had missed."[4] The "excellent women" are observers, too. In short, although the term has come to mean a socially useful spinster, inside that useful spinster is an unsociable, unconcessive individual who makes sense of life on her own terms—terms that may have little to do with popularity. As William tells Mildred, "We, my dear Mildred, are the observers of life" (*EW*, 70).

It is the triumph of *Excellent Women* that it takes a modest, pleasing, more or less philistine form of entertainment that absorbed English readers in the first half of the twentieth century, when Pym herself was young, and retains its virtues while making a work of art out of it. Pym's later fictions go further and sometimes deeper in ways that show that they are all in some degree of difficulty. The poise that characterizes *Excellent Women* could be held in this exact form only for one novel. The important art of observation, for instance, returns pervasively, always letting into the fictions the light and darkness of more troubling territories. In *Jane and Prudence*, the morally ambiguous, though interesting, Jessie Morrow spies and pries, as does her patroness, Miss Doggett, while even the wholly delightful Jane mildly questions Prudence about her sexual life (which is, in fact, clearly nonexistent). *Less than Angels* brings together a novelist and an unhappy anthropologist, Catherine and Alaric (to me, two of Pym's most engaging characters), both professional observers; and one of the book's superb minor characters, the exquisitely funny Jean-Pierre, studies all English bourgeois culture from the outside. The whole story of *A Glass of Blessings* is Wilmet's late learning that people need to be looked at. She at first misjudges her entire world, whereas Dulcie in *No Fond Return of Love* almost leaves research behind, moving straight into the practices of a private eye—a very private eye.

An Unsuitable Attachment, which was to have followed *No Fond Return of Love*, should, of course, never have been turned down by the publishers. The novel has good things in it, but a reader can see in these two later works that Pym had come to a turning point in her writing. There is something too curious, too personal in Dulcie's detective work. The whole trip to Taviscombe, masterful as are some of its details, gets out of hand. In *An Unsuitable Attachment*, those essential pit-props of the writer's romance world—love and the Church—are losing their complex utility, even their credibility. Nowhere do lovers or priests seem less effectual, less potent. Throughout the earlier works and beyond, romance and churchiness act as vital focusing points for what is lightly adored and mocked, for the believed and the unbelieved, the ruined church with the cup of coffee brewing outside its walls. The elements exist here in "an unsuitable attachment," but the contradictory energies are slackening. The materials of *Excellent Women* have exhausted, surely, their simple comic formula.

I began this paper by judging that the late work, particularly *Quartet in Autumn*, has a power and depth that the earlier fiction does not possess. That power and depth can perhaps be defined as a knowledge of the artistic problems, which are also difficulties of living, that we have been considering here. Loneliness, isolation, inarticulateness enter the art of popularity in forms that are quite new. Letty and Marcia, Norman and Edwin are also "out of hand," and have as human beings exhausted the little that their society offers them. The book, which starts in a public library, gives us, with extraordinary depth and lightness, four human beings who do not and cannot constitute a society, let alone a romantic love story. And yet there is a kind of happy ending for all four, even if there is death in the happiness. Traces of something that undoubtedly would be called love pervade the story. Letty and Norman, like Mildred, gain their power of choice, their open ending to the novel. Though it would be too much to say that *Quartet in Autumn* is *Excellent Women* rewritten, it deeply depends on a questioning and absolute understanding of the earlier fiction by a writer herself certainly excellent, and as certainly and finely a woman.

NOTES

1. Philip Larkin, *Selected Letters of Philip Larkin, 1940–1985*, ed. Anthony Thwaite (London: Farrar, Straus & Giroux, 1992); and *Required Writing: Miscellaneous Pieces, 1955–1982* (London: Faber & Faber, 1983).

2. Barbara Pym, *Excellent Women* (New York: E.P. Dutton, 1978), 37.

3. Pym, *Jane and Prudence* (New York: E.P. Dutton, 1981), 60.

4. Pym, *No Fond Return of Love* (New York: E.P. Dutton, 1982), 261.

A Suitable Detachment: Barbara Pym and the Romance of the Library

HELEN CLARE TAYLOR

In THE NOVELS OF BARBARA PYM THERE IS ALWAYS A TENSION between the dominant culture's social categories and the female protagonist's elected, though often covert, resistance to these conventions. Dulcie Mainwaring and Mildred Lathbury, for example, efface themselves within the public sphere while retaining in private a critical eye and a detached, even aloof, independence. *Crampton Hodnet's* Jessie Morrow laughs to herself at the romantic floundering around her, while confident that she has chosen the better part. She does not need "compensation" for her single status.[1] In fact, critics such as Jean Kennard and Barbara Bowman have discussed these tendencies as subversive,[2] especially as they seem to preclude traditional romantic love. Most of Pym's heroines actively choose their single, and thus inferior, status; they prefer to be on the margins of life, observing with humor the foibles of others. This detachment also allows them to assess the world of work, in which they take a secondary role, preferring to find satisfaction in the life of the mind.

One common theme and setting in Pym's novels—romance in a library—exemplifies this narrative tension between the independence of the educated, unmarried woman and the blandishments, even diminishments, of love and marriage offered by the men she meets. Many of Pym's novels take place in and around libraries. Flirtations there seem to undermine her heroines' serious work of study or research, forcing a choice between the head and the heart. The male protagonist often attempts to divert the heroine's serious work within the library, which stands for her intellectual independence, towards himself, as if his presence is the only object worthy of her attention. Or a male character may request indexing or proofreading as a task undertaken as proof of affection. However, these male figures do not often disrupt the female characters' sense of self. It is important to recognize that Pym does not cast her characters as victims. While Janice Rossen recognizes Pym's perspective as feminist, she asserts that

Pym's library-haunting female characters "exacerbate their own dependence on the men by uncritically applying much of their knowledge and many of the skills they acquired in their education."[3] I want to argue, in contrast, that the motif of the library and encounters within libraries occupy a crucial space in Pym's fiction. The library, in fact, stands as a gendered paradigm for her protagonists' dislocation from conventional roles. As a backdrop for serious reading, writing, and research, repressive in its silence and austerity—associated, at least in Pym's days at Oxford, with male academics and spinster librarians—the library seems a place as foreign to romance as are many of Pym's heroines. Yet in her work love flourishes there. Rather than offering "compensation," the romance of the library provides a catalogue of options for the heroine to secure her intellectual independence. Furthermore, we can find antecedents of the library's key tropological function in documents Pym left describing her own early experience in libraries. There is a clear connection between the formative episodes of Pym's life and the choices she gives to her protagonists. A study of the role of libraries in her life and in her novels reveals a perhaps surprising significance.

Most novelists write down their observations for later transmutation into fiction. For Pym, however, it is not only the observed details that we find lifted from life to art. In her notebooks we also find crucial events and attitudes that inform the broader context of a writer's work. This is especially true of Pym's attitude toward love, and in her diaries we see her carefully analyzing and charting the progress of her own relationships and then using these analyses in her novels. It is thus fairly easy to connect characters in Pym's novels with their real-life models as described in the notebooks. As Hazel Holt reveals in *A Lot to Ask*, Pym herself acknowledged that Henry Harvey served as the model for the Archdeacon in *Some Tame Gazelle*.[4] Gordon Glover, with whom she was in love during the war, is represented as Fabian Driver in *Jane and Prudence*. And Richard Roberts, or "Skipper," contributed a great deal to the characterization of James in *The Sweet Dove Died*. Only the men Pym met during her service in the Wrens during the war fail to make it into a novel as a romantic lead, although the character of Rocky Napier seems to be based on Rob Long, the handsome flag-lieutenant whom she encountered in Naples, and the marriages of Wilmet Forsyth and her friend Rowena in *A Glass of Blessings* can be traced to their days with the Wrens in Italy.

Of the romantic encounters we find in Pym's diaries, the most influential for her fiction in general seems to be one that took place in the Bodleian Library during the early 1930s. This affair provided material that she used and reused for the rest of her writing career. Because of the setting for this tumultuous and influential episode in her life, I would argue, libraries in general, but most especially the Bodleian, achieve a lasting place in Pym's work not only as settings but as symbols of the possibilities of romance. For it was in the Bodleian that Pym's long attachment to her fellow student Henry Harvey began, and her diaries, with some entries even written while supposedly studying in the English Reading Room, note her visits to the library in the hope of seeing him there. As a consequence of this youthful adventure, life becomes art, and the Bodleian, along with other libraries and librarians, appears in her fiction as the background for both excitement and despair. Her characters Belinda, Prudence, Dulcie, Deirdre, Ianthe, and Barbara Bird can all recall romantic interludes associated with a library. Important episodes in *Crampton Hodnet, Less than Angels, Civil to Strangers,* and *An Unsuitable Attachment* happen while the protagonists are (or more accurately, ought to be) working or studying in libraries. The contrast between intellectual work and frivolous flirtation sums up the personal dilemmas facing Pym's female characters.

In June 1971, Pym wrote to Philip Larkin, who was about to go on an extended visit to Oxford, that "[t]he English Reading Room of the Bodleian has many sentimental memories for me. I can remember deliberately not going there for fear of seeing a certain person or to hope my absence would be noted."[5] Actually, Pym's diaries for 1933 and 1934 document her many visits to the Bodleian in hope of seeing Henry Harvey and his friends, Robert Liddell and John Barnicot. Most of her time at the library in the early part of 1933, at least as she represents it in her diary, seems to have been taken up with observing Harvey (or "Lorenzo" as she called him) and trying to get him to notice her: "Went to the Bod. [He] was there. Our gazes meet, and he half smiles. But it is a cynical sort of smile"; (*ALTA,* 37); or "Bod. in the afternoon, but I did no work. Lorenzo was there . . ." (*VPE,* 19). Much of Pym's behavior during this period might strike us as typical of a love-smitten teenager seeking attention in obvious ways: "I went to the Dictionary and looked up a word (an entirely fatuous word) becoz [*sic*] he was there" (20). Nonetheless, Pym seems to have genuinely read a lot while frequenting the Bodleian, as well as making specious parades of study. Her lifelong interest in literature indicates both breadth and depth in her reading.

Pym's initial crush on Harvey allowed her to develop the skill of finding out about people she didn't know (later to become an asset to the novelist as well as a subject for her fiction), in this case by getting a friend to look at Harvey's pile of books to find out his name. Their first conversation, as Pym recalled it, took place on the steps on the way out of the Bodleian:

> Oh ever to be remembered day. Lorenzo spoke to me! I saw him in the Bod. and felt desperately thrilled about him so that I trembled and shivered and went sick. As I went out Lorenzo caught me up and said 'Well, and has Sandra finished her epic poem? . . . .' (20)

This episode and another two weeks later, in which Harvey actually asked Pym out while standing on the library steps, represent the apex of the Bodleian's role in her affair with Harvey. It finds its way almost unchanged into *Crampton Hodnet,* when Francis Cleveland meets his love-struck student, Barbara, in the Bodleian by chance:

> Mr. Cleveland wandered through the Upper Reading Room, brushed aside the dark mysterious curtain leading to the Tower Room, and hovered indecisively by the bookcase where the dictionaries and encyclopedias were kept.
>   'Oh, supposing he comes in here,' thought Barbara Bird in a great panic. So great was her agitation that she hardly knew whether she wanted him to come in or not. She crouched in her seat by the radiator, with her fur coat around her shoulders, trying desperately hard to concentrate on her work.[6]

The tone of mingled fear and desire that Pym captures here in the novel is familiar to the reader of her student diaries. Barbara Bird's ambivalence reflects her doubt, as an intellectual and independent woman, about exchanging the safe haven of the ivory tower for the male-dominated world of sexual relationships. Francis Cleveland can comfortably combine his role as Barbara's academic tutor with his aspirations to become her lover; as a man he can accommodate both functions. For Barbara, however, who like her creator had gained significant academic success in becoming one of the few women at Oxford at that time, it is not so easy to achieve a balance or to maintain her equanimity. Again, the scene in the library stages the tensions imposed on Pym's women by the intrusion of romance into the life of the mind.

Despite its exciting beginning, Pym's relationship with Harvey, although it grew into a lifelong friendship, was never satisfactory for her. Their affair seems to have been sexual, but Harvey, who married someone else in 1937, was not as serious about Pym as she about him. He was, however, willing to take advantage of her library-fueled longings. In fact, he used the Bodleian as a place where he could leave notes for her, inviting her to tea with sex as the second course. On May 9, 1934, for example, we find the following entry in her diary:

> In the morning I worked hard in Bodley. . . . Then Henry wrote in German on some of my Milton notes *'Kommst Du—Ja?'* and a few other things. I went and he was extremely nice. But Jockie came in and caught us reading 'Samson Agonistes' [*sic*] with nothing on. (*VPE*, 39–40)

Apparently reading Milton can be an aphrodisiac!

Several diary entries describe Pym's reluctance to go to Harvey's lodging for tea because of the inevitable consequences. Whatever we might think of his treatment of the young Pym (and her willingness to be used by him), these episodes in the Bodleian affected her very greatly. Her recollection of them is mostly nostalgic, although their sexual aspect casts a troubling shadow that is also reflected in her work.

The young Barbara Pym's ambivalence about sex and its connection in her mind with Oxford's great library appears, as we have seen, in *Crampton Hodnet*, a novel written in the late 1930s but not published until after Pym's death. Of all Pym's library novels, its plot represents the most complete and obvious transferal of Pym's romance with Henry Harvey in the Bodleian into fiction. Pym casts herself in several different roles. She is the detached and sardonic Miss Morrow, the faded companion who does not participate in life's dramas but chooses instead to observe the follies of mankind from behind her seemingly meek demeanor. She is also Anthea Cleveland, the don's daughter in love with the arrogant and narcissistic Simon Beddoes, who is a version both of Henry Harvey and of Julian Amery, the Oxford student whom Pym met after she had come down from Oxford. Most importantly, we can see Pym in Barbara Bird, the young student who has a crush on her tutor and who works in the Bodleian, sighing over romantic poetry and hoping that he will take notice of her.

Hazel Holt comments in *A Lot to Ask* that in Pym's description of Barbara Bird she is showing us how she was "coaxed and persuaded" into a sexual relationship with Henry Harvey (48). Its beginnings in the rarefied atmosphere of the English Reading Room allow Barbara Bird to assimilate her romantic feelings for her tutor with the poetry she is studying. She would rather that her relationship with Francis Cleveland stay literary and nonphysical. It is, in fact, the Reading Room in the British Museum (for Pym another great British library) and the manuscripts in cases outside it that cause Barbara and Francis to declare their love for each other. Barbara is emotionally moved by seeing Milton's signature (Milton again!), rather than by the proximity of Francis, but in typical Pym style, love for great books and their authors leads her to imagine this feeling as love for a person. Later, Francis Cleveland admits to himself that his outburst has been affected by the British Museum Reading Room, saying to himself, "Everyone knew that libraries had an unnatural atmosphere that made people behave oddly" (*CH*, 106). When they are "behaving" rather than reading, Pym's characters become confused about their conventional social roles. Although Rossen finds Barbara Bird's recalcitrance "unconvincing" and a signal of Pym's immaturity,[7] I would argue that Barbara's lack of real passion, like that of other, later characters, denotes instead her desire for intellectual integrity. For her, the Bodleian is a refuge, a gendered haven in which she can feel safe in a romantic poetic affair. Outside the library she is uprooted from the life of the mind that the library nourishes. Ultimately Barbara Bird refuses to be dragged from the ivory tower into an affair of the heart rather than the head.

Along with the romantic longings experienced by these central characters, Pym includes other details about the Bodleian in *Crampton Hodnet*. Edward Killigrew, a rather waspish character with a formidable mother, seems to be drawn from elements of Pym's friend, Robert Liddell, known as "Jock," who, like John Barnicot, actually worked in the library. Hazel Holt draws our attention to a letter from Liddell in which he tells Pym that he has bought a leather jacket as a protection against "draughts and readers" (*ALTA*, 56). Killigrew describes his own leather jacket and his soft-soled shoes, which are just right for creeping around the library without being heard by the readers. They also enable him to overhear the shocking declaration of love made in the British Museum. His authoritarian position as librarian makes him rightly scornful of many of the dons and the students whom he encounters at work.

Liddell's experiences in the Bodleian, as well as Pym's, also inform the plot of *Some Tame Gazelle*, Pym's first published novel, which she began writing in 1934 and features her Oxford friends projected thirty years into the future. Pym, as Belinda Bede, the former Oxford student, is still in love with Harvey, as the Archdeacon Henry Hoccleve, even though he has married someone else. The Archdeacon reminds Belinda of his reading to her in the old days and Belinda even reminisces about the time that he read *Samson Agonistes*; this allusion to the scene represented in her diary entry quoted above in which Jock found her in bed with Harvey reading this same poem would have been a rather daring reference to her sexual relationship, immediately recognizable to the original readers of her manuscript, the friends who were fictionalized in this *roman à clef* (*VPE*, 39–40).

Robert Liddell, as Dr. Nicholas Parnell, has become Bodley's librarian, and his visits elicit great awe from the quiet English village in which the novel is set. Belinda is conscious of his noble position, but Dr. Parnell's comments about the Bodleian seem to undermine her sense of its greatness: " 'Of course we have central heating there now. . . . There have been great improvements in the last ten years or so. We also have a Ladies' Cloakroom in the main building now,' he added, his voice rising to a clear ringing tone. 'That is a very great convenience.' "[8] Belinda affects to be shocked by this worldly aspect of Bodley's hallowed halls, but Dr. Parnell continues: "I do not approve of this hushed and reverent attitude towards our great library. After all, it is a place for human beings, isn't it?" (*STG*, 94). Pym, of course, is very well aware of how much the Bodleian was a "place for human beings," as the friends for whom the novel was written would recognize. As a setting for romance it would need to minister to the human comforts of lovers, as Dr. Parnell seems to acknowledge. In this private context, then, his words become a joke about the personal importance of the library to Pym and Harvey, a place not just for books and scholars but one that could foster love.

Another telling reference to the Bodleian comes in *Jane and Prudence*, which traces the post-Oxford life of two female graduates. Prudence, the younger protagonist, whom Pym claimed was most like herself, has a series of relationships with men, some of which are clearly sexual. She tells her mentor, Jane, that she remembers romances "in the idyllic surroundings of ancient stone walls, rivers, gardens, and even the reading-rooms of great libraries."[9] But Prudence, too, has retained her status as an independent woman.

It is perhaps in *Civil to Strangers*, a very early novel written in 1936 that remained unpublished until after Pym's death, that the Bodleian achieves its full grandeur as a place simultaneously representing romance, scholarly retreat from the world, and donnish eccentricity. The plot again represents the unsatisfactory romance between Pym and Harvey, although in this version they are a young married couple, Adam and Cassandra Marsh-Gibbon, who have reached a stage of complacency and lethargy in their marriage. Adam, like Henry Harvey, takes his partner for granted and spends his time worrying narcissistically about himself and his work. Cassandra, as a fictionalized version of Pym, however, takes a stronger stand than her model, escaping alone to Budapest in the hope that her husband will miss her. Adam's response, of course, is to retreat to the Bodleian, where his research will provide a restful refuge from his lonely house and unmet needs: "He would go and work in Duke Humphrey. There, enshrouded in history, he would find peace and contentment."[10] Pym's description of Adam's day at the Bodleian is familiar to us from her own descriptions in her diary. She mentions his walking up the steps, into the Picture Room, and of course into the English Reading Room, site of her own romantic agonies. Adam's somewhat unscholarly and dilettante-ish behavior reminds us of her own restlessness and of the looking-up of words in the dictionary:

[He] wandered about looking at various books and reading the *Dictionary of National Biography* to see if he could detect any mistakes in it. Then he went up to the Catalogue to look up several books that he might read. He also looked up his own novels and poems, and, for some reason, made a note of them. After that he leaned on a radiator and read several volumes of the *University Calendar.* Finally he went back to his seat and began a letter to Cassandra, but he found it difficult to write, as he really did not know what to say. He was glad when the bell tinkled, for this meant that all readers must leave the library, which closed at seven. (144)

This passage is typically Pym in its observed details and acknowledgment of human fragilities. It is also, however, a faithful portrait of a student troubled in love, with Adam's wanderings and specious attempts at research displaying the same kind of fitfulness that Pym describes in her own meanderings in the Bodleian.

However, here she has a final joke for us. As an antidote to Adam's frivolous and unscholarly behavior in the Bodleian, Pym presents us with a wonderful piece of academic comedy. As Adam is preparing to leave the library, he is addressed by a stranger, a clergyman, who initiates the following dialogue:

'I wonder, when you are working here, have you ever given a thought to all those who have died in Bodley's Library, or as a result of working there?'
Adam was forced to admit that he had not.
'You should, you know. It is quite an education.'
'It would surely do one more good to concentrate on one's work,' said Adam austerely.
'That is my work,' said the clergyman simply. 'I am preparing a thesis on that subject for the degree of Bachelor of Letters.' (144–45)

No doubt this humorous concept occurred to Pym herself during her many hours of contemplation in the Bodleian, and perhaps its sentiments are familiar to finals students, but in fiction its quirky irony impels Adam out of the library and onto a train to look for his wife.

The library usually stands in Pym's work as a setting for love, but here it also becomes associated with death. The eccentric clergyman suggests that those who cannot leave the library, who cannot tear themselves away from the ivory tower, are likely to find it has become their tomb. Adam leaves the Bodleian to reclaim his marriage; as a man he can adjust the balance of the head and the heart to combine his intellectual identity with his role as a husband. This symmetry is not so easy for the female characters to achieve. The dominant culture equates a devotion to the life of the mind in women with blue-stock-inged spinsterhood and sterility. Rather than resist all participation in the conventional world, Pym's female characters often leave the library, yet they remain connected to it. One such connection is work they perform on the fringes of academia. Another connection is the mental library of poetry to which they refer as touchstones or comforts. The "literariness" of Pym's work, the poetic allusions noted by most critics, afford her protagonists a liminal space between the cloisters of academe and the conventional world of love and marriage. They carry their libraries in their heads.

These early novels are the only ones in which Pym uses the Bodleian library as a specific setting. However, libraries still dominate Pym's later fiction as the background for romance. Love in a library forms the main plot in *An Unsuitable Attachment*, the novel that Cape would not accept in 1963, thus beginning the long period in which Pym could not get her work published. This novel plays again with the usual stereotype of the library as being a setting antithetical to romance, and subverts the idea of female librarians as unattractive spinsters. Ianthe falls in love with John in the library where they both work and in the face of opposition from the head librarian, who is more intent on their getting right the details of bibliographic cards. When in Italy, Ianthe thinks of John in his library setting and perhaps because of this realizes she's in love with him: "In her confusion it was a relief to think of John, so far away in the library, perhaps even at this moment compiling a bibliography or assisting a reader with a sociological query."[11] Later the issue of whether John is or is not a qualified librarian enters discussions of whether he is good enough for Ianthe; at their wedding Mervyn, the head librarian, goes about telling people definitively that his library was conducive to their romance.

In *Less than Angels* the action centers on the reading room of an anthropological institute, or "Felix's Folly," as Mark and Digby call it in mockery of the distinguished-looking Professor Mainwaring. In this novel, however, Pym does more than highlight the seductive possibilities of learned tomes. She again explores the gender issues associated with library romance and the strategies through which a woman must reconcile its intoxications with her intellectual identity. The main characters of the novel, Tom and Deirdre, first meet in the library—Deirdre is just leaving with her books. Tom introduces himself, and then "he beg[ins] walking about the room, taking books out of the shelves and making derogatory comments on them, as if he could not decide whether to go or stay."[12] Once again a female character falls in love in a library, and the beginnings of the affair follow the patterns familiar to us from Pym's student diary. Deirdre haunts the library in the hope that her first encounter with Tom will be repeated. She tells her aunt, "I thought I'd spend the morning at Felix's Folly," and thinks to herself that, "perhaps she might see Mark and Digby there and they might be able to tell her something about Tom Mallow. She hardly dared hope that she might see Tom himself" (61). But when none of her male friends are there, poor Deirdre is actually forced to study in the reading room, "settl[ing] down rather grimly with a pile of books" (61). Pym's choice of the word "grimly" indicates how different Deirdre's intentions at the library had been. When Tom actually arrives, Deirdre has her wish of having engineered a "chance" meeting. The trick, as Pym knew from her days at the Bodleian, was to turn this accidental meeting into an assignation. Pym approaches this problem with comic bathos: "Tom stood up and gathered his books together. In her eyes he read the unspoken question, that was so often in women's eyes, 'When shall I see you again?' His first impulse had been to ask 'Are you any good at typing?'. . ." (67).

Tom's words, amusing as they are in this context, reveal again the ambiguities inherent for Pym's heroines in library romance. While she previously came to the library only to study, Deirdre now comes to see Tom. He, however, has no problem mixing academic work with romance. Tom takes advantage of his female companions' intellectual abilities and assumes that their romantic feelings for him indicate their desire to support his academic career. Deirdre and Catherine are expected to relinquish their own work as the boundaries between exploitation and passion become vague and blurred.

This gendered exchange of intellectual skills forms a pattern in Pym's work. Like Aylwin Forbes in *No Fond Return of Love* and the young Henry Harvey, male characters in Pym's fiction often use a devoted woman's affection to help them in their research. Just as Pym helped Henry Harvey type his thesis on Gerard Langbaine in the summer of 1936, hoping that he would reward her hard work with his love, so Catherine and Deirdre in *Less than Angels* help Tom finish his thesis. Mark comments sardonically to Digby about this equation: "[I]t would be a reciprocal relationship—the woman giving the food and shelter and doing some typing for him and the man giving the priceless gift of himself" (76). Pym is well aware of what academics call a gendered commodity exchange. Its negotiations compel women to give up so much in a relationship that her heroines choose the margins rather than adopting the expected conventions of their culture. Their detachment is cultivated.

The pattern is noted from a different perspective by *Less than Angels'* Minnie Foresight, who is glad to come upon Tom and Deirdre in a little anteroom off the library, and remarks to Felix Mainwaring about "that charming couple, so obviously in love, well, the girl anyway. Perhaps women show it more than men. Romance among all these books—however much education of women there is, you can't keep it out, can you . . ." (125). The aptly named Minnie Foresight highlights the problems of library romance, presenting romance and education as two different goals, each occluding the other. In her conventional view, women's desire for love and marriage ought to be privileged over their education. Symbolically, when women fall in love they should leave the library. Certainly Pym's female characters often seem to sell out their feminist impulses and education by allowing themselves to be used as secretaries or helpmates. Mildred Lathbury, Belinda Bede, and Dulcie Mainwaring are all typically "excellent women," but they are ready to squander their education to assist men. Yet they make the decision knowingly. Dulcie in *No Fond Return of Love* judges Viola's rather pathetic slaving for Aylwin Forbes and yet does not seem above this kind of work herself. Pym's diaries confirm this pattern in her own life, yet, as I have argued, she was aware of the sexism inherent in the arrangement. Her ironic and detached viewpoint allowed her to reproduce this academic inequality in order to draw the reader's attention to it. After all, as she writes in her diary at the end of 1935, she would rather get a novel published than have Love, and of course that was the choice she made in her own life. Like their author, Pym's characters remain on the margins so that they can avoid the gender stereotypes that seem to govern social roles. While the work they undertake as "excellent women" may seem trivial, it is what George Herbert called "drudgery divine," as the Archdeacon notes in *Some Tame Gazelle* (68). Pym's heroines remain intellectually faithful in a culture that forces them to choose between romance and the life of the mind.

The examples I have cited above are clear evidence of the important role that libraries, particularly the Bodleian, play in the fiction of Barbara Pym. There is a curious self-referential quality about the prominence of the Bodleian for the student of Pym's work. As I was reading the manuscripts of Pym's diaries in the Bodleian, I became aware of the irony of sitting in the place that Pym was writing about with such vivid detail. And what made this even more odd was reading, while in the library, about Pym's own awareness of this very possibility. She had written to Robert Liddell: "All my love letters—no young woman should be without 50 of these. Could I deposit them in Bodley and order them when I felt inclined to reread them?" (*ALTA*, 57). Similarly, Liddell had written to her: "How immensely valuable our correspondence ought to be to the Department of Western Manuscripts—only we don't leave enough margin and I can't think how it will ever be bound." (56). In 1978, Philip Larkin, himself the librarian of Hull University who had regaled Pym with the absurdities of his own university reading room, suggested, among other possibilities, that she might deposit her "literary remains," that is, manuscripts and typescripts of her work, with the Bodleian. Her sister Hilary carried through this commission after her death.

Libraries, for Barbara Pym, were an integral part of existence. They provided her with a great deal of material for her fiction—including, in addition to her escapades in the English Reading Room, her years of work for the International Africa Institute and its library. Her correspondence over many years with Larkin is full of joking references to catalogue problems and other issues pertinent to libraries. When Larkin's university built a new wing to its library in 1968, the poet sent Pym a picture, evoking a typical pithy comment in her diary: "Philip Larkin sent me a photograph of his new Library extension. Was ever a stranger photo sent by a man to a woman (in a novel she might be disappointed)" (*VPE*, 246). Yet again a library was the focus of her sense of the oddities of life, which she celebrated with great affection in her fiction.

Barbara Pym, then, can be counted as a "library novelist," whose youthful experiences in one of the world's great libraries gave it a lasting place in her work. An exploration of her use of the library reveals its role in her treatment of gender and her mediation of life with art. While Pym herself admitted that her usual subject matter was concerned with the trivial and the ordinary, her treatment of libraries clearly shows her witty reverence for both the building and the books, which culminated after her death, fittingly and in fulfillment of her own wishes, in her own important place upon the Bodleian's shelves.

NOTES

1. Janice Rossen, *The World of Barbara Pym* (New York: St. Martin's Press, 1987), 30.

2. Jean Kennard, "Barbara Pym and Romantic Love," *Contemporary Literature* 33, no. 1 (1993): 44–61; Barbara Bowman, "Barbara Pym's Subversive Subtext: Private Irony and Shared Detachment," in *Independent Women: The Function of Gender in Barbara Pym*, ed. Janice Rossen (New York: St. Martin's Press, 1988), 82–94.

3. Rossen, *The World of Barbara Pym*, 22.

4. Hazel Holt, *A Lot to Ask: A Life of Barbara Pym* (New York: E. P. Dutton, 1991), 151.

5. Barbara Pym, *A Very Private Eye: An Autobiography in Diaries and Letters,* ed. Hazel Holt and Hilary Pym (New York: E. P. Dutton, 1984), 262.

6. Pym, *Crampton Hodnet* (New York: E. P. Dutton, 1987), 50–51.

7. Rossen, *The World of Barbara Pym*, 32.

8. Pym, *Some Tame Gazelle* (New York: E. P. Dutton, 1978), 94.

9. Pym, *Jane and Prudence* (New York: E. P. Dutton, 1981), 13.

10. Pym, *Civil to Strangers and Other Writings*, ed. Hazel Holt (New York: E. P. Dutton, 1987), 144.

11. Pym, *An Unsuitable Attachment* (New York: E. P. Dutton, 1982), 191.

12. Pym, *Less than Angels* (New York: E. P. Dutton, 1980), 50.

"Love Like Bedsocks":
Barbara Pym's *Some Tame Gazelle*

ANTHONY KAUFMAN

SOME TAME GAZELLE IS BARBARA PYM'S FIRST IMPORTANT NOVEL, and it is brilliantly successful. In many ways it is revealing of what is to follow: similar or identical concerns and characters interweave through fictional worlds at once recognizable as Pym's. Like all of her novels, *Some Tame Gazelle* is at once funny and serious, offering the detached, amused observation and mild sense of irony and absurdity that is Pym's specialty. Pym's first novel transmutes elements of her own life story through the forms of traditional social comedy, so that the sense of rejection and hostility seen so clearly in her diary is distanced and alleviated for both reader and author. I will argue that in the writing of *Some Tame Gazelle* Pym was able to transform her feelings of rejection, anger, and depression, and her sense of negligibility into brilliant social comedy. Her diaries, begun at Oxford, serve as a revealing prototype for her first published work of fiction. Central to the novel, written while quite young, are her feelings of premature middle age, transience, and mortality.

Large excerpts from Pym's diary entries, notebooks, and letters were published in 1984 as *A Very Private Eye*. It is clear upon reading these excerpts and the entirety of Pym's papers at the New Bodleian Library that her diaries were meant for publication and contain heightened and fictionalized renditions of the people and events in her life. As I have argued elsewhere more fully, the diaries, when read chronologically, form a "kind of a novel" which Pym herself referred to as "my own story."[1] The story Pym tells in her semi-fictional diaries is one of early joy and a sense of exciting possibility crushed by the traumatic rejection of the diarist by her Oxford lover, whom she calls in her diaries "Lorenzo." Pym understood that her "own story" was the semi-fictionalized narrative of a rejected woman whose search for "something to love" is frustrated and whose feelings of youth, possibility, and excitement are permanently (it seems) terminated. However, from this traumatic wound comes new purpose: to tell her

story publicly and in another form. She will become a writer and her
fictions will explore her frustration, anger, and depression through
brilliant, ironic comedy. Her vulnerable sense of self will be protected
and expressed through laughter, which will serve as a means of defense and aggression. So Pym writes as "one of the rejected," to use
her own phrase, and in telling her master plot over and over in her
novels she gains a measure of catharsis and revenge.[2] The triumph of
Pym is to transmute her negative and destructive feelings into a series
of brilliant novels.

To tell her story in the diaries Pym very quickly adopted the per-
sona of "The Spinster," a middle-aged woman, one of the rejected,
who copes with feelings of abandonment and loss, a sense of the self
as negligible. She feels also a disturbing sense of transience. The Spinster, Pym herself, finds everywhere intimations of mortality: her own
aging, privation, the shutting down of possibility and the approach of
death.

Very soon after leaving Oxford in 1934 Pym began writing a novel,
which at one time she thought she might call *Some Sad Turtle*. Fortu-
nately she thought better of this and called her book *Some Tame Gazelle*. In it Pym tells "My Story," brilliantly distanced from her own
life and a masterpiece of ironic comedy. Yet this first published work
obliquely reveals her intimate inward motivation. Pym maintained
that the process of writing *Some Tame Gazelle* was therapeutic, and
by writing she gained relief from feelings she could not well articulate
in any other form:

> Sometime in July I began writing a story about Hilary [Pym's sister] and
> me as spinsters of fiftyish. Henry [the Oxford lover], Jock and all of us
> appeared in it. I sent it to them and they liked it very much. So I am going
> on with it and one day it may become a book. It is interesting in more
> ways than one. It is of course 'for Henry,' and in it I seem able to say what
> I cannot in the ordinary course of events. Barbara [who becomes Belinda
> in the novel] keeps looking back to her youth, and so I have an excuse for
> revealing my present feelings about Henry.[3]

In *Some Tame Gazelle* Pym elaborates The Spinster character of
the diaries into Belinda, the first of her heroines, retaining The Spinster's "how did all this happen to me" puzzlement, the feelings of
middle age and transience, the importance of memory, the sense of
the absurdity of it all. Henry Harvey becomes Archdeacon Henry
Hoccleve, a comic figure who reappears in one form or another in
most of Pym's fiction. The transformation of The Spinster of the diaries into Belinda is marvelously successful, and *Some Tame Gazelle*,
as several critics have maintained, is one of Pym's best.

Fresh from her study of English literature at Oxford, a formative influence in her life, Pym takes the crucial step of mediating a deeply personal situation through a well-established literary mode, thus distancing her fiction from herself and making it highly accessible to those responsive to the conventions of English social comedy. Indeed, *Some Tame Gazelle* is the most consciously literary of her works, a novel filled with literary quotation. The immediate (but not the only) reward of her study of literature was her increased facility in translating her painful personal situation into comedy.

That Barbara Pym should convey in this novel a sense of detachment is remarkable, for it is perhaps the most personal of her novels. Earlier she had completed her unpublished novel "Young Men in Fancy Dress," written between August 1925 and April 1930. This awkward, immature work can be regarded as little more than practice. Here her aspiring artist, Denis Feverel, intends to write a novel that will be autobiographical: "Don't you think first novels nearly always are?"[4] In a radio talk given in 1978, Pym described the inception of *Some Tame Gazelle* and suggested how Lorenzo provided her immediate motivation:

> When I was eighteen, I went up to Oxford to read English. Most aspiring novelists write at the University, but I didn't though I *did* start to write something in my third year, a description of a man who meant a lot to me. I tore it up, but this person did appear later in a very different guise as one of my best comic male characters. There was nothing comic to me about him at the time but memory is a great transformer of pain into amusement.[5]

Virginia Woolf noted in her essay "Women Novelists" that "no doubt the desire and the capacity to criticize the other sex has its share in deciding women to write novels, for indeed, that particular vein of comedy has been but slightly worked and promises great richness."[6] Although in the diaries Pym's relationship to Lorenzo is painful, *Some Tame Gazelle* is considerably distanced from her situation and is thus highly amusing.

Much was changed in the novel between its beginning in July 1934 (when Pym was just down from Oxford), its revisions after World War II, and its final publication in 1950 (when Pym was thirty-seven, had experienced the war, and was working in London). The version finally accepted by Jonathan Cape in 1950 is radically different from the original drafts. The twenty-two-year-old graduate projects herself, her sister, her former lover, and indeed several of her college friends and acquaintances some thirty years into the future, picturing them as middle-aged.

She sets her novel in a nameless, featureless village, a kind of pleasant never-never land, where a few houses are grouped around the church and vicarage. There are references to Miss Jenner's yarn shop and the Crown and Pinion public house, but the world is as generalized and timeless as the New York/London of P. G. Wodehouse or the Riseholme or Tilling of E. F. Benson. Indeed the rivalry of Belinda and Agatha may recall the humor of Mapp and Lucia. Critics have observed a pastoral quality in *Some Tame Gazelle*, but here the pastoral is mock. Although the subject of love is central, Pym's shepherds and shepherdesses are mostly middle-aged eccentrics. Nevertheless, a sense of a world apart from the here and now is important in the novel. Its fictional world lacks the sense of postwar limitations and shabbiness, shortages and making-do that are a part of Pym's later books set in the 1950s.

It is remarkable that we come to care for Belinda, this somewhat befuddled, ineffectual, rather dim English gentlewoman in her late fifties, who for some thirty years has been in not-so-secret love with Archdeacon Hoccleve, her married neighbor, whom Belinda first met at Oxford. As in Pym's own experience, her love for him was immediate and irrevocable. But she met with rejection: he married the practical and ambitious Agatha, who could further his ecclesiastical career. The result for Belinda is one typical of the rejected central character of all Pym's fiction: she feels insignificance, a sense of "not having," and submerged anger, together with a tendency to dwell in memory and a heightened awareness of her own transience and mortality.

Belinda is a curious and sympathetic mix of abstractedness, timidity, gentleness, and loyalty. Her intellectual foundation is a comfortably soft and shapeless pillow of Anglicanism and English literature, which together provide "sentiments to which every bosom returns an echo"—a cloud of platitudes provided by The Greater Poetic Thinkers. Her life is undergirded by her belief, or perhaps it is more of a hope, that "an English gentlewoman can never come to any harm," and she notes that she has the "long English gentlewoman's feet" of her kind. The demands of her emotional life are similarly vague, if occasionally demanding, and they are at the center of the book. They focus of course on Henry; the Archdeacon is a fine comic character, an egotistical and lazy cleric in the great English tradition of comic clergy.

Living in adoring proximity to Henry, Belinda is circumscribed by the daily round of village life. Her response to rejection is service and nurture. She is one of that legion of devoted or semi-devoted church workers, carriers of soup to those sick or in need, readers of *The Church Times* and the parish newsletter, workers for "the poor in

Pimlico," makers of coffee for the male members of the various committees, decorators of the church at the Harvest Festival. The first of Pym's celebrated "excellent women," she thinks of herself as a middle-aged spinster, devoted perforce to "the trivial round, the common task."

But does the common task indeed furnish all we ought to ask, as the old hymn suggests? Belinda is aware of the limitations, the futility, the obscurity of all this: the vicar's foolishness and complacency, the bickering always present in small-town life, the dreary sameness of it all. While Belinda and her successors are hardly Cleopatras, they do have "immortal longings". And central to them all is the need for "Some tame gazelle, or some gentle dove: / Something to love, oh, something to love!" in the words of poet Thomas Haynes Bayly. Here is the Pymian subject. The need to love and nurture is presented in Pym as uniquely that of the woman; there is a marked and irreducible division between the sexes. Men are seen as needing not so much to be loved as to be admired, cared for, and assisted. There is in Pym little intimacy or intercourse between the sexes. In such a novel as *Jane and Prudence* the sexes are seen almost as different species.

The unsatisfactory, even bizarre, consequences of the woman's need to love is essential to Pym's comedy. We understand the strength of this need and what curious and inadequate forms it must at times take. Such is the centrality of the need to love that often its victims, almost always female, are both sad and laughable in their single-minded and inevitably ill-fated pursuit of their particular gazelle. They become self-enclosed, not entirely aware of the reality of their situation, unrealistic in their expectations—in short, figures both sad and comic. They are all the more so in that Pym's men, the objects of pursuit, are invariably portrayed as inadequate. These fictional women are the literary products of Pym's own transformation of pain into literary comedy and reflect her own ambivalence toward her emotional situation. In short, they recapitulate the Pymian master plot of unrequited love, which appears from *Some Tame Gazelle* to her last novel, *A Few Green Leaves*, in which Emma Howick is the spinster figure.

Belinda is fully aware of Hoccleve's absurdities, his slackness, his affectation, his confident and negligent use of her. But for over thirty years she has loved him and he fills a central need in her life. Her love for the complacent Henry is mildly absurd, but it is at the center of Belinda's emotional life. To her eyes, the eyes of thirty years' devotion, he is still handsome and charming. There is a humorous solipsism here; though not herself one of the novel's many and wonderfully realized egotists, she too is self-enclosed within her con-

stant need to orient herself in relationship to the Archdeacon. Indeed,
Belinda's most intense pleasure is simple proximity to dear Henry—
conversation with him, listening to him reading poetry as he did in
"the old days." She finds compensation in the smallest tokens from
Henry.

So for Belinda passivity, proximity, and nurture largely overcome
her feelings of negligibility, of "not having." The characters of the
novel are nearing the end of life; they lead lives without great possibilities (although Harriet, Belinda's lively younger sister, would indignantly dismiss such an idea). It is remarkable that Pym, writing at the
beginning of her career, could foresee and dramatize a sense of joy
and contentment evolving out of what is so nearly a melancholy situation. All these characters, not just Belinda, need something to love,
and much of the comedy of the novel concerns the strange forms this
need takes. For example, the ongoing melancholy love of the Count
for Harriet; of the Count for his late friend, Akenside; the love of the
two sisters for each other; even the rough dominance of Edith over
Connie seem necessary forms of human relationship. This is the delicate center of Pym's novels: the need for love, or a form of it, and the
consequences (sometimes sad or bizarre) of "not having." Isolation is
not possible. Those characters who are truly isolated in Pym are mad
or enfeebled—Marcia of *Quartet in Autumn* is the fullest and most
terrible portrait of the isolated woman. When relationships are *deliberately* diminished or denied, as in the case of Leonora Eyre of *The
Sweet Dove Died*, the effect is disturbing.

Some Tame Gazelle is to a great extent about the selectivity of
memory, how memory is transformed by current emotional needs.
Belinda's seemingly clear memory of what so much of her life has
been—her relationship with Henry—is deceptive, in that we understand Henry's selfish use of her, his lack of real interest, his need for
her applause and loyalty. One's emotional needs make for falsified
recollection. Belinda has shaped her memories into a satisfying fantasy. Her life is filtered through emotional imperatives formed largely
by literature and the fund of artificial dreams that she herself has developed to meet the reality of "not having." In creating Belinda, Pym
develops the satisfactory analogue to her own relationship with
Henry Harvey, diminishing him and avenging herself upon him by
transforming him into an indolent, egotistical, pompous windbag.

But Belinda does return repeatedly in her abstracted musings to the
fact of aging and death, and her awareness of this becomes a central
preoccupation of the novel. The awareness of time past and passing,
of one's own middle age and that of others, causes Belinda to reflect
on death. Depressed by a slight chill, Belinda takes to her bed (having

called for *The Oxford Book of Victorian Verse*), and is visited by the formidable Agatha. She, in the midst of conversation, reminds Belinda that it has been some thirty years since Belinda met a visiting bishop, Theo Grote:

> 'Oh, yes, about thirty years I think. We none of us grow any younger, do we? *Timor mortis conturbat me*,' murmured Belinda, staring straight in front of her. Agatha looked at her sharply. Sometimes she wondered whether Belinda was quite all there. She said such odd things. (190–91)

Belinda is aware that age should mean an end to the anxieties of youth: to the absurd self-consciousness, the passion, and the foolishness. But it doesn't. Dressing for a garden party at the vicarage, Belinda and Harriet discuss clothes: "With the years one ought to have grown beyond such thoughts but somehow one never did. . . ." (32). The absurdity, if not the opportunities, linger on, and Belinda's inward life is constantly thrown into turmoil by the sudden unexpected upsurge of disturbing emotions. She is intensely shocked and exhilarated by the sudden possibility that Agatha actually proposed to Henry, which alters the very foundation of her emotional life.

Belinda's awareness of her middle age and of death is kept in focus throughout the novel by continual reference to English literature, especially the poetry of the seventeenth and eighteenth centuries. Perhaps the key reference in *Some Tame Gazelle* is to Gray's *Elegy in a Country Churchyard*, one well-known stanza of which appears at the beginning of chapter 5:

> Far from the madding crowd's ignoble strife,
> Their sober wishes never learn'd to stray;
> Along the cool sequester'd vale of life
> They kept the noiseless tenor of their way.

One understands that Belinda and Harriet live far from the world's center, although the village has its share of low-key ignoble strife: the unpleasantness between Miss Jenner and Miss Beard about the decorations for the Harvest Festival, or the muted contention between Harriet and Agatha about just whom Count Bianco is to marry. But far more important is the theme of the elegy and its reflection on death. Belinda, Harriet, Henry, Agatha, Ricardo—all of these figures on Pym's urn are, to a greater or lesser extent, subject to the difficulties of aging and the approach of death. If Belinda muses on transience, Harriet most emphatically does not. Hoccleve, despite his penchant for loitering in the country churchyard, contemplating the

Universal End, does not seem especially concerned with his own death, but only about socks without holes and a proper tea.

Literary references to mortality form a network of allusion throughout the novel. One of Belinda's favorite poets, and certainly Hoccleve's, is Edward Young, the poet of *Night Thoughts*, that grandiose compendium of eighteenth-century sentiments. Young's lines, "We take no note of time / But from its loss. To give it then a Tongue / Is wise in man," are twice quoted, both times by Hoccleve, whose tastes run to melancholy. Both times, as one would expect from the Archdeacon, the quotations are quite unsuitable to the occasion. Stopping Belinda as he wanders in the churchyard, he tells her with characteristic affectation that

> 'I was thinking out my sermon for Sunday. . . . I find the atmosphere so helpful. Looking at these tombs, I am reminded of my own mortality. . . .'
>
> Belinda waited. She doubted now whether it would be possible to be back for tea at four o'clock. She could hardly break away when the Archdeacon was about to deliver an address on the mortality of man.
>
> He began to quote: 'We take no note of time / But from its loss. . . .' 'I thought of those lines when I heard the clock strike just now.' (85)

In context the quotation is ludicrous, yet the note of transience remains. Here Pym suggests the inadequacy of literature to define individual human experience. There is something comic about Young's sonorous lines; their elaborate artificiality seems to give the speaker a touch of the *poseur*. When the slightly ill Belinda calls for *The Oxford Book of Victorian Verse*, then lays it aside, surely the implication is that poetry, even Victorian, cannot stand up to the common cold, that literature may not be as immediately satisfying as a hot milky drink. The very act of calling for it in such a situation seems artificial, itself a situation out of Victorian literature.

When for the second time Young's lines are quoted, this motif is amplified. Here the quotation is almost monstrously inappropriate to the occasion, a wedding. At the presentation of a gift to Mr. Donne and his fiancée, Olivia Berridge, Hoccleve recites the quote and flings aside the cloth covering a clock, "with a dramatic gesture that Belinda thought very fine, if a little too theatrical for the occasion" (234). Indeed, the maladroit quotation is a Hoccleve specialty, and in both instances the comic element plays off against and alleviates the sober undertones of Young. The lines are part of the network of allusion that repeatedly evoke an awareness of aging and death on the part of Belinda. She does not brood—the comic is always present and the novel is not melancholy. Still the allusions reinforce our impression that Belinda's musings, her continual abstraction, define her basic need for "something to love" and her sense of transience and "not having."

When Agatha is about to return from Karlsbad, Belinda, predictably perhaps, feels some melancholy. Harriet believes that Belinda has not made the most of her time with Agatha away. She points out what Belinda feels only too keenly: "We none of us get any younger."

> Ah yes, thought Belinda, as she turned to knitting the dull grey jumper that might have been a pullover for the Archdeacon, that was it. She thought about it so seldom but now she became melancholy at the realization that the fine madness of her youth had gone. She was no longer an original shining like a comet, indeed, it would have been unsuitable if she had been. *Change and decay in all around I see . . . All, all are gone, the old familiar faces. . . .* (160)

There is a suggestion of the mock-heroic in "shining like a comet." The fragments of Charles Lamb ("Old Familiar Faces") and Henry Francis Lyte ("Abide with Me") once again illustrate how Belinda typically turns to The Greats (or semi-greats) to make concrete her emotional disturbance: she expresses herself through them and gains consolation from them. There is irony in that her emotions must be channeled through male poets. Her situation, Pym implies, is characteristically female—but both institutions to which she unthinkingly gives allegiance, English literature and the Church of England, are largely male constructs and unable to offer guidance and real consolation.

The deep-seated love of Belinda for Hoccleve, however compromised by her sentimentalism, and that of Ricardo for Harriet, contrast with the cool and self-interested purposes of two ludicrous lovers who enter the village, causing much consternation before their departure. Here is the ostensible hinge of the novel's plot: at the conclusion the intruders will have retreated from the village and the situation of the principal characters will be unchanged. But at the entrance of the two purposeful suitors, Belinda is bothered by the possibility that the even tenor of her life with Harriet will change. She thinks of Dr. Johnson's notion that "all change is of itself an evil and ought not to be hazarded but for evident advantage," a sentiment even truer when one reaches middle age. But with the departure of Mr. Mold and Theo Grote, Bishop of Mbawawa, nothing is changed: a curate has been found for Harriet to replace Mr. Donne, Ricardo is constant in his devotion to Harriet, and of course Belinda will always have dear Henry to moon over. Belinda realizes as the novel ends "that she too was happier than she had been for a long time":

For now everything would be as it had been before those two disturbing characters Mr. Mold and Bishop Grote appeared in the village. In the future Belinda would continue to find such consolation as she needed in our greater English poets, when she was not gardening or making vests for the poor in Pimlico. (250–51)

Although a strain of melancholy runs throughout this pastoral romance, its central character is finally content. Belinda is conscious of aging, desirous of keeping her dignity—one doesn't want to "act silly," as Miss Jenner does with the traveling salesmen. She senses that she, and women like her, are somewhat absurd. But she is contented nevertheless in her love for Henry and Harriet, both of whom she knows to be selfish, self-absorbed, and silly. She serves them dutifully, darning and cooking, thus validating Herbert's lines after all: "Who sweeps a room as for Thy Laws, / Makes that and the action fine." Her response to rejection is service and nurture.

Belinda's inward and abstracted musings are very much at the heart of the book, and the observations of a female character will continue to be central throughout Pym's novels. *Some Tame Gazelle* is an anatomy of its creator's art. There will be sharper, more decisive observers than Belinda, characters quite different, but her consciousness, playing digressively over the vicissitudes of village life, over past and present, character and motive, will be typical. Pym continually retells "My Story," the story of rejection and attempts at compensation, usually resulting in an unsatisfactory compromise between the heart's desire and an uncomfortable reality. Although there is a darker tone to *Quartet in Autumn* and *The Sweet Dove Died*, her subject and her methods of fictionalizing it remain constant. Her fictive projections of herself in the diaries—"I am a spinster," "I am a writer"—always reflect her commitment to writing, her need to present imaginative variations of her own situation and to transform them into fiction.

NOTES

1. I have discussed Pym's deliberate fictionalization of her life in "A Life Like a Novel: Pym's 'Autobiography' as Fiction," *Journal of Modern Literature* 20, no. 2 (1996): 187–97.

2. Pym's tendency to transmute her negative emotions into comic fiction is well discussed by Janice Rossen, *The World of Barbara Pym* (New York: St. Martin's Press, 1987) and Anne M. Wyatt-Brown, *Barbara Pym: A Critical Biography* (Columbia: University of Missouri Press, 1992).

3. Barbara Pym, *A Very Private Eye: An Autobiography in Diaries and Letters*, ed. Hazel Holt and Hilary Pym (New York: E. P. Dutton, 1984), 44.

4. See MS Pym 1, fol. 263, Bodleian Library, Oxford.

5. Pym, "Finding a Voice: A Radio Talk," in *Civil to Strangers*, ed. Hazel Holt (New York: E. P. Dutton, 1987), 382–83.

6. Virginia Woolf, "Women Novelists" (1918), in *Contemporary Writers* (New York: Harcourt, Brace & World, 1965), 26–27.

7. Pym, *Some Tame Gazelle* (New York: E. P. Dutton, 1983), 73, 32.

Reading Barbara Pym Autobiographically: Metaphors of Aging and Death in *The Sweet Dove Died, Quartet in Autumn,* and *A Few Green Leaves*

ORPHIA JANE ALLEN

> *By their metaphors shall you know them. And . . . by the same metaphors, if they are used by an artist, shall you know yourselves.*
> —James Olney, *Metaphors of Self*

Barbara Pym's novels, from the early *SOME TAME GAZELLE* (1950) to *A Few Green Leaves*, written as she was dying from cancer and published after her death in 1980, provide a metaphorical account of her personal development. These highly autobiographical novels, as her diaries and letters indicate, trace her development from her days as a young college graduate through nearly forty years that include military service in the Wrens and work in the British censorship offices during World War II, some twenty-five years as an editor with the International African Institute (IAI), and retirement and ill health in the 1970s.[1] Read autobiographically, the novels support Paul John Eakin's claim that "the writing of autobiography is properly understood as an integral part of a lifelong process of identity formation in which acts of self-narration play a major part." Self and story, Eakin writes, are "complementary, mutually constituting aspects of a single process of identity formation."[2]

The close connection between Pym's life and her fiction is especially apparent in the last three novels she prepared for publication, *The Sweet Dove Died, Quartet in Autumn,* and *A Few Green Leaves.*[3] These three novels provide a metaphorical record of a woman coming to terms with aging and impending death. If one accepts the claims of Eakin and of James Olney (whose work ranks among the formative studies of autobiography as a literary genre) about the nature of autobiographical writing—that it can take many forms from that of professed autobiography to philosophy or poetry—these novels may indeed be seen as the vehicle through which Pym came to understand herself.[4] Further, they may provide a metaphorical guide for many of her readers in the process of self-identification.

Olney's reluctance to define autobiography is important here, as is his insistence on the autobiographical metaphor as a means toward understanding the self. To define autobiography as a literary genre, he writes, is "virtually impossible, because the definition must either include so much as to be no definition, or exclude so much as to deprive us of most relevant texts."[5] Art is sometimes presented as autobiography, as in the *Essays* of Montaigne or John Henry Newman's *Apologia pro vita sua*; and autobiography may present itself as a work of art, as in Yeats's *Collected Poems* or T. S. Eliot's *Four Quartets*.[6] "[T]here is no history of autobiography to trace nor any form that a book must observe in order to be autobiography," Olney writes; the works of artists are more than "account[s] of an isolated life without pattern," they are "metaphors for our selves."[7]

Part of the appeal of autobiographical writing is that it meets a human need for order and meaning in life. For Olney, metaphor is a vehicle, "something known and of our making, or at least of our choosing, that we put to stand for, and so to help us understand, something unknown and not of our making." It is "the point through which the individual succeeds in making the universe take on his own order," providing the connections that the individual needs "to sense that there is meaning in something—in a poem, in experience." Metaphor is a way of knowing. We "grasp the unknown through the known" and in so doing are able to organize experience, find "new relational patterns" and transform the self "into a new and richer entity." In autobiographical writing the individual brings to consciousness "the nature of one's own existence."[8] Furthermore, "the study of how autobiographers have . . . discovered, asserted, created a self in the process of writing it out . . . requires the reader or student of autobiography to participate fully in the process," so that metaphors of the autobiography elicit in the reader a fuller understanding of the self.[9]

Olney distinguishes between autobiography simplex and autobiography duplex. The former is the product of the individual who reaches a "clearly defined end point in development . . . well before the composition of the autobiography." The latter is the work of a writer who, through the creation of metaphor, changes and develops throughout life—the autobiography, in other words, becomes a vehicle for change.[10] Pym's novels fall into the second group, as evidenced by the evolution of thought that can be traced in her work, particularly *The Sweet Dove Died, Quartet in Autumn,* and *A Few Green Leaves.*

Pym wrote *The Sweet Dove Died* in the 1960s during the publishing hiatus that followed the rejection of *An Unsuitable Attachment* (published posthumously in 1982 with revisions by Hazel Holt, her literary executor). In fact, both *The Sweet Dove Died* and *Quartet in Autumn* were written with little hope of publication, possibly because Pym needed to write as a way of seeking order and meaning in her life. Hazel Holt writes that during this period Pym wrote for "her own enjoyment and for that of her friends," with little expectation of publication.[11]

The Sweet Dove Died, completed in 1968, was inspired in part by her fondness for Richard Roberts, a young Bahamian antiques dealer (*VPE,* 213), reflected in the character of the youthful James, who works for his uncle Humphrey, owner of an antiques shop. The fifty-ish women of the novel, among them the narcissistic Leonora Eyre and her friends Meg and Liz, represent some of the issues that concerned Pym as she entered her fifties.

The antiques shop setting, the prevalence of aging characters, and repeated allusions to death set the mood of the novel. Its title derives from a poem by John Keats, cited in the novel by Ned, the young American academic who is writing a thesis on Keats's minor poems and competes with Leonora for James's attention.

> 'I had a dove and the sweet dove died;
>   And I have thought it died of grieving . . .
> O, what could it *grieve* for? Its feet were *tied*
>   With a single thread of my *own hand's* weaving.'[12]

The quotation provides the novel's controlling metaphor. The death of the dove is symbolic of the death of the self that comes from the inability to act in the interest of others, a characteristic that applies to Ned as well as Leonora.

Through an array of women characters Pym resolves some of the issues she faces as she finds herself past middle age, never married, and with an uncertain future as a novelist. Leonora Eyre, whose "disquieting" name recalls Beethoven's Leonora overtures and Jane Eyre (85), is a paragon of narcissism, so engaged in perfection and possessions she cannot relate to others. She covets the twentyish James because he is safe, and holds Humphrey, more nearly her own age, at a distance because she dreads sexual contact. Leonora's most obvious foils are Meg and Liz. Meg mothers Colin, her twentyish counterpart to James, entertaining him and his male lover and agonizing over him when he is not spending time with her. However, unlike Leonora, she exists on a level of self-awareness that permits her to feel affection for Colin and causes her to openly reveal, in spite of Leonora's revulsion, her "present state of health and the difficulties experienced by women of 'their' age" (164). "You mustn't expect things to be perfect," she tells Leonora, "they never are" (202).

Liz, unlike Leonora and Meg, doesn't covet young males. Liz breeds Siamese cats, and because her "husband had 'behaved so appallingly,'" now loves cats more than people (26). Liz's interest in breeding cats introduces a metaphor of possession and imprisonment into the narrative that Pym uses to expand on the consequences of Leonora's narcissism and interest in possessions.

Cats and imprisonment are especially relevant to the relationship between James and Ned. James's furtive affair with Phoebe, a woman closer to his age, offers him escape and freedom from the oversight of his uncle and from Leonora's hovering. After James has spent the night with Phoebe, she meditates on a neighborhood stray cat that has wandered into her apartment, fancying "its spreading body was like a great empty wineskin or bladder being filled with Mendelssohn" and writes a poem for James (64). Pym juxtaposes this image of freedom and inspiration with James and Leonora's visit to a cat show that involves only "kittens and neuter cats" (65). Here James feels his maleness is questioned. He refuses Leonora's suggestion that he should have a cat, "imagining the malevolent creature ruling his life" (66), and then finds himself identifying with caged neutered kittens:

> They had stopped in front of a cage where a cat-like shape shrouded in a cloth lay fast asleep. How much wiser to contract out altogether, James felt, as this creature had evidently done. Or to sit stolidly in one's earth tray, unmoved by the comments of passers-by. Yet too often, like some of the more exotic breeds, one prowled uneasily round one's cage uttering loud plaintive cries. (68)

Pym repeats the cage imagery in James's involvement with Ned, whom he picks up on a tour of Spain and Portugal. James's "sensation of freedom, almost of escape" on the plane is short-lived when Ned, whose "gnat-like" voice teases and probes, becomes a male counterpart to Leonora, a malevolent creature who rules his life (83). In the hotel room where he and Ned stay in Lisbon, James reads a letter from Leonora (telling him she is looking for a flat for him to occupy when he returns) and stares at the hotel room wall "covered in a kind of striped paper, like the inside of an old-fashioned suitcase." He imagines himself in a suitcase "with the heat and general feeling of constriction which Ned's presence and his American voice gave" (106). Pym uses prison imagery again to describe the flat Leonora "finds," an apartment with barred windows in her own house. And the malevolent Ned's flat, its sitting room with olive-leaf-patterned walls, synthetic fur rug, and divan of a fur-like material, and its bedroom walls covered with striped paper, is both prison and lair. The freedom that Phoebe represents is lost to James, who seems unable to escape the prisons of his relationships with Ned and Leonora.

Leonora, narcissistic, proud, and possessive, does experience some change in the course of the novel. She loses the "pleasure of being alone" and comes to almost welcome "Liz's interruptions or Meg's cozy chats about Colin" (201). She even breaks down in tears in front of Meg, though her tearful display embarrasses her and she finds the contact of Meg's comforting embrace distasteful. In the end, when James returns to her, she finds "something humiliating about the idea of wooing" him "in this way, like an animal being enticed back into its cage" (207). Yet the sweet dove of her self remains tied with the thread of her narcissistic perfectionism as she watches Humphrey arrive with a sheaf of peonies—perfect flowers, because they "went so well with one's charming room" and "possessed the added grace of having been presented to oneself" (208).

Pym's journal entries and letters during the years she was writing *The Sweet Dove Died* reveal numerous parallels between her life and the novel. Already noted is Hazel Holt's recognition of the inspiration provided by her fondness for the young antiques dealer Richard Roberts. In August 1963, Pym visited Keats's house on a "wet day" (*VPE,* 218). In May 1964 she sat in the Crush Bar at Covent Garden with Richard Roberts and imagined her characters Leonora and Quinton, who became James in the novel, in action. On June 2, 1964, her birthday, Roberts gave her a Victorian china cup and saucer illustrated with "a lady and her cat" (227). As early as March 1962, she wrote in her journal:

> In Gamage's basement I buy (for 1/—) a little Italian bowl with a lemon and leaves painted inside it. It really pleases me, although it is chipped and I begin to wonder if I am getting to the stage when objects could please more than people or (specifically) men. (206)

It would be a mistake, however, to read Leonora literally as Pym. Leonora represents instead one of the directions an aging, unmarried woman's life could take. Pym was aware that she could permit herself to become like Leonora; she recognized in herself aspects of Leonora's concern with aging and preoccupation with possessions.

In addition to Meg and Liz, Pym uses several other minor characters who are fifty or approaching fifty as foils for Leonora in the novel. One is Miss Caton, who works with Humphrey and James in the antiques shop, a plain woman who drinks her coffee from a "thick, serviceable cup" that is an embarrassment to Humphrey and James (*SDD*, 71). Miss Caton is one of the few characters in the novel with a connection to the church. On returning from a holiday tour, she expresses her "relief at the eventual return to good plain food and the Anglican Church" (132). Miss Caton could almost be Pym talking, as could Ba, an "unattached woman" with a "toothy, ruddy face," who suggests that Leonora "could do voluntary work" (176–77).

Another who seems to echo Pym is Rose Culver, "a typical English spinster" and model of propriety who openly confronts Leonora before offering tea when Leonora attempts to retrieve the furniture James lent Phoebe. Her wise words sound as though they could have derived from Pym's own experience: "The odd thing about men is that one never really knows. . . . Just when you think they're close they suddenly go off" (118). Perhaps the woman who comes closest to articulating Pym's preferred resolution to Leonora's predicament is Leonora's cousin Daphne, "a kind woman and perhaps as one grew older there was something to be said for kindness" (185). Daphne takes Leonora to lunch at her club, where men are noticeably absent and where Leonora feels "an absurd desire to confide" (186), suggesting perhaps that aging women have much to offer one another. Leonora's resolution, in other words, might best be found in the company of other women and not in younger (or perhaps even older) men. But Leonora is impervious to help. Her fears of closeness and intimacy prevent her from reaching out with compassion to others or accepting sympathy from them. In short, being Leonora means imprisoning oneself and others, killing the sweet dove with "a single thread of [her] own hand's weaving."

Pym finished writing *The Sweet Dove Died* in 1968 and started almost immediately on another novel, *Quartet in Autumn,* which again uses prison metaphors to illustrate the difficulties its four primary characters have in forming relationships. In May 1971 she had surgery for breast cancer. While in recovery, she had a stroke in 1974 that left her with mild dyslexia and prompted her retirement from the IAI. She settled in with her sister Hilary, who had retired from the BBC in 1971, in a cottage in Finstock, near Oxford, where she joined in the village activities, including the Local History Society. With little hope of ever publishing it, she completed *Quartet in Autumn* (*VPE*, 213–14).

The quartet consists of four older, unmarried people, two women and two men, who work together in an office. Their office conversation frequently turns on modes of dying, such as hypothermia and starvation, which the four are made aware of through their own imaginations, the media, and obituaries in *The Times* and the *Telegraph*, or through upsetting sights on the way to work. Midway through the novel, two of the quartet retire, providing the opportunity for Pym to contemplate the consequences of her own retirement as she returns to the theme of self-imprisonment, concentrating on the alienation that sometimes overwhelms the aging. In *Quartet in Autumn*, Pym uses the mummy as a metaphor for the isolation her characters experience.

Norman, his coarse, bristly hair cut in a "medieval or pudding-basin style," spends his lunch hour in the library, which is "nearer than the British Museum . . . another of his lunchtime stamping-grounds."[13] When he visits his brother-in-law Ken, in hospital with a duodenal ulcer, the two men sit in silence and are both relieved when Norman leaves. Ken is a driving instructor, and Norman, who cannot drive, hates motor cars and feels gratification at the sight of a wrecked one being towed. He rides a bus "like a visitor to London," and observes "the roads men engaged in the rituals concerned with the motor car" (145), indicating perhaps his rejection not only of motor cars but also of ritual in general.

Marcia, her short hair stiff, lifeless, and dyed dark brown, collects milk bottles, plastic bags, and, ironically, leaflets about services available to the elderly. She goes to the library at lunch time for warmth, to collect leaflets, and sometimes to dispose of unwanted objects, including milk bottles that do not fit into her collection. Marcia has been hospitalized for cancer and has developed a fixation for her surgeon, Mr. Strong, that becomes her reason for being. She rejects the help offered by the social worker, Janice Brabner, and by her neighbors, Nigel and Priscilla, and succumbs in the end to anorexia nervosa when she has no strength to open a tin to eat and sustain herself.

Marcia and Norman come close to a reciprocal relationship. When they first meet, Marcia "experience[s] a faint stirring of interest" in Norman that "occupie[s] her thoughts briefly," and once at lunchtime she follows him into the British Museum where she watches him contemplating mummified crocodiles. But her feelings for him wane after Mr. Strong enters her life and fills her thoughts (23). When Norman aimlessly takes a bus into her neighborhood and wanders down her street, he gazes at her house "in stunned fascination, very much as he had gazed at the mummified animals in the British Museum" (145). When Marcia returns his stare, "again it was like the British Museum encounter with the mummified animals—giving no sign of mutual recognition" (146). Pym uses mummy imagery again in describing the bed cover where Marcia's dead cat, Snowy, spent his last days. Mummification becomes a metaphor for the alienation that imprisons both Norman and Marcia.

Letty, her too-long hair a faded light brown, is the only member of the group who goes to the library at lunchtime to read. She is an "unashamed reader of novels" but has come to "realize that the position of an unmarried, unattached, ageing woman is of no interest whatever to the writer of modern fiction" (3). The one member of the quartet who can still appreciate nature, who can quote Wordsworth's "One impulse from a vernal wood . . . ," Letty plans on retirement to "devote herself to some serious reading" (112). But "frozen with boredom, baffled and bogged down by incomprehensible jargon," she comes to the "conclusion that sociology was not quite all that she had hoped for" (117). Letty has the advantage of awareness of her isolation. Watching pigeons "picking at each other, presumably removing insects," she thinks, "Perhaps this is all that we as human beings can do for each other" (9). Unmarried because she believed love should be a part of marriage and "love was a mystery she had never experienced" (54), Letty's plans for living with her friend Marjorie after retirement go awry when Marjorie responds to a proposal from vicar David Lydell, who seeks the unmarried woman who best meets his culinary/digestive needs. Marjorie's solution for Letty is Holmhurst, the old people's home that has periodic vacancies ("due to *death*, of course!)" (53). Letty, deciding she need no longer trail behind her friend, resolves that it would be "better to lie down in the wood under the beech leaves and bracken and wait quietly for death" than move to Holmhurst (151). Consequently, when her bed-sitting room becomes intolerable because of the noise made by a new landlord, Mr. Olatunde, and his exuberant religious followers, Letty, with Edwin's help finds a room with the bleak and silent eighty-year-old Mrs. Pope.

Edwin, his thin grey hair cut in a "sort of bob" (1), spends his lunch break in the library doing research on the background of a clergyman whose parish he sometimes frequents. Edwin's church association provides a somewhat stable background. Because of his interest in Church of England ritual, he attends a memorial service for a man he doesn't even know. Only Edwin is able to empathize with Letty enough to help her find the room with Mrs. Pope, where her life might be "governed by the soothing rhythm of the church's year" (73).

Through Edwin and Marcia, Pym expresses her concern with a social system that lets people slip through the cracks, and with a church community that no longer addresses the needs of its older parishioners. The retirement party for Marcia and Letty is presided over by an "(acting) deputy assistant director" who doesn't even know what the two women do—"something to do with records or filing . . . women's work . . . that could easily be replaced by a computer." Their coworkers assume that "the State would provide for their basic needs which could not be all that great. . . . [S]ocial services were so much better now, there was no need for anyone to starve or freeze" (101). Social worker Janice Brabner, who tries without success to break through Marcia's façade, is Pym's representative of an intrusive social system that makes "*contact*, by force, if necessary. Believe me, it can be *most* rewarding" (32).

Letty and Edwin are the only members of the quartet connected in any way with religion, and through them we can perhaps make some assumptions about Pym's religious sense at the time she was writing *Quartet in Autumn*. Letty's concept of religion contrasts with the loud, religious exuberance of Mr. Olatunde's followers. Her religion is "a grey, formal, respectable thing of measured observances and mild general undemanding kindness to all" (66). When Edwin settles on Mrs. Pope's room as suitable for Letty, his imagination carries him through the long list of church observances: "how it had always been and how it would go on in spite of trendy clergy trying to introduce so-called up-to-date forms of worship, rock and roll and guitars and discussions about the Third World" (74). The church, though caught up in social transition, still provided the patterned ritual Pym valued, though by now, like Letty, what she valued most seemed grey, formal, respectable.

Pym's clergymen in *Quartet in Autumn*—Father Gellibrand, David Lydell, and Mr. Olatunde—go a long way toward reflecting Pym's concerns about the church and religion at this point in her life. Father Gellibrand, who does "not much care for the aged, the elderly, or just 'old people,' whatever you liked to call them" (192–93), remarks about a well-known local vicar, "Trendy Tony," who represents the younger generation and goes in for "Rock-and-roll and extempore prayers" (162). Gellibrand prefers visiting "houses where people were on the point of death or had already died" to "normal parish visiting, with its awkward conversation and the inevitable cups of tea and sweet biscuits" (164). Lydell seems preoccupied with his digestive system, and Mr. Olatunde's exuberant religion is out of step with Letty's more formal needs, and presumably also with Pym's.

What seems most significant about this strange quartet of elderly people is their inability to extend themselves toward one another. Like the mummies in the British Museum, dead inside, they remain isolated from one another until Marcia's death brings them at last into somewhat meaningful communication and leads to Norman's and Letty's discoveries that they can still influence their own and other people's lives.

This ending, like the ending of *The Sweet Dove Died* that finds the little-changed Leonora still self-centered and seeking perfection, seems unsatisfactory, without real resolution. The discoveries of Norman and Letty border on illusion, perhaps Pym's nod to the imperfect world referred to by Leonora's friend Meg. The closest Pym comes to resolution is through Edwin, who seems more realistic than the others and genuinely concerned for the future of both Norman and Letty. Significantly, Edwin is the only one of the quartet overtly connected with the church. That grounding is imperfect, but he takes from his religion what works for him, going to Mrs. Pope's church only when "there's something special going on" (112). Nevertheless, he succeeds in extending himself to others by helping Letty find lodging in Mrs. Pope's house and standing in as next of kin to arrange Marcia's funeral service. His actions bear out Letty's recognition in watching the pigeons that there may be limits to what humans can do for one another. In *Quartet in Autumn*, Pym wrote a novel about her own concerns with aging, one that is indeed relevant to the "unmarried, unattached, ageing woman" (3). Confronting the isolation that many older people experience, she seems to be questioning the extent to which the boundaries that separate and alienate are a part of the aging process.

Pym finished *Quartet in Autumn* in time to receive rejection letters from Jonathan Cape before her "rediscovery" and new popularity in January 1977. Macmillan then published *Quartet in Autumn* and *The Sweet Dove Died*, and Cape reissued her earlier novels. She continued to write, completing *A Few Green Leaves* and revising it for publication (*VPE*, 291).

There is little doubt that Pym used this final novel to come to terms with dying and to resolve the issues she struggled with metaphorically in *The Sweet Dove Died* and *Quartet in Autumn*. Janice Rossen has suggested that *A Few Green Leaves* can be read as "an *apologia pro vita sua,* offering a summary of all Pym's essential novelistic themes and a comment—however indirect—on her personal life."[14] The themes of Pym's earlier novels pass in review in this final one, while the significance of historical time becomes a factor that must be weighed in finding a balance between anthropological writing and the romantic novel. A journal entry in October 1979, written when she was "not feeling well . . . (more fluid)," finds her "reflecting on the mystery of life and death and the way we all pass through this world in a kind of procession" (*VPE*, 331).

The passing of time is a controlling theme for this novel. Time extends over centuries from the medieval era, represented by rector Tom Dagnall's interest in the search for the Deserted Medieval Village, into the future, represented by Tom's suggestion as the novel closes that Emma Howick talk to the village history society about her experience there, relating it to the past and speculating about " 'what *might* happen in years to come,' " and by Emma's anticipation of the novel she will write and the love affair on which she will embark.[15] Time also includes the seventeenth century, reflected in allusions to time passing in the annual walk in the park and woods surrounding the de Tankerville manor, "a right dating from the seventeenth century" (*FGL*, 1), and in the rector's desire to write his diary in the manner of the seventeenth-century antiquarian Anthony à Wood.[16] It includes the eighteenth and nineteenth centuries, represented by Beatrice Howick's specialization in the novels of that period and by the de Tankerville mausoleum, constructed in the early nineteenth century. And it extends into the twentieth century in the nostalgic preoccupation of the history society members with early twentieth-century events that revolve around the de Tankerville family and Miss Vereker, their former governess.

In *A Few Green Leaves,* Pym returns to a village setting much like the setting of her first published novel, *Some Tame Gazelle,* a setting that draws heavily on the village of Finstock, where she lived at the time with Hilary, and suggesting an almost uncanny prescience—that Pym may have anticipated the course of her own life in writing that first novel about "real people." Her use of carry-over characters, typical of her novels, extends into *A Few Green Leaves.* Two of the carry-over characters in this novel about death and time passing, Fabian Driver and Miss Clovis, are there as participants in their own funerals. Images of death are as prevalent in *A Few Green Leaves* as they were in *The Sweet Dove Died* and *Quartet in Autumn,* but the overall tone of the novel is much lighter, with more of Pym's characteristic irony and wit. Its major themes are the ones she has developed throughout her work, having to do with literature and her role as a writer, social change and the church, and relationships between men and women. But here she brings them together to deliver a complex metaphorical statement about the mystery of life and death.

Emma Howick, Pym's protagonist in *A Few Green Leaves*, namesake of both Jane Austen's title character and Thomas Hardy's first wife, and whose mother studies eighteenth- and nineteenth-century novels, is an anthropologist who has come to the village to write up her anthropological studies. Pym uses Emma and her relationship with the anthropologist Graham Pettifer to revise her earlier treatment of the phenomenon of romantic love. As late as *Quartet in Autumn*, Pym has Letty's friend Marjorie give up her own plans to live with Letty in retirement following David Lydell's proposal, only to have Lydell leave her for a woman with a more suitable table. Throughout the novels Pym's unmarried women, from Belinda Bede of *Some Tame Gazelle* on, seem willing to make great sacrifices for romantic attachments. However, Emma is not quite so willing. She provides Graham with food and other household needs and is hopeful of lovemaking in return. But she is also aware of the sacrifices she is making, commenting to herself that though "there may be an unlimited number of things that can happen to the ordinary person, . . . there are only a few twists to the man-woman story" (*FGL*, 120). In spite of her assistance to Graham, she muses that it "was a mistaken and old-fashioned concept, the helplessness of men" (145), and as she carries food through the woods to his cottage she decides "she couldn't always be carrying food to Graham," but that "sometimes he would have to be content with her company only" (146). When Graham invites her to come in for a drink, and she discovers the invitation has nothing to do with a desire to make love but is rather to include Robbie and Tamsin Barraclough talking academic shop, she decisively leaves to "get on with her own work" (174).

Emma's primary male counterpart, however, is the widowed rector Tom Dagnall, who seems more concerned with organizing the ladies of the Local History Society to pursue his historical interests than in what some might consider his more relevant duties as rector. Ironically, his sister Daphne, who came to live with him immediately after his wife's death, is described as "living entirely in the present with no memory of any kind of past" (118). She and the rectory housekeeper, the dire Mrs. Dyer, whose son Jason runs an antiques business called "Deceased Effects Cleared," are more concerned with cleaning schedules than with parish affairs, evicting Tom from his study at inconvenient hours.

Tom and the rectory are pitted against the village physicians and their office, where Dr. Luke Gellibrand and Dr. Martin Shrubsole issue "ritual" scraps of paper—prescriptions—on Mondays to residents who visit the office in atonement for their failure to attend church the day before. Not only does attendance there outstrip church attendance, but the young Dr. Shrubsole, whose interest is in geriatrics, covets the rectory because it offers more space for his family. Significantly, Shrubsole does not move into the rectory, but that doesn't keep him from imagining that "Dr. Martin Shrubsole, The Old Rectory" would be "a highly suitable address for a rising young physician" (183). The older Dr. Gellibrand, who does "not much like the elderly" but loves "the whole idea of life burgeoning and going on," is said to look "more like a clergyman than the rector did" (18). A confrontation between Tom and Dr. G. raises the question of who has more right to the mausoleum—in fact, who has precedence in the village—the doctor or the rector. Tom, however, gains control when he invites the doctor to give a talk on "Death in the olden days" at a winter meeting of the history society (107). In the end it is death that ensures the rector's precedence over the doctor.

Death pervades *A Few Green Leaves*. The de Tankerville mausoleum and church burial grounds stand as monuments to death. Tom encourages his history society ladies to make notes on the graves and the kind of stone used, and to write down the inscriptions when possible "for the county historical record of graveyards" (182). He is preoccupied with the 1678 edict requiring burial in woolens. Miss Lickerish dies without attention one evening during a power outage, yet it is with her death that Tom feels "that he came into his own" (229). The Sunday after her funeral, when Emma notes that one of the front church pews is occupied by relatives of Miss Lickerish who ordinarily did not come to church, Tom tells her that

> it was customary for the mourners to be present in church on the Sunday after the funeral. These particular people would not be seen at a service again until the next funeral, marriage or christening. When Emma expressed indignation, Tom, in his kinder and more tolerant way, pointed out that it gave a kind of continuity to village life, like the seasons—the cutting and harvesting of crops, then the new sowing and the springing up again. (233)

Through Tom, Pym seems to be acknowledging the evolution of the church in community affairs, perhaps even commenting on her own recognition of the fundamental significance of religion in her life. The novels reflect an evolution from the gray, formal respectability of Letty's religion and Edwin's marking of the church calendar in *Quartet in Autumn* to an even more fundamental marking of the seasons, the sowing and harvesting, the recognition of a continuity in village life connected with the natural cycle.

The final chapter of *A Few Green Leaves* brings the community

together for a meeting of the history society that takes place in the
rectory. Dr. G. is there to give his promised "informal talk about the
history of medicine, starting in the seventeenth century and working
up to date" (241). But he speaks instead about "the 'good old days' of
the nineteen thirties" when motorcars were less prevalent and people
walked to the office, turning his talk into a lecture on the health ad-
vantages of walking and jogging (243). Tom is disappointed, but most
of the villagers, like the ladies of the history society, for whom history exists primarily in what they can nostalgically summon from
memories of their own lives, are satisfied.

The novel ends with Emma's acceptance of Tom's proposal that she
speak to the history society, and her determination to write a novel
and embark on a "love affair which need not necessarily be an unhappy one" (250). The implied marriage between Emma and Tom,
however, has little to do with romantic love. It is instead a metaphorical marriage that joins Emma's anthropological objectivity and sense
of romantic idealism with Tom's sense of history. Emma represents
Pym's anthropological experience, gained from her work with the
IAI, and her turn to novel-writing affirms Pym's role as a novelist.
Emma's implied marriage to Tom points to Pym's recognition that
her sense of history, derived at least in part from her literary background, permitted her to live her life symbolically.

Throughout these three novels Pym's metaphors become increasingly complex, as she comes to accept the symbolic meaning of her
own life seen on a grander scale of historical time. Through her metaphors she is able to organize, understand, and universalize her experience. In *The Sweet Dove Died*, Leonora's spirit, the sweet dove of her
inner self, was caged and bound, preventing her participation in the
lives of others. Similarly, in *Quartet in Autumn* the characters are im-
prisoned within themselves—like mummies, dead inside. Communion comes only when Marcia's friends experience her death. Up to
this point aging and dying are tragic and isolating. In *A Few Green
Leaves*, her final creative act, Pym finds her peace with death. As time
takes on symbolic proportions, death becomes a natural phenomenon. The discovery of the Deserted Medieval Village marks Tom's
success as a historian and extends the time represented in the novel
from the medieval period into the twentieth century. Discovery of the
ancient ruins signifies Tom's victory over the limitations represented
by the members of the local history society, who could not see beyond their own nostalgic reminiscences. Emma's union with Tom,
who represents the vastness of history, marks Pym's symbolic acceptance of her own place in the mysterious procession of time. Writing
her self, Pym found a pattern "greater than any of us or all of us" that

would permit her to live "the symbolic life."[17] Through her metaphors she provides her readers a similar opportunity, for by integrating her metaphors with our selves through the study of her art, we create ourselves anew.

NOTES

1. See, for example, Orphia Jane Allen, *Barbara Pym: Writing a Life* (Metuchen, N.J.: Scarecrow Press, 1994), and Anne M. Wyatt-Brown, *Barbara Pym: A Critical Biography* (Columbia: University of Missouri Press, 1992).

2. Paul John Eakin, *How Our Lives Become Stories: Making Stories* (Ithaca: Cornell University Press, 1999), 101, 100.

3. Pym also wrote several short stories, including "Across a Crowded Room," published in the *New Yorker*, 16 July 1979, and reprinted in *Civil to Strangers* (New York: E. P. Dutton, 1987), 367–80. She worked on other novels during this period, but I have chosen to concentrate here on the novels she personally revised and prepared for publication. Pym frequently wrote about aging and death. Wyatt-Brown counts references to death in 66 of 116 manuscripts, and notes that while death was important in her work, it never became the "core of a plot until *Quartet in Autumn*" (148).

4. See James Olney, *Metaphors of Self: The Meaning of Autobiography* (Princeton: Princeton University Press, 1972).

5. Olney, *Metaphors*, 38–39. See also Olney's discussion of his reluctance to define autobiography in his "prelude" to *Memory and Narrative: The Weave of Life-Writing* (Chicago: University of Chicago Press, 1998), xv–xvi.

6. See Olney, "Autobiography and the Cultural Moment: A Thematic, Historical, and Bibliographical Introduction," in *Autobiography: Essays Theoretical and Critical*, ed. Olney (Princeton: Princeton University Press, 1980), 9.

7. Olney, *Metaphors*, 4, 50.

8. Ibid., 30–32, 44.

9. Olney, "Autobiography," 24.

10. Olney, *Metaphors*, 39–42.

11. See Barbara Pym, *A Very Private Eye: An Autobiography in Diaries and Letters*, ed. Hazel Holt and Hilary Pym (New York: E. P. Dutton, 1984), 214.

12. Keats, cited in Pym, *The Sweet Dove Died* (New York: E. P. Dutton, 1979), 146. The Keats poem is entitled "I Had a Dove and the Sweet Dove Died."

13. Pym, *Quartet in Autumn* (New York: E. P. Dutton, 1978), 1, 2.

14. Janice Rossen, *The World of Barbara Pym* (New York: St. Martin's Press, 1987), 156.

15. Pym, *A Few Green Leaves* (New York: E. P. Dutton, 1980), 249.

16. Pym wrote in her diary in July 1976, "Anthony à Wood died at 63, my present age" (*VPE*, 287).

17. Olney, *Metaphors*, 103.

The Quest for Ritual and Celebration in the Comedic World of Barbara Pym

ELLIE WYMARD

THE ELEVEN NOVELS OF BARBARA PYM ARE MUCH ADMIRED AND widely read as well-crafted entertainments. Overlooked are their existentialist mood and Pym's sense of disappointment that organized religion is not more of a help when men and women feel alone and suffer privately, left on their own to devise quiet rituals of self-renewal. Her canon evolves toward one certainty: a woman rescues herself from chaos and affirms herself in a leap of faith only when willing to confront the terms of her own life, which Catherine Oliphant describes as "comic and sad and indefinite—dull, sometimes, but seldom really tragic or deliriously happy, except when one's very young."[1]

At first, the world of Barbara Pym seems strangely insular. The diminutive scale of English village life with the humdrum experiences of spinsters, rectors, and vicars' wives appears to camouflage any serious definition of the human condition. Pym's essential questions are further disguised by the tone of high comedy, for her characters are often ambivalent about learning the true meaning of their lives. In the early novel *Jane and Prudence*, Jane Cleveland, a vicar's wife, ruminates:

> one's life followed a kind of pattern, with the same things cropping up again and again, but it seemed to [her], floundering among the books, that the question was not one that could be lightly dismissed now. 'No, thank you, I was just looking around,' was what one usually said. Just looking round the Anglican Church, from one extreme to the other, perhaps climbing higher and higher, peeping over the top to have a look at Rome on the other side, and then quickly drawing back.[2]

Like Jane, other characters surprise themselves with questions from which they tentatively withdraw, as if to probe them would demand too much. Alaric Lydgate, one of the many anthropologists throughout Pym's novels, "often avoided looking into people's eyes when he spoke to them, fearful of what he might see there, for life was very terrible whatever sort of front one might put on it" (*LTA*, 57).

But ultimately, the characters in the situational microcosm of Pym's country village do not escape or just endure their experience. Rather, they become more human by trying to live with it, affirming their lot in private ritualized gestures or formal ceremonies. Pym's essential subject is the incommunicable uniqueness of each ordinary person: "After all, life was like that . . . for most of us [life is] the small unpleasantness rather than the great tragedies, the little useless languages rather than the great renunciations and dramatic love affairs of history or fiction," notes Mildred Lathbury.[3] From this perspective, Pym accentuates the commonplace, even the banal. While her characters do not confront irrevocable decisions, they do shape their lives through very personal choices. Moreover, they celebrate themselves in ceremonies that have private, and sometimes communal, significance.

The act of writing is itself a ceremonial act for Pym. In *No Fond Return of Love*, she acknowledges that both the novelist and the sociologist may perceive those moments that are "very near the heart of reality."[4] But Emma Howick, the social anthropologist in Pym's last novel, *A Few Green Leaves,* gradually forsakes accumulating data on the "Social Patterns of the West Oxfordshire Community" to write a novel using the same setting. According to Pym, the novelist who involves the emotions of readers in the rhythm of everyday living invites their participation in the very continuity of being. Since "we all came to the same thing in the end—dust and/or ashes, however you liked to think of it,"[5] it is the writer, not the anthropologist or the historian, who can preserve "a few green leaves" for future generations.

Tom Dagnall, the village vicar in *A Few Green Leaves*, is particularly aware of historic time. His goal is to discover the ruins of a deserted medieval village in the woods of Oxfordshire. On the first Sunday after Easter, he also rallies the villagers to participate in a walk through the park and woods surrounding the ancient manor and mausoleum on the fringe of town, a variation on an annual rite dating from the seventeenth century. Preoccupied with local history, he keeps a record of his own daily life: "What was he to write about the events of the morning? 'My sister Daphne made a gooseberry tart . . . ?' Could that possibly be of interest to readers of the next century?" (137).

Life for Pym is a social enterprise. Natural ceremonies must be preserved if one is to live fully in the present. Funerals, marriages, christenings "gave a kind of continuity to village life, like the seasons—the cutting and harvesting of the crops, then the new sowing and the springing up again" (233). Such affirmation risks sentimentality, for it may seem that Pym is yearning for simpler times. Her sense of ritual, the most important organizing principle of her fiction, reveals, in fact, the evolving complexity of her work and brings us closer to its significance.

The early novels, *Some Tame Gazelle, Excellent Women,* and *Jane and Prudence,* are grounded in unquestioned values. Jane Cleveland, forty-one and a former English tutor at Oxford, had once "taken great pleasure in imagining herself as a clergyman's wife . . . but she ha[d] been quickly disillusioned" (*JP,* 81). Nonetheless, she grows in personal identity to the point of being able to confide in her husband: "We can only go blundering along in that state of life unto which it shall please God to call us. . . . I was going to be such a splendid clergyman's wife when I married you, but somehow it hasn't turned out like *The Daisy Chain* or *The Last Chronicles of Barset*" (212). But by continuing to carry out the ritual duties expected of her role, she restores herself:

> 'I wanted some little books suitable for Confirmation candidates,' said Jane in a surprisingly firm and thoughtful tone. 'Not too High, you know'. . . .
> By now it was almost teatime. . . . [but] she would go without [it] as a kind of penance for all the time she had failed as a vicar's wife. (218–19)

In *Excellent Women,* Mildred Lathbury, the "just over thirty," unmarried daughter of a country clergyman, is drawn to worship at St. Mary's Church "on the wrong side of Victoria Station," because it is relatively "High." This mild rebellion against the wishes of her dead parents involves Mildred in the lives of Father Julian Malory, his sister Winifred, and their boarder, Mrs. Allegra Gray, who has romantic designs on the unmarried rector. Mildred has more opportunities than most of the "excellent women" of the parish to meet men and possibly marry. But she exercises a firm sense of choice, clarified for her through simple domestic ritual: "As I moved about the kitchen getting china and cutlery, I thought, not for the first time, how pleasant it was to be living alone" (*EW,* 19).

Although Pym's early characters are not moved to profound meditation, they experience the joy of making quiet decisions about their own lives in the presence of ordinary human reality. In *Less than Angels,* a young anthropology student, Deirdre Swan, draws insight for us:

> Yes, I suppose it's comforting to see people going about their humdrum
> business. . . . At home her mother would be laying the breakfast and later
> her aunt would creep down to see if she had done it correctly. And they
> would probably go on doing this all of their lives. (53)

Pym keeps faith with life itself, even its trivialities.

One never hears the actual sound of terror in Pym's early novels.
Her first heroine, Belinda Bede in *Some Tame Gazelle,* only suggests
unspoken depths by ruminating, "If only one could clear out one's
mind and heart as ruthlessly as one did one's wardrobe."[6] But two
later heroines, Letty Crowe in *Quartet in Autumn* and Leonora Eyre
in *The Sweet Dove Died,* encounter nothingness and the horror of
being. The quartet in autumn are lonely government clerks—Letty,
Marcia, Norman, and Edwin—who have worked together many years
in an airless London office, but have shared very little of themselves.
When facing retirement, Letty awakens from a dream about her
youth: "All gone, that time, those people . . . [she] lay for some time
meditating on the strangeness of life slipping away like this."[7] At the
office retirement party for Letty and Marcia, the host does not even
know what their jobs were, only that he has no reason to replace
them. At this point, Letty experiences utter helplessness: "It seemed
to Letty that what cannot now be justified has perhaps never existed,
and it gave her the feeling that she and Marcia had been swept away
as if they had never been. With this sensation of nothingness she entered the library" (114).

The quartet hesitantly tries to redefine itself when Norman and
Edwin plan a reunion luncheon. Shortly after, when Marcia, the most
eccentric member of the group, dies, the three survivors follow her to
the crematorium and afterward share their second meal. Returning
that night to her eighty-year-old landlady, Letty is renewed with another cup of tea: "There was something to be said for tea and a comfortable chat about crematoria" (195). At the end of the novel, she
looks forward to a day in the country with Edwin, Norman, and Marjorie, her only sustaining friend. Planning such a day "made one realize that life still held infinite possibilities for change" (218). To rescue
herself from emotional deprivation, Letty must find significant forms
and ceremonies. Pym insists that rituals preserve one from experiencing chaos, but such actions must spring from the ability of the character to admit to the realities of her own existence. Letty's picnic is an
affirmation of life, a free act of faith.

One of Pym's most complex heroines, Leonora Eyre of *The Sweet
Dove Died,* is unappealingly selfish and snobbish. A collector of Vic-
toriana, she admits to insulating herself against disagreeable realities:

"Life is only tolerable if one takes a romantic view of it. . . . And yet it's wicked, really, when there's all this misery and that sort of thing, but one feels so helpless—I mean, what can one do?"[8] Approaching fifty, Leonora rejects a wealthy antiques dealer, Humphrey Boyce, in favor of his twenty-four-year-old bisexual nephew James, whom she loses to the malicious Ned. James feels that Leonora would have been able to deal with his relationship with Ned had she the ability to lose her perfect control and "been just a little angry" (205). But unknown to James, Leonora does experience disintegration. She enters into a cycle of despair, suffering migraines and sleeping fitfully. Her first crisis occurs in a Knightsbridge tearoom where she is conscious of belonging

> with the sad jewellery and the old woman and the air of things that had seen better days. Even the cast off crusts, the ruined cream cakes and the cigarette ends had their significance. . . . [Leonora felt] debased, diminished, crushed and trodden into the ground, indeed 'brought to a certain point of dilapidation'. I am utterly alone, she thought. (184–85)

Later, she humiliates herself further by sobbing uncontrollably in front of Meg, a younger friend who has been tormented in her love for a homosexual man. Up to this point, Leonora had offered her little comfort. During these two crises, Leonora creates new meaning for herself by relinquishing her false pride and dignity; shallow refinements, at the beginning of the novel, now deepen into a kind of courage. But even though Leonora grows in sympathy and sensitivity, Pym still does not claim too much for her. After all, the mode of *The Sweet Dove Died* is essentially ironic. Yet for Pym style is a way of coping with modern pressures, even if it cannot resolve them.

Other characters, too, relieve their isolation by discovering their own private ceremonies—for contemporary life, according to Pym's later fiction, is very unfestive. Even in a world of structured social effort, the individual is more isolated than ever. For example, the social worker assigned to Marcia in *Quartet in Autumn* has little insight into the old woman's profound loneliness, let alone her peculiar habit of collecting, washing, and stacking discarded milk bottles. The geriatrician's mother-in-law in *A Few Green Leaves* finds more comfort participating in parish coffees than in adhering to diet charts and exercise schedules. In comparison to the present, the past is rich with natural rituals that provide assurance and connection.

If Pym's characters are in search of order and ceremony, it is ironic that the Anglican Church, so central to their social life, is never the source of inspiration for their renewal of faith. The churches are, in fact, half empty, but the ineffectual, often ludicrous vicars hardly know what to do except muse:

> One morning Tom went into the church, as he often did, to spend half an hour or so, not exactly to meditate or pray but to wander in a random fashion round the aisles, letting his thoughts dwell on various people in the village. This was in its way a kind of prayer, like bringing them into the church which so few of them actually visited, or never darkened its doors, as a more dramatic phrase had it. (*FGL*, 62)

Even though Catherine Oliphant in *Less than Angels* and Rupert Stonebird in *An Unsuitable Attachment* want to return to church, it offers little for them except the comfort of nostalgia. In *The Pleasure of Miss Pym,* Charles Burkhart asks why Pym's men and women even bother to go to church. For him, the only character who comes close to experiencing "inner as opposed to outer religion is Rupert Stonebird," who, after eighteen years of separation, "amid clouds of strong incense [in a North London church] . . . seem[s] to have regained that faith. It had been an uncomfortable and disturbing sensation. . . ."[9]

On the contrary, many of Pym's characters share a religious spirit while being disenchanted with institutional religion. In their search for coherence between spirit and institutionalism, they are, indeed, in crisis. They keep returning to Anglican services because they have been conditioned to think that rejecting church is the same as denying the spiritual realities of life. They are discontent with the church and discontent without it. In Pym's parish, the church is as ineffectual in nurturing the inner lives of men and women as it is in inspiring social reform.

After her retirement, Letty Crowe tries to discover what churchgoing held for people, apart from habit and convention, wondering if it would hold anything for her and if so what form this would take. Attending the Stations of the Cross, she hears the litany, " 'From pain to pain, from woe to woe' . . . but Letty's thoughts had been on herself and how she should arrange the rest of her life" (*QIA*, 143). Letty finds hope, not in church liturgy, but in the promise of planning a picnic for herself and the remaining trio of her retired friends. When each day does not follow an ordered pattern, Pym's characters create informal rituals to save them from defeat. Jill Rubenstein notes that a few of Pym's characters find in "the very familiarity of their religion . . . true consolation."[10] But Rubenstein does not explore the fact that they choose to affirm their spirituality in other rituals outside the church. Pym is not iconoclastic in her attitude toward religion, but has more trust in finding grace within the communion of people.

Even within the church, Pym's characters are still left to discover their own rites of affirmation. Tom Dagnall casually ponders if one of the "excellent women" of his parish ever

> asked herself what she was doing there, Sunday after Sunday and even some weekdays, subscribing to something she wasn't sure about. Could he possibly ask her? . . . Of course Miss Lee never had doubts! And if she had, she was much too well-bred ever to dream of troubling the rector with such a thing. (*FGL*, 201–2)

With stoic strategy, Pym never judges such remarks. Unlike Jane Austen, with whom she is inevitably compared, Pym does not achieve her irony through language that says one thing and means another. Rather, her silence reverberates with tension, exposing, in this case, how church ministers are remote from the lives of those they are intended to serve. Pym shouts out only once in her canon, but in doing so, she achieves a startling effect worthy of Flannery O'Connor. The incident occurs when Letty Crowe's apartment building has been sold to a Nigerian, Mr. Olatunde, the father of a large family and a "priest of a religious sect" (*QIA*, 65). One evening Letty finds courage to ask him to tone down the hymn singing because

> '. . . some of us find it rather disturbing.'
> 'Christianity *is* disturbing,' said Mr. Olatunde.
> It was difficult to know how to answer this. Indeed Letty found it impossible so Mr. Olatunde continued, smiling, 'You are a Christian lady?'
> Letty hesitated. Her first instinct had been to say 'yes', for of course one was a Christian lady, even if one would not have put it quite like that. . . . 'I'm sorry,' she said, drawing back, 'I didn't mean . . . ' What had she meant? (66)

From Barbara Pym's viewpoint, the church is never disturbed nor disturbing. By treating religion itself as a secular phenomenon, she seems to be challenging its decline as a mere product of human culture. If Pym's vicars continue in their limited vision and lame leadership, the church risks becoming even more superfluous than her novels reveal it to be. "Did people then only go [to church] for the light and warmth, the coffee after the Sunday morning service and a friendly word from the vicar?" (143).

Pym expresses disappointment rather than bitterness that the church fails to offer sustenance to those who search for an expression of faith. In fact, she is radically protestant, wanting to discover in church tradition a meaning for the new. She seems to wonder wistfully whether religion may have more to say about life than she is even able to imagine. For example, Mildred Lathbury parcels her day according to the church bells: "The bell of St. Mary's began to ring for Evensong. . . . It was too early to go to the vicarage, so I hurried into the church and took my place with the half-dozen middle-aged and elderly women who made up the weekday evening congregation" (*EW*, 12). More importantly, Edwin, one member of the quartet in autumn, does measure time by the liturgical season:

> Everybody knew about Lent, of course, even if they didn't do anything about it, with Palm Sunday ushering in the services of Holy Week—not what they used to be, certainly, but there was still something left of Maundy Thursday, Good Friday and Holy Saturday with the ceremonies, the prelude to Easter Day. Low Sunday always seemed a bit of an anticlimax after all that had gone before, but it wasn't long before Ascension Day and then Whit Sunday or Pentecost as it was properly called. After that you had Corpus Christi, with a procession out of doors if fine, and then Trinity Sunday, followed by all those long hot summer Sundays, with the green vestments and the occasional saint's day. . . . That was how it had always been and how it would go on. . . . (*QIA*, 74)

Pym recognizes a deep human need for liturgical feasts, but in her fiction they continue as solitary celebrations, an ironic contradiction in terms. Her perspective is therefore in the best liturgical tradition, which stresses that liturgy should bring one into communion with the realities of life—joy, death, pain, and evil. Instead, her characters feel separation, not communion, during church ritual.

Although it would be false to claim that Pym is in the profound theological literary tradition of Graham Greene, Evelyn Waugh, and Muriel Spark, she does suggest that the church can distance one from integrating religion as a meaningful part of life. The problems raised by Graham Greene, for example, of whether or not his alienated characters achieve salvation according to the teachings of the church, are not within Pym's realm of speculation. Neither is she beguiled by the theological complexities typical of Waugh and Spark regarding the presence of grace in human activity. While her stylistic affinities are with Jane Austen and Anthony Trollope, Pym quarrels with the Victorian assumption that the world that really counts is the human world. Even though the novels of Austen and Trollope are filled with ministers, their characters do not see a relationship with God as the way to bring meaning to their lives. Pym suggests, on the other hand, that the individual does require spiritual sustenance, but that outmoded religious forms and the supercilious attitudes of lethargic vicars cannot provide it.

When Caroline Grimstone of *An Academic Question* leaves her husband Alan to visit her mother, hoping that in a week or two the problems of their marriage might have resolved themselves in one way or the other, she helps to arrange flowers in the village church. Alone with her thoughts and the flowers, Caroline is startled by the vicar, who asks, "Can I help?"[11]

> For a moment I thought of taking his offer at its face value, as if he were a marriage guidance counsellor, and asking him to help me make it up with Alan. But of course it was unfair of me to expect that he had meant anything more than to hold the beech branches while I tried to arrange the flowers around them. (119–20)

The next morning, while attending the high church service at which the "vicar had three servers assisting him," Caroline wishes she "could feel something" (120). In no way do Barbara Pym's characters expect that the clergy will be involved with the pathos and tragedies of their lives. Furthermore, liturgical worship becomes irrelevant to her characters' deepest concerns, even when, like Letty and Caroline, they are present for it.

Pym's disappointment with formalized religion is a consistent theme throughout her work. When Edwin asks his friend Father G., for example, to visit the dying Marcia, his first response is "she's not in my parish. . . . You know what these parish boundaries are—one road's in, the next one isn't" (QIA, 162). Pym sees ordinary life in religious but noninstitutional terms. Many of her characters validate their lives by the rhythm of the liturgical calendar. The liturgy practiced by the church, however, is without social commitment, causing worship to be alienating and almost self-destructive. The church that once dignified human beings by supposing them worthy of salvation or damnation now contributes to their diminution by taking little account of their most fundamental problems. This essential folly contributes to the tension as well as the comedy of Pym's identifiable world. In her view, only the resiliency of human nature generates the rebirth of a dead soul. Celebration will occur, if only with a "cup of tea . . . and a comfortable chat about crematoria." Acknowledging that "life bruises one,"[12] Wilmet Forsyth elevates her own life "in a glass of blessings," and looks forward to dinner with "Sybil and Arnold, a happy and suitable ending to a good day" (256).

Such ordinary characters are at home in the literary imagination of Barbara Pym. They put small things in order, even if life is not. To minimize this aspect of Pym's high comedy would be to deny the core of her vision. But her novels also share in the existential temper of twentieth-century fiction, where human beings, motivated by a desire for salvation, must ultimately redeem and save themselves.

Notes

1. Barbara Pym, *Less than Angels* (New York: E. P. Dutton, 1980), 89.
2. Pym, *Jane and Prudence* (New York: E. P. Dutton, 1981), 218.
3. Pym, *Excellent Women* (New York: E. P. Dutton, 1978), 101.
4. Pym, *No Fond Return of Love* (New York: E. P. Dutton, 1982), 141.
5. Pym, *A Few Green Leaves* (New York: E. P. Dutton, 1980), 116.
6. Pym, *Some Tame Gazelle* (New York: E. P. Dutton, 1983), 220.
7. Pym, *Quartet in Autumn* (New York: E. P. Dutton, 1978), 27.
8. Pym, *The Sweet Dove Died* (New York: E. P. Dutton, 1979), 91.
9. Pym, *An Unsuitable Attachment* (New York: E. P. Dutton, 1982), 35. Rupert Stonebird's faith is discussed in Charles Burkhart, *The Pleasure of Miss Pym* (Austin: University of Texas Press, 1987), 108.
10. Jill Rubenstein, "Comedy and Consolation in the Novels of Barbara Pym," *Renascence* 42 (1990): 183.
11. Pym, *An Academic Question* (New York: E. P. Dutton, 1986), 119.
12. Pym, *A Glass of Blessings* (New York: E. P. Dutton, 1980), 242.

Full of Quotations, Like *Hamlet*:
Literary Quotations and Allusions
in *Some Tame Gazelle*

ANNE PILGRIM

LIKE MANY FIRST NOVELS, *SOME TAME GAZELLE* IS PYM'S MOST DI-
rectly autobiographical work, one that originated in the playful impulse of a twenty-one-year-old author imagining herself, her sister,
and her closest friends as they might be thirty years in the future.[1] It
is also her most literary, as gauged by the remarkable frequency in
it of quotations from and allusions to literature of many kinds. An
atmosphere of literature and learning is established from the outset in
the evocative naming of her characters and in their preoccupations.
They have been educated at the University (*i.e.*, Oxford, though it is
never so named), either in their distant youth, as in the case of Belinda
Bede and her sister Harriet, Archdeacon Hoccleve and his wife Agatha, and the librarian Nicholas Parnell, or much more recently as in
the case of Father Plowman and the successive curates assigned to assist the Archdeacon.

The characters are not only educated and well read, but apt to rec-
ollect bits of their reading at every juncture, and more than willing to
share them, in the form of quotations, with others. Given the leisurely
style of village life, quotation becomes an activity in itself. Archdeacon Hoccleve is the undoubted champion in this regard (though he
spares his memory by reading literary extracts to captive audiences
whenever possible) and is jealous of his preeminence. When Count
Bianco, Harriet's perpetual suitor, seems "on the point of bursting
into a flow of Dante" at the mention of Venice, "the Archdeacon [is]
too quick for him and [gets] in first with Byron."[2]

So used to quoting and hearing quotations is he that he assumes
that any striking phrase, such as a remark by Harriet about the Apes
of Brazil, must have a poetic source, and thus worries for days about
the "elusive quotation" (77). The same confusion about the originality of familiar expressions, or those that just sound familiar, informs

Edith Liversidge's joke at the expense of the Archdeacon's Judgment Day sermon: "I couldn't make much of the sermon this morning," she complains. "Too full of quotations, like *Hamlet*" (118). Male characters, such as the Archdeacon, his house guest Bishop Grote, and Count Bianco, often use poetic quotations in private in an attempt to stir the admiration of female listeners. Harriet, flirting with the young curate, flings at him a line of Latin verse, "the last remnants of her classical education." (17). Belinda, who is more modest and introspective, hardly ever quotes aloud, but silently recollects and meditates upon scores of passages, many of them quite obscure.

Pym provides few attributions for the borrowed material introduced into *Some Tame Gazelle*, and no translation for the Greek and Latin. Whatever the language, the words imported are set in italic type. Some quotations are as long as four or even six lines of verse, and are centered on the page, but most, whether prose or poetry, are integrated into longer sentences. Some, especially those associated with Belinda, are quite fragmentary, little more than echoes of the original, buried in interior monologue, and thus in danger of not being noticed at all, much less correctly identified and appreciated by the reader. This is a problem exacerbated by Pym's practice of abandoning italics on occasion to signal that a character, usually Belinda, is quoting while unconscious of doing so.

Were it not for the successive revisions of the text of *Some Tame Gazelle* between its first being offered for publication to Chatto and Windus in 1935 and its acceptance by Jonathan Cape in 1949, one might dismiss the proliferation of quotation as the self-indulgence of a schoolgirl author just down from Oxford, her head over-stocked with passages left over after cramming for exams, and intent perhaps on diverting such absent friends as Henry Harvey and Robert Liddell (the models for Archdeacon Hoccleve and Nicholas Parnell) by embedding private literary jokes in her fiction. We know, however, that through the years Pym retained this feature of the work, even in the face of criticism. As early as 1936 a publisher's reader was asking doubtfully, "Have all the quotations been verified? The quotation from Lyly's Endimion?"[3] When Pym made extensive notes for a "second version" of the novel in the summer of 1945, she asked herself as a preliminary, "If you want quotation [*sic*], why not have them at the beginning of the chapters?" and recommended to herself a page later that the reworked novel have "More plot, less quotation. . . ."[4] But she promptly rejected both restrictions. The novel accepted by Cape in 1949 had been drastically cut down in length, from about 135,000 words in the 1935 version now in the Bodleian Library archive to about 90,000, and many too-extensive quotations that slowed the narrative had been condensed along the way, if not removed altogether.

Yet despite the outright deletion of many quotations and allusions, Pym freely introduced new ones into the sections of the novel that were revised or freshly invented, and she maintained their frequency at an average of one per page. What then was their value to her? An unsympathetic critic might see them as a device for the author to show off her own learning. But this claim is undermined by the fact that by the final revision Pym had subtilized this element of the work, removing most of the explicit references to writers and to the titles of works. It seems more likely that Pym had in mind, in 1949 and later—for she never altogether relinquished literary quotation as a component of her style—a mixed audience for her fiction. She wrote for readers who appreciate the stories her novels unfold without taking much notice of the literary-historical element, but partly also of those other, ideal readers, those able not only to recognize all the quotations and allusions, but to identify their sources and understand their relevance, often richly productive of ironies, to the dramatic context in which they appear. It is my contention that such an informed reading—no matter how achieved—enhances awareness of the wit and humor of *Some Tame Gazelle*, supporting its categorization as a work of "high comedy," and also tends to bring Pym's portraits of certain characters, including the protagonist Belinda, into much sharper focus than could otherwise be achieved. I shall deal with these two claims in turn.

A rare but telling example of a character using a quotation for consciously humorous effect (the full impact of which depends on knowing its source) comes when Dr. Parnell, on his first morning in the village, complains to Belinda that his host, the Archdeacon, has been trying to make him donate to the church-roof fund. Shifting into blank verse, he "solemnly" quotes, ". . . but perforated sore, / And drill'd in holes the solid oak is found / By worms voracious, eating through and through" and provokes Belinda into smiling, "although she knew it was very naughty of her" (95). Belinda's guilty conscience arises from her knowledge that they are colluding in deflation of the Archdeacon's self-importance and perhaps even of his worthy cause, for Parnell's sonorous words come from the opening mock-heroic section of William Cowper's poem *The Task* (1803), which describes the lamentable state of the few surviving three-legged joint stools in the course of listing all the things the human race has sat on.

Frequently, the humor attached to quotations arises inadvertently. The Archdeacon, who is too lazy to plan ahead or to get things straight, introduces the inappropriate at every turn. An early gaffe is his choice of prayer to open the vicarage garden party: "O Lord God, who seest that we put not our trust in anything that we do, mercifully grant that by Thy Power we may be defended against all adversity . . ." (33). Even ever-loyal Belinda suspects him of saying "the first prayer that came into his head" (34); she does not seem to recognize it, however, as the Collect for Sexagesima, the second Sunday before Lent, and so chronologically and liturgically, as well as intrinsically, unsuited to this late-September occasion. At the evening concert that follows, small children from the Sunday school recite passages of poetry that the Archdeacon has just as arbitrarily chosen for them, including unidentified extracts that prove upon investigation to be from Michael Drayton's extremely obscure poem of 1630, *The Muses Elizium,* and from Edward Young's lugubrious eighteenth-century meditative poem sequence, *Night Thoughts on Life, Death, and Immortality.* Father Plowman, sitting in the audience, is presumably not alone in finding the recitations "rather heavy going" (42). The absurd repetition by rote, and "rather too fast" (41), by uncomprehending children is followed by the Archdeacon's leisurely explanation of "the history of the rare word dingle" as it occurs in English literary works before and after Drayton's employment of it in the lines "In dingles deep and mountains hoar / They combatted the tusky boar." In an act of comic self-exposure, the Archdeacon's pretentiousness and his insensitivity to his hearers combine in this display of his learning to "an audience not really interested in such linguistic niceties" (42), just as they do in his sermons.

A lifelong churchgoer and a writer of forthrightly churchy novels, Pym delights in the humorous mismatch of sermon texts with the ensuing sermon. The most notorious instance here is that of the Archdeacon's sermon on the Judgment Day, which begins with his text, "quite a usual one from the Revelation. 'And I saw a new heaven and a new earth, for the first heaven and the first earth were passed away'" (108).[5] However, he gives the text a most unusual treatment, not just because the sermon itself ignores John's vision of the holy city and places emphasis instead on the world ending abruptly in a Day of Wrath, but also because it consists of little more than "a long string of quotations" (109) from poets of the seventeenth and eighteenth centuries, including "bits of Restoration drama" (113), and concludes with a series of abusive-sounding if poetic threats of eternal damnation. Similarly, when Bishop Grote is given the opportunity to preach on the Sunday just before Christmas, he ignores the season altogether and delivers a sermon very much like the slide lecture he had given earlier on his work among the Mbawawa tribe in Africa, minus the slides. For his text he chooses "a verse from the psalms: 'In them hath he set a tabernacle for the sun, which cometh forth as a bridegroom out of his chamber, and rejoiceth as a giant to run his course'" (201),[6] which "seemed to have little reference to the sermon, although the more intelligent of the congregation saw it as referring to the Bishop himself. He was the giant and his course was the Mission Field" (202). They are right about his egotistical sense of his own eminence, but it is not until some weeks later, when he has proposed unsuccessfully to Belinda and successfully, after the briefest of intervals, to Connie Aspinall, that it becomes clear what has been on his mind, and that the key word in his text was actually "bridegroom." A less familiar passage of Scripture than these two is the one taken by the impressively dim Mr. Donne for his appearance that same Sunday evening at Father Plowman's church: "We heard of the same at Ephrata and found it in the wood" (203). So inscrutable, so unpromising a quotation—could it be an invention? Not at all. Pym has picked out verse 6 of Psalm 132, though she was evidently unwilling or unable to imagine any details of the accompanying sermon; we learn only, tantalizingly, that it was "most successful" (203).

Dozens of little jokes are scattered through the text of *Some Tame Gazelle*, there to be enjoyed by any reader with a reasonably full knowledge of the Bible or English canonical texts. Reporting on the arrival of Dr. Parnell and Mr. Mold at the vicarage, Harriet brightly tells her sister, "They came by night, like Nicodemus" (93). It is for the informed reader (clearly not for Harriet) to register how ludicrous is the comparison of two train-riding librarians to the member of the Jewish Sanhedrin who appears in the Gospel of John as a secret follower of Jesus making nocturnal visits to talk with Him.[7] Readers with some literary background often have occasion to enjoy Harriet's slips, as when she wrongfully attributes Goldsmith's verses to Shakespeare: "You remember what Shakespeare said about when lovely woman stoops to folly . . ." (142)—this somewhat immodest remark in explanation of her own reasons for not committing the folly of marrying Mr. Mold.[8] She does not recognize Shakespeare's lines when she hears them, either, not even when they are part of Hamlet's most famous soliloquy: "Harriet remembered Belinda once saying something about people preferring to bear those ills they had, rather than flying to others that they knew not of, or something like that. It had been quite one of Belinda's most sensible observations" (136). When the Archdeacon hears that Belinda, in bed with a cold, has asked for *The Oxford Book of Victorian Verse*, he betrays a somewhat surprising acquaintance with Ernest Dowson's 1891 lyric of dissipation, "Cynara," exclaiming, "She called for madder music and for stronger wine." The joke is lost on Harriet, who replies severely that strong wine is "the last thing that should be given to an invalid" (187).

Unlike Harriet, who tends to be oblivious to literary references, Belinda has an almost over-developed literary curiosity, a trait that contributes much to the memorably comic scene in which Bishop Grote proposes marriage to her (223–25). Maladroit and insincere, the Bishop calls quotation to his aid in a way that only exposes his inadequacies as a suitor. When Belinda first tries to fend off his attentions by protesting that there is "nothing very special" about her, he replies, "Ah well, one hardly looks for beauty at our time of life. 'She is not fair to outward view' . . . how does Wordsworth put it?" Annoyed at the insult to her looks, Belinda nonetheless feels a duty to set him straight: "Not Wordsworth. . . . Coleridge, Hartley Coleridge, I think." (Of course she is right.) An allusion to *Paradise Lost*—"a man does need a helpmeet, you remember in *Paradise Lost* . . ."—does not advance his cause at all, as Belinda recalls only too well the subservience of Eve in the epic: "'*Paradise Lost!*' she echoed in horror. '*Milton*. . . .'" Growing desperate, she hints at a lover who died, and the Bishop, easing away, makes one last stab at literature, beginning, "Of course, as Lord Byron says," but evidently drawing a blank in searching for an appropriate verse, for he remains silent even when the irrepressible Belinda demands, "Do tell me. What *did* Lord Byron say?" (she silently speculates about and rejects as "not really applicable" Byron's "When we two parted in silence and tears"). In full retreat, Bishop Grote falls back on a clerical standby, a hymn, proclaiming somewhat ambiguously, "After all, we must remember that 'God moves in a mysterious way, His wonders to perform,'" but even here he has trespassed on Belinda's territory, for he has appropriated Belinda's favorite among Cowper's *Olney Hymns*—that she has been found humming on three earlier occasions. The whole scene is an anti-romantic set piece much enlivened by the play of literary references.

In her last year of reading English at St. Hilda's, Pym learned that her younger sister Hilary had been admitted to Oxford in her turn and was to enroll at Lady Margaret Hall to read classics. Her still-studying sister was much on her mind in 1934 as she worked at home on the first version of *Some Tame Gazelle*, which she described in her diary as "a story about Hilary and me as spinsters of fiftyish."[9] The teasingly affectionate portrait of Hilary/Harriet and her foibles is one of the charms of the book, along with the continuous interplay between the contrasting yet complementary traits of the two sisters. As we have seen, there is a running joke whose premise is the classically educated Harriet's ignorance of English literature, and Pym, to be fair, made Belinda equally at sea with the ancients; ill at ease with the seamstress Miss Prior, who is "very nearly a gentlewoman," Belinda realizes that she has two feelings about her: "Pity and Fear, like Aristotle's *Poetics*, she thought confusedly" (46). The difference in their education accounts for only one aspect of the contrast between the sisters, however. Temperamentally they are opposites, in a way that recalls such literary models as Elinor and Marianne Dashwood, or even the grave owl and the gay nightingale in the Middle English poem that Agatha Hoccleve's bluestocking niece is studying. Where Belinda is decorous, cerebral, and prudish, Harriet is impulsive, instinctual, and earthy. Harriet is not much of a reader and cannot quote with the facility of some other characters, but there are still many deft touches of characterization in Harriet's use of literary, or quasi-literary, references.

Harriet's down-to-earth physicality introduces a welcome note of comic reality into the genteel atmosphere of village life. Harriet judges others by externals: having looked into *Harmsworth's Encyclopaedia* on the subject, she breezily announces that the Archdeacon's "odd sloping forehead" is "a sign of mental deficiency" (58). She has a fund of folk wisdom and distresses the curate with her hearty reminder, "They say a green Christmas means a full churchyard" (200). Earlier, while planning a trip to pick blackberries with Belinda, she warns, "in October the devil will be in them. You know what the country people say" (79). Belinda only smiles indulgently, probably aware of the proverb asserting that after Michaelmas, the devil defiles the remaining blackberries; in one version he spits on them. Moments later, when Belinda wistfully imagines the serenity of having been born "like Milton's first wife, an image of earth and phlegm," Harriet, with her mind still running in less elevated channels, replies, "Oh, Belinda, don't be disgusting!" (80).

As its title and poetic epigraph from Thomas Haynes Bayly suggest, this novel concerns the universal need for "something to love" (17), whether it be a gazelle, a dove, or in Harriet's case a curate to dote on. There is no shortage of evidence of her affection for curates, though Pym saw fit to slip in a further clue when revealing Harriet's favorite prayer. Bothered, like Belinda, by the Archdeacon's unfortunate choice of prayer at the garden party, Harriet mentally substitutes "the obviously correct one . . . 'Prevent us O Lord in all our doings,'" (34)—none other than the closing Collect from the service for the Ordering of Deacons, presumably also Harriet's favorite service.

Mr. Donne's first visit to the Bede sisters in the novel's opening chapter is viewed through Belinda's eyes and accompanied by her reflections on Harriet's fondness for curates. To Belinda the fondness is innocent enough; though aware that Harriet is "especially given to cherishing *young* clergymen" and that her visits to their lodgings "have often given rise to talk" (7), she concludes that there is "naturally nothing scandalous" about the visits (8). She sees Harriet as behaving "like a motherly hen" when she fusses around Mr. Donne at his leave-taking (17). Not all readers may accept the characterization of Harriet's interest in the curates as maternal, however, especially not those alert to her flamboyant dress, flirtatious behavior and habit of speaking "roguishly" (12), in this and subsequent episodes. Those who find Harriet's attentions to the young men more forward than motherly will find their perceptions validated by a series of allusions, blithely and perhaps unwittingly made by Harriet herself, to sexual relationships in literature.

Harriet, who loses one curate after another to other parishes, the Mission Field, or marriage, clearly identifies with historical lustful women spurned by lovers, or potential lovers, who leave them. In one rapid exchange (which Pym added in revision as though to underscore the point) Belinda raises the idea of being turned into a pillar of salt, and Harriet immediately concludes that she is talking about "Potiphar's wife . . . in the Old Testament somewhere" (80). It was not Potiphar's wife who was thus punished, though perhaps she should have been after her determined attempts to seduce the handsome young Hebrew slave Joseph when he was first brought into her Egyptian household.[10] Lot's wife is a more familiar Biblical figure, so the closeness of Potiphar's wife to the surface of Harriet's consciousness seems more than a little incriminating, although not to Belinda, who blandly makes the necessary correction. Two other examples, from Harriet's highly selective recollection of the Latin poets she once studied, hint at her identification with mistresses who are abandoned. In the first scene with Mr. Donne, Harriet exclaims as proof of her knowledge of Latin, "*Ah quotiens illum doluit properare Calypso*" (*STG*, 17). This is a line from that manual of seduction, *The Art of Love*,[11] in which Ovid recalls the extended affair of Ulysses and Calypso, and the despair of the goddess when Ulysses finally tears himself away from her. In English it would read, "Ah, how many times did Calypso grieve at his hastening." (The bemused curate only wonders whether this is a hint for him to go home.) Later on, when Belinda is unwell, Harriet tries to press on her the Fourth Book of Virgil's *Aeneid*, saying, "I know you like the part about Dido and Aeneas" (186). Even in her feeble state Belinda has the strength to point out that she can't read Latin. Presumably then it is Harriet who lingers over the text, in which the proper widow Dido is inflamed with love for her guest, the godlike Aeneas, enters into a scandalous affair with him, and then, like Calypso, "grieves at his hastening."

It would be too bold to suggest that Harriet makes overt sexual advances to curates thirty years her junior (though Mr. Donne does seem extremely relieved when Belinda's return from the vicarage releases him from his place on the sofa, construing with Harriet the erotic poetry of Catullus), but the reader's sense of the sensuality in her nature—so different from Belinda's—can only be intensified by comprehension of the allusions to the ancient texts. Even Harriet's recollection of such a dry history as the *Germania* of Tacitus is tinged with impropriety: in an after-dinner discussion of the dress of the ancients, Harriet launches joyfully into a remembered sentence in Latin, one which translated means, "The wealthiest are distinguished by a dress which is not flowing but is tight, and exhibits each limb" (*STG*, 126).[12] Harriet may be a spinster, but she is a racy spinster, and in the light of these quotations and allusions it is all the more understandable that near the end of the novel her own sister, speculating to herself on the age at which Harriet might safely have a curate to live with her without fear of scandal, concludes that "whatever the age might be . . . it would be many years before Harriet would attain it" (217).

Harriet is reliably comic, a flat character according to E. M. Forster's definition, who is the same whenever she appears. Of much greater complexity and serious interest to the reader is Belinda, the novel's protagonist and central consciousness. This is a novel in which little happens, at least outwardly, and in which the moral of the story, as articulated by Belinda to herself on two occasions, is supposedly that "all change is of itself an evil" (145). Both sisters decline proposals of marriage, and the plot in fact has to do with Belinda's growth, with change in the direction of an enhanced self-knowledge and self-confidence. No accurate assessment of her character and her personal evolution can be made without taking into account her habits of quotation and allusion.

Throughout the novel, the reader witnesses Belinda's habitual alternation, often from moment to moment, between self-doubt (expressed in her diffidence, timidity, and constant anxiety lest she do what is "not quite the thing") and self-confidence. The major movement, however, is toward renewed self-esteem, symbolically marked in the closing chapter by the new, more closely fitting blue dress she wears to Mr. Donne's wedding reception, and the "rather large sip of champagne" she boldly takes before looking round the parish hall "with renewed courage" (248). Her progress is made possible, in the traditional way of such novels of formation, by a series of discoveries about herself and others. Belinda as we last glimpse her has learned that she will not, as she thought, have to go through life without having received at least one proposal of marriage (and from a bishop at that); she will be a spinster by choice rather than necessity. She has learned that the ever-pretentious Agatha can on occasion appear "pathetic" (226)—her warm feelings for Bishop Grote unreturned and her gift of hand-knitted socks ungallantly sneered at. In some amazement, Belinda realizes "that she had been offered and refused something that Agatha wanted" (225). Most importantly, Belinda has discovered that her own loss of the Archdeacon as a suitor thirty years before was more in the nature of a theft, that he was in fact stolen away by Agatha, who in her commanding way proposed to him. She will no longer have to blame herself but can believe that she was his first choice then, as she is Bishop Grote's now. All of these discoveries, however, come near the end of the novel, and perhaps a bit late to undo the casual reader's impression that Belinda is inferior and inadequate. In part because of the filtering of the narrative through her consciousness, Belinda's tendency to self-deprecation may mislead readers who accept at face value her over-modest reflections; for instance, on the very first page of the novel she describes herself in midlife as having "retained some smattering of the culture acquired in her college days" (7). Too easily overlooked are her exceptional qualities of heart and mind, including—of most interest here—the impressive erudition revealed in her thoughts, if not in her speech. "[S]mattering" proves to be a considerable understatement.

Ever circumspect, Belinda quotes aloud from or speaks about literature only half a dozen times in all of *Some Tame Gazelle*, but she is continually thinking about it, to the point of selecting quotations she might use in a certain situation, or which others might appositely use. She can lose track of where she is and what she is talking about when a key word in her thoughts sets her off mentally locating a literary source. In addition to Belinda's demonstrated familiarity with Church of England hymns, the Bible, and the *Book of Common Prayer*, the list of English authors whose work she gives proof of knowing includes the following, in chronological order: William Dunbar, John Lyly, Michael Drayton, Thomas Campion, William Shakespeare, Ben Jonson, John Donne, Thomas Carew, Abraham Cowley, John Cleveland, Thomas Browne, John Milton, the Earl of Rochester, Thomas Southerne, Alexander Pope, Edward Young, Samuel Johnson, George Crabbe, Charles Lamb, Lord Byron, John Keats, Hartley Coleridge, Thomas Haynes Bayly, Leigh Hunt, Alfred Lord Tennyson, Christina Rossetti, Samuel Butler, and T. S. Eliot.

Not only is Belinda's learning extensive, but it tends to the esoteric. Beyond the "greater English poets," she knows minor ones (though "minor" hardly does justice to the status of Thomas Haynes Bayly). As well as recalling works of poetry, she displays an impressive knowledge of lesser-known prose discourses by the same authors: where the Archdeacon is content to quote from *Night Thoughts* or *Samson Agonistes*, Belinda recollects phrases from Young's *Conjectures on Original Composition*, echoed in her hopes that despite the aging process she is still "an original shining like a comet, mingling no water with her wine,"[13] and from Milton's *Doctrine and Discipline of Divorce*, whence the description of the burdensome wife as "an image of earth and phlegm."[14] Where others quote from prose works, she shows herself familiar with more obscure prose works by the same author, as in the case of Dr. Johnson. Nicholas Parnell likes to cite, "Love is only one of many passions and it has no great influence on the sum of life" (144), from Johnson's *Preface to Shakespeare*, and the Archdeacon makes repeated reference to the phrase "sentiments to which every bosom returns an echo" from Johnson's *Life of Gray*, but Belinda's almost letter-perfect recollection of Johnson's statement that "all change is of itself an evil [and] ought not to be hazarded but for evident advantage" (*STG*, 145) is drawn from his 1747 *Plan*, or prospectus, for the *Dictionary*.[15] Belinda refers only once to her literary knowledge, and then it is with a note of apology, as she tells the Bishop, "I'm afraid I like what I remember from my student days" (207). Readers aware of her range and depth of reference may well take a more positive view and reach a conclusion unavailable to those in Belinda's circle: that she alone is truly educated, in that her university studies have had a lasting effect on her inner life.

Belinda not only reads and recollects, but actually thinks about the passages that come to mind with a critical intelligence—a habit that sets her above the other quoters of literature. She continually tests the validity of literary statements against her own experience, questioning, doubting, and struggling to find where the truth lies. Her contemplation of poetry provides not just consolation, but a series of revelations that lead on to and illuminate for the reader Belinda's recovery of self-confidence, which is achieved despite her being so isolated among and undervalued by the foolish. Four examples will demonstrate this process. Standing in the church pew just before the Judgment Day sermon begins, Belinda concentrates on the words of the morning hymn penned by John Keble in 1827, "Through sleep and darkness safely brought, / Restored to life, and power and thought," and weighs their applicability: "Not that she ever thought of herself as having much *power*, but she was certainly alive and might be considered capable of a small amount of thought. She could at least thank God for that" (106).

As Belinda grows in assurance near the end of the novel, she becomes more aggressively critical; the next three examples crop up over
100 pages later. When the curate sings the Elizabethan lyric "Love is
a fancie, / Love is a frenzie, / Let not a toy then breed thee such
annoy,"[16] Belinda silently queries the term "toy," but then accepts it,
and decides that the poet is giving "excellent advice" (208). By now,
she suspects that her love for the Archdeacon will never be returned,
and she has begun to detect ominous signs of Bishop Grote's interest
in her. Another instance of rapid second thought comes as she con-
soles Count Bianco for his lack of success with Harriet by quoting to
him Tennyson's "it is better to have loved and lost than never to have
loved at all."[17] Out loud she testifies to the comfort in those lines,
saying, "so many of us have loved and lost," but inwardly she rebels
against "this picture of herself, only one of a great crowd of dreary
women." In a sudden act of disassociation from past views, she decides that "perhaps Tennyson was rather hackneyed after all" (214).
    In the immediate aftermath of having firmly refused the Bishop's
patronizing proposal, the resurgent Belinda examines Keble's morning hymn one more time, and dismisses both Keble and by implication the Archdeacon in a flash of feminist insight. In an earlier scene,
the Archdeacon had arrived unannounced at the Bede household and
patronizingly told Belinda and Harriet how glad he is to find them
engaged in "the trivial round, the common task"—words that roll off
his tongue as a mere cliché. Now, as Belinda returns to the labor of
kneading ravioli, they recur to her mind. As she contemplates Keble's
original claim in the hymn's sixth stanza that "The trivial round, the
common task / Will furnish all we ought to ask," she imagines the
lines being penned by a gentleman in his paneled study, "well dusted
that morning by an efficient servant." "Had Keble *really* understood?
Sometimes one almost doubted it" (227). Keble's experience lies too
far away from the efficient servant's, and from Belinda's own ("standing at the sink with aching back and hands plunged into the washing-
up water" [227]), for his words to carry any authority. She has in fact
all the "power" she needs, especially the emotional power to liberate
herself from past dependencies, and although once she identified with
the faithful slave who "had grown to love its [*sic*] chains," (130), she
has by novel's end set about casting off her own.
    In delineating Belinda's consciousness, and particularly her evident
reluctance to regard her own memory as trustworthy, Pym boldly
runs the risk of creating misunderstanding in her readers even while
offering the richest rewards to those whose familiarity with the
poetry and prose of several centuries allows them to be undeceived
by Belinda's chronic diffidence. Readers who too readily accept the

fallibility of her memory as a given may undervalue the character's insights and even her intelligence. Belinda is keenly aware of the years that separate her from her student days and betrays some concern about loss of mental acuity: the reader observes her quoting "vaguely," remembering "something about" a poetical statement or "whatever it was" a poet said, and worrying if she had "made it up herself." While these hesitations are no doubt in character, one ought to note that they all occur in the first fourteen chapters, before Belinda begins to revive in confidence, and that Pym has ensured that they then— fittingly—die out altogether.

Moreover, a close examination of the quoted matter proves her tentativeness entirely unwarranted. In Chapter 11, Belinda declines to heed Harriet's advice to put on lipstick with a heavier hand: "Oh no, Harriet, I don't think I can use any more. I shouldn't really feel natural if I did. 'Thou art not fair for all thy red and white,' she quoted vaguely" (115). Belinda's manner may be distracted, and her use of the words in discussing makeup rather far removed from Thomas Campion's original anti-Petrarchan conceit, but she has perfectly recalled the first line of his lyric of 1601.[18]

Similarly, her wondering whether the poet Young had not "said something about his heart becoming the convert of his head" (129) belies her quite precise knowledge of the pentameter line near the end of Night IV of *Night Thoughts*.[19] Reflecting on her continuing though hopeless love for the Archdeacon, Belinda thinks, "Perhaps the slave had grown to love its chains, or whatever it was that the dear Earl of Rochester had said on that subject" (130). Here the question is only which of two "songs" using slave/chain imagery informs her thoughts. Since there are references elsewhere in the novel to the *Poems on Several Occasions, with Valentinian: A Tragedy*, it may be the lines sung in Rochester's adaptation of the play, concluding "Kindness only can persuade; / It gilds the lover's servile chain / And makes the slave grow pleased and vain," that are meant, rather than (or in addition to) the declaration by the enslaved lover in the verse eventually collected in *Examen Poeticum* in 1693, "I triumph in my chain."[20] The final example of Belinda's being right, and not guilty (as she speculates) of having "made it up herself," comes when she asks herself, "hadn't one of our greater English poets said something about Pity being akin to Love?" (155). The dramatic poet, "greater" or not, is Thomas Southerne, whose title character in *Oroonoko* does declare, "Pity's akin to Love."[21]

These examples of Belinda's undervaluing of her own knowledge all arise from her grand preoccupation, her unrequited love for Henry Hoccleve, and demonstrate what damage has been done to her self-esteem by her unqualified admiration of one who is in mind and character her inferior. In this early phase, in the first fourteen chapters, she doubts that she can be fair to his eyes and suspects that his smiles are those of pity. She feels herself enslaved, even if comfortably so, and she despairs of achieving a calm rationalism. Where the Archdeacon regards literary learning as merely the wherewithal for pretentious and public display, Belinda, who knows as much or more about poetry, elects to keep her knowledge to herself—worse, as we have just seen, she tends to keep it *from* herself. Still, for readers who know their Campion, Young, Rochester, and Southerne, Pym has left useful clues to Belinda's mental and moral strengths. The most alertly perceptive of readers may thus be able to anticipate early on Belinda's insight, in the anagnorisis of the late chapters, that her self-doubt is largely unwarranted.

The final version of *Some Tame Gazelle* had the double advantage of Pym's accumulated years of experience as a writer of fiction and of the very careful reworkings she had given it, especially in the later 1940s. "After the war (about 1948)," she recalled, "I took up the manuscript of *Some Tame Gazelle* again and decided to rewrite and improve it, which I did."[22] As far as the use of quotations and allusions is concerned, the nature and degree of the improvement is made clear by comparison of the 1935 typescript version with the ultimate one. The well over 200 literary references that appear in the latter are without exception under firm artistic control, integrated with care into the fabric of the novel. Pym's manipulation of literary quotations and allusions serves, as I have shown, to intensify the comic effects and to illuminate character traits in the novel, and ought to draw the attention of readers to the often unacknowledged erudition, and the developed artistry, of Barbara Pym herself.

NOTES

1. I would like to thank York University for grants supporting my research. All biblical references are to the 1662 text of the Church of England *Book of Common Prayer* and to the Holy Bible, Revised Standard Version.

2. Barbara Pym, *Some Tame Gazelle* (New York: E. P. Dutton, 1983), 124.

3. MS Pym 163, fol. 45, Bodleian Library, Oxford.

4. MS Pym 3, fol. 1r, 2.

5. The text is Revelation 21:1.

6. Psalm 19:5, as Englished for the *Prayer Book* Psalter.

7. John 3:2.

8. Oliver Goldsmith, *The Vicar of Wakefield* (1766) (Harmondsworth, Middlesex: Penguin Books, 1982), 148.

9. Pym, *A Very Private Eye: An Autobiography in Diaries and Letters*, ed. Hazel Holt and Hilary Pym (New York: E. P. Dutton, 1984), 44.

10. Genesis 39:7–20.

11. Ovid, *Ars Amatoria* 2.125. See *Ovid: The Art of Love*, trans. Rolfe Humphries (Bloomington: Indiana University Press, 1957), 134.

12. The Latin sentence reads "Locupletissimi veste distinguuntur, non fluitante ... sed stricto et singulos artus exprimente." For the passage in English see *The Complete Works of Tacitus*, ed. Moses Hadas (New York: Modern Library, 1942), 717.

13. See *The Complete Works of Edward Young*, ed. James Nichols (London, 1854), 2:547–86.

14. See *The Doctrine and Discipline of Divorce*, in *The Complete Prose Works of John Milton*, ed. Douglas Bush et al., vol. 2 (New Haven: Yale University Press; London: Oxford University Press, 1959).

15. Johnson's assertion is quoted by Donald J. Greene in *The Politics of Samuel Johnson* (New Haven: Yale University Press, 1960), 33.

16. Robert Jones, "Goe to Bed, Sweete Muze" (1601); see *Lyrics from English Airs*, ed. Edward Doughtie (Cambridge: Harvard University Press, 1970) 206.

17. Alfred, Lord Tennyson, *In Memoriam A.H.H.*, 27.15–16; see *Tennyson: In Memoriam*, ed. Susan Shatto and Marion Shaw (Oxford: Clarendon Press, 1982), 59.

18. Thomas Campion, "Thou Art Not Fair" (1601); see *The Works of Thomas Campion*, ed. Walter R. Davis (New York: Doubleday, 1967), 34.

19. Young, *Night Thoughts*, IV, line 740 in *Complete Works* 1:64.

20. David M. Vieth has described both songs as "prentice work" in his edition of *The Complete Poems of John Wilmot, Earl of Rochester* (New Haven: Yale University Press, 1968), where they appear on pages 10 and 11.

21. Thomas Southerne, *Oroonoko* 2.2.58; see *Oroonoko*, ed. Maximillian E. Novak and David Stuart Rodes (London: Edward Arnold, 1977), 44.

22. MS Pym 98, fol. 123.

Part II
Literary Encounters

My First Reader

HAZEL HOLT

To Hazel—my first reader, the author's love and thanks.
—Barbara, 17ᵗʰ October 1955 (inscription in Less than Angels)

I SUPPOSE I'D BEEN WORKING IN THE LIBRARY OF THE INTERNA-
tional African Institute for about two months when Mrs. Wyatt, the
secretary, said to me, "I must lend you Miss Pym's novel. I'm sure
you'll enjoy it." Miss Pym worked in the chaotic office downstairs
labeled Publications, and I'd occasionally been sent down there by
Miss Jones, the librarian, to take a manuscript or a book for review in
Africa. These had been acknowledged with a brief smile and a polite
murmur. We had had no conversation. Tall, rather austere-looking,
Miss Pym was certainly not my idea of what a novelist should look
like—well, not the sort of novelist *I* would want to read. When Mrs.
Wyatt gave me the book, my heart sank. *Some Tame Gazelle*: a book
about Africa, even worse, a novel about Africa. Very much *not* my
sort of book.

"Thank you very much," I said, and took it away thinking I'd just
glance through it and try to find something polite to say. With some
reluctance I opened it and read, "The curate seemed quite a nice
young man, but what a pity it was that his combinations showed,
tucked carelessly into his socks, when he sat down."[1] And, of course,
I was lost.

After that I found myself making excuses to go down to the office
marked Publications, and I discovered that Miss Pym was not austere
at all but shy, and that when she realized that you were, as our friend
Ailsa Currie used to say, "on the same wavelength," she was friendly
and full of chat. By the time *Excellent Women* was published in 1952,
I, too, was working in that downstairs office, and I had made a friend.

Excellent Women was even more appealing to me because, although
I loved to read about the lives of the Misses Bede, I had spent my
childhood prewar years in a city and not in a country village. Mildred's London was my London—a place still littered with unrecon-

143

structed bomb sites, with austerity, shortages, and that strange *fin de guerre* feeling that still hung on, even though the war had finished seven years before. I, too, had attended Lenten services in the ruins of St. Ermin's (St. James's Piccadilly), and I often had lunch with Barbara in Lyons Corner House, with our trays rattling along that moving belt. Now I could really respond to the acute observation, the delicate irony, and the splendid felicities of style.

By the time *Jane and Prudence* was published in 1953, Barbara and her sister Hilary were my friends, and I knew enough of Barbara's life and surroundings to appreciate the various themes in the book, while the scenes with Miss Trapnell and Miss Clothier were, of course, part of our daily office life:

> 'I wonder if we might have one bar of the fire on?' asked Miss Clothier at last.
> 'Oh, it isn't cold,' said Miss Trapnell. 'Do you find it cold, Miss Bates?'
> 'No, it doesn't seem cold,' she said.
> 'Well, of course I have been sitting here since a quarter to ten,' said Miss Clothier. 'So perhaps I have got cold sitting.'
> 'Ah, yes; you may have got cold sitting,' agreed Miss Trapnell. 'I have only been here since *five* to ten.'[2]

But it was with *Less than Angels* that my position as merely a faithful reader changed. Barbara asked me to read the book in manuscript. Years before, she'd asked Robert Liddell's opinion of the first draft of *Some Tame Gazelle*, but now he was living abroad and, in any case, they were not as close as they had been; he was no longer the published author and Barbara the young tyro. Hilary always preferred to read Barbara's books when they were actually in print, so I was the very first person to read them. She asked my opinion. I suggested a few very minor alterations of structure and style, and from then on she always gave me her manuscripts to read before she sent them to the publisher, and I always read the proof. In the Publications Department of the Institute Barbara taught me how to be a good editor and I tried to apply to her novels the principles that she had shown me. (A function, incidentally, that I still perform for my son Tom's novels all these years later. Barbara would be pleased about that.) It is always exciting to be the first person to read anything, like making new footsteps on a clean, tide-washed beach, and I loved it. The world of anthropology was now my world and I, too, had followed breathlessly all the details of the "saga" that she and Hilary had created about their neighbors, had watched the prototype of Keith from the window of their flat, longing for more details: "*Well*, Little Thing is certainly here. . . . Hilary and I saw him coming from the bus stop about 10:30 last night. We had come from Hammersmith, he from the other stop (I think) as if he'd been seeing a friend off."[3] Now I felt that I was really part of the Pym world.

The novels appeared regularly every couple of years: *A Glass of Blessings, No Fond Return of Love* (which Barbara dedicated to me—a great pleasure), and it seemed that that was how it would be until she left the Institute and could write full-time. But it wasn't to be, for in March 1963, Cape rejected her new novel, *An Unsuitable Attachment*. It was a bitter blow. I have written elsewhere about those long, miserable years—the "Wilderness Years," as they have been called—when it seemed that nothing she wrote would ever be published again. I can still feel the pain of that time and I don't believe that Barbara, in spite of her later spectacular success, ever got over it. I can remember her setting out from the office with a neatly wrapped package and a brave smile to deliver one or other of her manuscripts to some publisher's office. I can also remember the mornings she came in with an expression of weary resignation to tell me that she had received yet another rejection. "My novel has had its umpteenth rejection (from Cassell). After lunch . . . I go to Red Lion Square and I enter the portals of Cassell's to collect the nicely done-up MS. Where next? Up to Faber in Queen's Square?"[4]

At first she rewrote *An Unsuitable Attachment*, and we both read it again and again, trying so hard to see what could be done to "improve" it. After a while she accepted that the time was out of joint for such a novel and abandoned it, going to work on a book she had had in her mind for some time about the relationship of a young, bisexual man and an older woman: *The Sweet Dove Died*. That was a fascinating manuscript to read, especially since I knew it contained, more than any of her other books, so much of her own overt feelings. But even a book on such a fashionable theme was deemed by the publishers to be not of a kind "to which people are turning," and it was despair once more. In 1971 she developed breast cancer, but, as she always did, she found something of value even in such a horrible experience, making notes in her notebooks to be fleshed out in her books and finding the inspiration for Marcia, one of her most complex characters: "I used to mingle with people in the ward and had lots of talks. I discovered that all you need to do is make some enquiry and you will get a whole life story" (*VPE*, 263).

Towards the end of her time at the Institute, Barbara had the idea of writing a novel set in an office (as it might be the Institute's new office in the more depressing part of Holborn) about four "old, crabby characters, petty and obsessive, bad tempered" (267). When I first read the manuscript of *Quartet in Autumn*, I was dismayed by its bleakness, but as I read it again and yet again the humor (though of a different kind from Barbara's earlier humor), its absolute truthfulness and what Philip Larkin called the courage of all the characters (an echo, of course, of Barbara's own courage) took hold of me and I realized that it was, indeed, a remarkable book.

On St. Valentine's Day, 1977, Macmillan accepted *Quartet* and in September Barbara sent me a copy of the book suitably inscribed: "To Hazel with love and grateful thanks (1961–1977!) From Barbara." For once I wasn't eager to read one of Barbara's books in manuscript. What I passionately wanted to do once more was to read one of Barbara's books *in print*. Then came the fame and the glory, and it was so good to see her quiet pleasure, especially when Macmillan (forgetting that it had ever been rejected by them) published *Sweet Dove,* which was received by the critics with even greater rapture—"highly distinctive". . . "teasing wit" . . . "this faultless novel."

But, alas, the pleasure was to be all too short. The cancer came back, and although Barbara completed *A Few Green Leaves* and knew that it had been accepted by Macmillan, she also knew that she would probably not live to see it published. She gave me the manuscript and asked me to see it through the press for her. This book, then, for many reasons, has always seemed to me to have an elegiac quality. Robert Liddell called it "Barbara's farewell to her readers." The books had come full circle, from village setting to village setting, but what a world of experience, both of life and of writing, lay between.

Some years before she died, Barbara had said that she wanted me to be her literary executor and so, after her death, the cardboard boxes of letters and manuscripts piled up in a corner of my sitting room, waiting to be sorted out before the little white van from Oxford's Bodleian Library came to collect them. At that time my son was up at Oxford and it was, therefore, convenient and agreeable for me to read through Barbara's papers in the New Bodleian. Under the helpful and friendly eye of Colin Harris, the Bodleian librarian, it was a pleasant place to work. At times I almost felt I was a student again, reading for an essay, as Barbara herself used to read in the Bodleian. I felt this most strongly in the Michaelmas term when dusk was falling and I could imagine myself going back to my college for crumpets and tea!

It was a strange voyage of discovery I embarked upon in Room 132. There is always, I think, a tinge of guilt in our pleasure in reading other people's published diaries and letters. How much greater, therefore, was that feeling, a sense of intrusion in fact, as I opened the files and looked at the familiar handwriting on those yellowing pages. I found that there was so much about Barbara's life that I didn't know. Gordon Glover, for instance, was to me only the name of a radio presenter. Barbara had never told me about the part he had played in her life. She hadn't consciously concealed it, but, as people nowadays don't seem to understand, friends—close friends, even—didn't, in those days, feel it necessary to confide every last detail of their lives. There was a restraint, a formality almost, in most relationships. For example, I had known and liked the assistant bookkeeper at the Institute for twenty-five years, but in all that time we were always Mrs. Holt and Mrs. Fisher to each other. *Autre temps, autre moeurs*, better perhaps than this promiscuous flinging about of Christian names.

As I read through the letters I found strong echoes, hitherto unrealized, of Barbara's life in her novels. Now that I knew about the eager young Barbara, Prudence, with her youthful affairs, sprang more vividly to life, as did the Wrens at Naples in their crumpled white uniforms, and, above all, Belinda and her unswerving devotion to the Archdeacon. But glimpses of Barbara's life had been transmuted in the novels, made *smoother*, Barbara would have said. They had been viewed almost objectively—recollected, as Wordsworth said, in tranquility.

But when I came to read the unpublished manuscripts—finished and unfinished—and the short stories, it was a different matter. Here was raw material indeed, not refined into literature, but quite simply large chunks of Barbara's life laid out for inspection and appraisal in a way she never would have allowed when she was alive.

That was really my main problem as her literary executor. Although I knew that these riches, and they were riches indeed, should be made available to her many admirers, I felt that Barbara would have hated them to be presented to her readers (readers who expected the very highest standards from her) without being edited into the kind of finished product that she would have approved of. I realized, too, that the letters and diaries, giving as they did the key to so much of her writing, should also be published. Again I tried, with Hilary's invaluable help and as we both knew Barbara would have wished, not to use material that would cause pain or embarrassment to the people involved. Her letters and diaries, when they were published, came as a great surprise to many of her readers, who had thought of her as an "old brown spinster," one of the more desiccated of her own characters. "You have destroyed a legend," Philip Larkin wrote reproachfully to me when *A Very Private Eye* first came out. "No," I replied. "I have simply destroyed a myth." And, remembering the vivacity of her letters to him, he agreed that was indeed what I had done.

The posthumously published novels were well received—so very well, in fact, that it was difficult to resist pressure to publish everything, even the juvenilia, but both Hilary and I knew that was not what Barbara would have wanted. I read through the unpublished material many times before we made the final decision not to publish any more, but to give permission for all the material in the Bodleian to be "open," that is, available to any scholar who wants to see it.

One thing that gave me more pleasure than almost anything else was to read the notebooks. For many years I had seen Barbara pull out a small spiral-backed notebook from her handbag and jot down some *trouvaille*, some incident, something she had seen or overheard. It was, therefore, with great anticipation that I opened the first one:

> Mission meeting. Prayers are difficult when choir practice interrupts them—the organist making jokes. We pray for streets. 'Warwick Square,' says the Vicar, his tone seeming to gain in fullness. (*VPE*, 185)

> Read some of Jane Austen's last chapters and find out how she manages all those loose ends. (188)

> The Riviera Café, St. Austell is decorated in shades of chocolate brown. Very tasteless, as are the cakes. (188)

Here was the very essence of Barbara, not only an invaluable insight into her method of work but also a sheer joy to read in their own right.

And then there was no more Barbara left to read. Every last word, every last scrap, had been perused—with interest, with astonishment, with joy. But I was glad that I had been able to give a little more Barbara to those faithful readers (many of whom wrote to me and some of whom have since become dear friends) whose overwhelming feeling for Barbara herself, as well as for her novels, is one of great affection. And I know she would have been proud of that.

I no longer read Barbara. I don't need to. If I want to renew my acquaintance with any of her characters or situations, I simply reach back into my memory and they are all there. That's how it is with Barbara—once you've read the novels, she is with you forever.

NOTES

1. Barbara Pym, *Some Tame Gazelle* (New York: E. P. Dutton, 1983), 1.

2. Pym, *Jane and Prudence* (New York: E. P. Dutton, 1981), 36.

3. Hazel Holt, *A Lot to Ask: A Life of Barbara Pym* (New York: E. P. Dutton, 1991), 178.

4. Pym, *A Very Private Eye* (New York: E. P. Dutton, 1984), 272.

Autumn Leaves: Publishing Barbara Pym

PAUL DE ANGELIS

IN THE OLD DAYS—I WON'T SAY "GOOD OLD DAYS," BECAUSE THEY really weren't that—I worked at E. P. Dutton, an old-fashioned firm struggling to come to terms with the changing economics of American literary culture. Not surprisingly, E. P. Dutton did not survive the transition, though a corporate entity called plain old Dutton still lurks in the bowels of the British-owned Pearson-Penguin-Putnam publishing conglomerate. But the old Dutton, the publisher of A. A. Milne, Gore Vidal, Borges, and Barbara Pym, bit the dust a little less than a decade ago, on Halloween Day, 1989, just as the Berlin Wall was tumbling down.

Though publishers die all the time—almost as frequently as bookstores, it seems—publishing doesn't. Just as obviously, authors die, though great literature does not. In the case of Barbara Pym and me, we are mostly talking about a relationship between an editor/publisher and a deceased author. It was by no means what could be called a close relationship. I never met Barbara Pym, and I did not know her personally. Certainly her death in 1980, though it saddened and sorrowed me, and was in many ways a surprise, was a rather abstract thing, soon overtaken by the course of publishing events. Though we had conducted a polite publishing correspondence for nearly two years, this was nothing compared to the friendship that would evolve between me and her surviving sister Hilary and her literary executor, Hazel Holt.

Soon after her death and my publishing disappointment over the relative quiet—and dip in sales—of her posthumous novel, *A Few Green Leaves,* I decided that, rather than be depressed about the fact that potentially the greatest literary author of my career was never going to produce another novel, I ought rather to embark on reading her backlist. Might there not be one acceptable novel out of the (probably drab) half dozen that had never been accepted by American publishers in the '50s (with the exception of *Less than Angels*)? Over the decade that followed Barbara Pym's death, E. P. Dutton, usually in collaboration with various powers-that-were at Macmillan London, proceeded to publish eleven further books by Barbara Pym in addition to the three we had published while she was alive.

The excitement of watching Pym's readership grow was like a magnified echo of the rediscovery that had lifted her out of the obscurity of unpublished novelist in the last three years of her life. To me, Barbara Pym was never more alive than in those days—long after she had already passed away. The Barbara Pym party stopped for me on Halloween Day, 1989, the day I was fired and E. P. Dutton was no more.

Death and Barbara Pym are inextricably intertwined. This has never been more true than in these last few months. The files I pulled out of my drawer to prepare a talk I was to give at the 1999 inaugural meeting of the North American chapter of the Barbara Pym Society were in the tall black filing cabinet I reserve for my "dead files." The thoughts about Barbara Pym that started to take shape that New Year's took their cue from my confession to her that *Quartet in Autumn*, the first book of hers I ever read, was still the one I favored most. So I decided that it was the one I would reread before participating in the conference. I was curious to find out how it felt to reread it, some twenty years later, at a very different stage of life.

Before I could get to it, illness and death struck closer to home. A few days after New Year's I found out that my father's chronic preleukemic condition was transforming into acute leukemia. I began a series of trips to Washington, D.C., for what seemed then to be a process that might last several months. I wrote to Ellen Miller, the conference organizer, that I could not guarantee being in Cambridge for Barbara Pym's special day. I was lucky no longer to have an employer and to have among my clients many understanding writers. Thus I could afford to take the time to be with my father—and perhaps more importantly, to be with myself—during those days. As it turned out, the disease progressed rapidly, and my father died, with only a few days of severe suffering, on February 14, 1999. Instead of a talk for the conference, I found myself preparing a speech for his memorial service.

I had toyed with the idea of taking *Quartet* along with me on several of those trips to be with him, but it was not the book I could read in the heat of those emotions. I even began to wonder whether Barbara Pym really did have something to say to me about the "major" things in life, about death and dying. What would the poet of the forgotten and lonely, the single and unattached, the dull daily routine of the lives of the washed-out English middle class have to say to me in my grief?

A month later I went on vacation to the beach with my family to try to "clean out" my mind and soul after the winter's loss; *Quartet* came along with me. It was not a consoling book. It was not the book I would have taken, or would have read, for a catharsis of any kind, an emotional purging—but at this particular stage in my mourning, I wasn't looking for that. For the first time in my life, I had experienced the death of a parent . . . of *the* parent who, for better or worse, most mirrored me, whatever "me" really consists of in spirit, flesh, and soul. What I seemed to be looking for, and finding, in long walks on the beach, was a way of being alone in a more intense way than ever before. *Quartet* offered reassurance. For isn't *being alone* the very subject of the novel?

These are a few of my perceptions about the principal actors in *Quartet in Autumn*: Letty, Marcia, Edwin, and Norman. The four work in an indistinct office performing indistinct office work. The word *super*annuated comes to mind, though in point of fact they are only in their sixties. They live perhaps *super*ficial lives, at least according to psychological dictates of the times (or the code of the social worker who attempts to bring "relationship" into Marcia's life after her bout with breast cancer). They live without mates or children or family or relatives, though one, Edwin, as a widower with a married daughter whom he visits during holidays, provides a vicarious link to the world of the ongoing, the *still*-living, the world of renewal and change.

They live in urban London, itself changing at a furious pace, the London long since turned upside down by pop culture, immigration, and the loss of empire, but that had yet to find its polyglot voice in writers such as Salmon Rushdie, Kazuo Ishiguro, Martin Amis, or Angela Carter. The heroes of *Quartet* are being displaced by a new world they hardly understand, a city that is not yet conscious of itself, a London typified by Letty's new landlord, Mr. Olatunde, the Nigerian priest who likes to gather his sect of pearly-teethed followers for raucous revival meetings in the downstairs flat of her building.

These Nigerians are Christians too, Letty thinks later, and—if she had dared stay in her old building—they might well have provided warmer and more interesting company than Mrs. Pope, the busybody church lady found by Edwin to "save" Letty from her distressing living conditions. But no one in this quartet ever dares anything. They are fast becoming *super*fluous, even in their own workplace, a department that will be phased out entirely as soon as these four retire.

Norman is an archetypal grouch. His sole tie to the world outside work is his brother-in-law, who puts up with him because he feels sorry for Norman, while Norman believes it is he who suffers most from the curse of brotherly togetherness. Until recently, Marcia's sole tie to the world outside work was her mother and her mother's cat. Then mother dies, followed by mother's cat. Marcia is a collector of milk bottles (only the finest), and though nothing else in her house is dusted or cleaned, her milk bottles are spotless and carefully arranged in a specific order. All her bags are numbered and filed away in drawers. Other odd bottles, bags, and containers that are not suitable for either the dustbin or the milk-bottle collection have to be abandoned in choice shelves at the library.

When the inevitable comes and the two women must retire, Marcia becomes obsessed by the unwanted milk bottle that Letty once gave her in the office and which has unexpectedly found its way into her own home. It is too obvious to leave in the library. That bottle must be disposed of—everything must be ready and in order for Mr. Strong. For Marcia has had an operation, years before. The doctor cut into her most intimate parts. Marcia had once vowed she would "never let the surgeon's knife touch her body, a woman's body being such a private thing."[1] But that was before she met Mr. Strong, the surgeon. Now she has given herself to the doctor. She takes the bus to his house and lingers outside while the surgeon and his wife are giving a party, watching the guests come and go. Soon she will be offering herself to him again. In her obsession, Marcia never eats. One day she collapses, goes into hospital. Mr. Strong registers his disapproval, but Marcia dies.

And now we come to the gift: the great surprise in Marcia's will. She leaves the house to the old grouch, that practical, unimaginative misanthrope, Norman. This gift changes the life of each and every one of the four. The three survivors, who had never before been inside each other's houses, come together at last in the house of the deceased friend. They are visiting Norman, the man of property, admiring the neatly stacked and sorted and arranged milk bottles, the closets upon closets full of old and newly bought clothes, the cupboards crammed full of tins of every sort. Letty suddenly realizes that she has a choice about things, that it is up to her now to decide whether to move to the country or not. Anything is possible. She can even extend the invitation of her country friend Marjorie to bring along Norman and Edwin next time she comes: "Any new interest . . . was to be encouraged, though it was difficult to think of Edwin and Norman as objects of romantic speculation, and two less country-loving people could hardly be imagined. But at least it made one realise that life still held infinite possibilities for change" (218). Marcia's gift has reopened the opportunity of choice. She is the unknown self-sacrificer, the bearer of new life. She who could say nothing in real life or make a real impact can in death render meaning and renewal to all of her friends, about whom she had nothing good to say, and did not even, while in her last days, remember. Could there ever be a novel that more dispassionately reflects the truths of human solitude? Reading and reflecting on it, on the beach and afterward, I found it an oddly comforting meditation on the gifts of the dying. The reading experience was reassuring in an impersonal yet affecting way, the way a religious ritual can sometimes be.

Of course, knowing about Barbara Pym's own struggle with breast cancer in 1971, it isn't hard to see Marcia as a partial reflection of the author. But then, strong aspects of Barbara Pym can clearly be found in all four of the protagonists: in the churchly ritual and calm solicitousness of Edwin; in the hermit-like reclusiveness and critical voyeurism of Norman; in the shy charm, vague romantic urges, and bookishness of Letty; in the aberrant self-abnegating behavior of Marcia.

Did Barbara Pym at some level see herself as Marcia taken to an extreme? The parallel between Marcia's gift to her coworkers and Barbara's to her readers, a gift neither character nor author ever lived to fully see, is intriguing. Of course we must be careful not to make anything too grand out of this literary bequest to us, not some vision of "art for art's sake"; we need to understand it like her characters and her prose, as something pared down and understated, homely and everyday. Like the tins the three survivors lovingly sort according to their own individual tastes after Marcia has passed away—Edwin choosing "spam and stewing steak, Letty prawns and peach halves, Norman sardines, soup, butter beans and the macaroni cheese" (216).

We know that by the time Barbara Pym wrote *Quartet*, she had given up hope of being published. She was writing not for a public, but in my view for part of herself, for a particular part that she wished to "improve," in much the same way she liked to "improve" her novels as she put them once more through the typewriter. I think she wrote *Quartet* as a gift from Marcia, the aberrant one, to that part of herself who was Norman, the critic and misanthrope. And lo and behold, the bequest that *Quartet* represents turned out to be a way out of the woods not just for Norman, and for Letty and Edwin, but for Barbara Pym herself. Whatever Barbara Pym exactly intended with *Quartet* (and I'm sure she knew no more than we), it has always seemed slightly ironic that it was such an apparently bleak novel, the most somber of all her comedies, that propelled her rediscovery and acclamation after several years of the purgatory of being an unpublished novelist.

∽

As far back as 1970, before Barbara Pym had ever had a hint of cancer in her life, James Wright at Macmillan London had read and rather liked *The Sweet Dove Died*. At that time he had not been willing or able to risk publishing it. But in 1977 he was ready to pounce as soon as the *Times Literary Supplement* came out with their famous list mentioning Barbara Pym twice as one of the most underrated novelists of the century. At this point in my life I had just left St. Martin's Press, the American-owned subsidiary of Macmillan London, for the more literary old American publisher, E. P. Dutton. St. Martin's basic function was to make money for Macmillan London in the enlarged marketplace that was America, and any cultural pretensions would have to play second fiddle.

I went to Dutton despite knowing that it was a publishing company in severe identity crisis, a family firm recently sold to a Dutch reference-book publisher that had brought in enough financial resources to buy itself a wonderful editor-in-chief, Henry Robbins, once of Farrar, Straus & Giroux. Henry was literary, but he knew things were changing, and knew he'd have to change with them, and that Farrar Straus was no place to stay if he wanted to do that. Before coming to Dutton, he had briefly had a fling with "big time" publishing at Simon & Schuster, though all it had earned him was a heart attack.

The day of the middle-sized American publishing house was slowly coming to an end, and the last member of the old publishing family, the indecisive Jack Macrae, had had *Quartet in Autumn* sitting on his desk for nearly six months. Like almost every other vaguely literary publishing house in New York, he wondered if he could ever sell more than 1,500 copies of such a title. Would anything *so English* really work in the U.S.? Ironically, the only publisher who didn't care if it sold so few copies was my former employer, Tom McCormack, the head of Macmillan's own subsidiary, St. Martin's Press. (And it was precisely that *indifference* to sales—reflected in their meager advance offers for book rights—that made them a court of last resort even for their owner, Macmillan.)

On my first or second day in my new job, Henry Robbins handed me *Quartet in Autumn*. After I read the newspaper accounts of Barbara Pym's rediscovery in the U.K., I told him that if possible we should publish two books, not one, and try to repeat Macmillan's success in making her rediscovery "a publishing event." I called up the agent for Jonathan Cape, Barbara Pym's former publisher, to ask for some of the older titles. In the back of my mind lingered my ex-boss Tom McCormack's story about how he had made a best-seller out of James Herriott's British veterinarian's tales by putting together two thin British volumes with humorous but incomprehensible U.K. titles such as *If Vets Could Fly* and rechristening the enlarged volume with the second line from a famous Protestant hymn, "All Creatures Great and Small."

It was a sunny day in October 1977 when Henry Robbins told me to come to lunch with him and rights director Tess Sacco of Macmillan. When I told Tess Sacco and Henry over lunch how much I was moved by *Quartet in Autumn* and how much I laughed over *Excellent Women*, she said, "So don't make me sell it to your ex-boss!"—a reference to St. Martin's stingy advances and the low expectations for the books it published. Henry said, "Okay, Paul, make an offer." I said, "Here, at lunch?" He said, sure. I offered a few thousand, Tess wanted a few more, and we compromised. Was it because I was so new to my job and simply needed to sign up some noteworthy titles that I was given the go-ahead? Or was it that I was so unlikely an enthusiast for Barbara Pym's work that my bosses decided that the books stood a chance of becoming popular? Whatever the case, a deal was made. Back at the office I phoned in an offer for *Excellent Women* to Georges Borchardt at Barbara Pym's former publisher, Jonathan Cape. We had decided to try to create our own little revival on this side of the Atlantic.

So began my correspondence with Miss Pym:

31st March 1978

Dear Mr. De Angelis,

Thank you for your letter of 15th February which I am now answering as quickly as possible and returning the publicity form. I expect you already know most of what you need. (I fear it is too late for my age to remain confidential now—I should have thought of that when I was in my twenties!)

Let me say first how thrilled I am that Dutton are to publish *Quartet in Autumn* and *Excellent Women.* It is a good idea to bring them out simultaneously, I feel, because the two books are rather different and may attract different kinds of readers, one hopes. . . .

You ask about Pamela Hansford Johnson and other writers who might say a word for me. It was she who saw *Quartet* in MS. and advised me to send it to Macmillan and she gave me a very good review of my first novel. I know she hasn't been too well lately but James Wright thinks she is better now and could be approached. I have no idea whether Margaret Drabble or Jean Rhys have ever read me. Beryl Bainbridge chose *Quartet* in her list of books of the year, and Jilly Cooper . . . is also a fan. But are either of these well-known enough for your purpose? Iris Murdoch's husband, John Bayley, likes my books, I know, so perhaps she also does—it might be worth trying.

American writers: I was really delighted to see the quote from Shirley Hazzard—it gives me a glow of pleasure to think of it—because she is a writer I very much admire and to think that she likes my books is a won-

der 'testimonial.' I was in Italy during the war and she writes so beautifully about Naples. Another writer I have greatly enjoyed is Louise Field
Cooper (but is she still alive?)—I don't feel she has been appreciated here
as much as she should have been. . . . I don't read much American fiction
but feel that there are probably many writers I should like if I came across
them. A couple of years ago Cape published a novel by Gail Godwin,
The Odd Woman, which I liked, but I haven't read anything else of hers.
(Incidentally do we count Henry James as yours or ours?!)

I hope this will be of some help.

Yours sincerely,
Barbara Pym

1st June 1978

Dear Mr. De Angelis,

Thank you so much for your two letters, the last one containing the
kind and flattering things said about my work by other novelists. It is
most pleasing to know that Louise Field Cooper liked my books, . . . and
I'm so glad to know that she is still writing.

About my trip to South America! This was really a joke, based on a
remark I made when Caroline Moorehead of *The Times* came to interview
me and I happened to have seen a friend who had been somewhere on
Concorde the previous day. . . . But of course if I ever did come to the
United States I should certainly call on you. Possibly we may meet in
London or Oxford some time?

With all good wishes,

Yours sincerely,
Barbara Pym

15th August 1978

Dear Mr. De Angelis,

Thank you very much for the exciting parcel which came today and for
your letter with the photocopies of the reviews of *Quartet in Autumn* and
Excellent Women. I think the books look most attractive and you have
certainly done me proud with the nice bits on the jacket. I do hope readers
will agree with all that or at least some of it.

James Wright has just told me that you have made an offer for *The
Sweet Dove Died*, which is very good news. It is rather different from *Q.
in A.*, and has been gratifyingly well received here. I never thought I would
ever find a book of mine in the *Sunday Times* best seller list, but so it has
been. (Of course we are apt to say that it doesn't mean a thing, but it's
different when you get in it yourself!)

With best wishes,

Yours sincerely,
Barbara Pym

16th October 1978

Dear Mr. De Angelis,

Most encouraging on a Monday morning to receive that splendid *Chicago Tribune* review! . . .

I must now get back to my typewriter, or rather put another sort of paper in it and try to get on with what I'm writing at the moment. The trouble is that a good review of a previous book makes you feel you'll never write anything again, but I suppose a bad one would have an even worse effect, so you can't win anyway when it comes to literary effort.

With all good wishes,

Yours sincerely,
Barbara Pym

I received another similar letter on the 5th of December 1978 in response to my having sent her, in search of a jacket blurb, a copy of Doris Grumbach's new novel, *Chamber Music*. She was not only tactful as always, but alert and generous. She seemed to have really liked the novel, but perhaps more interesting, she was curious to find out about the author: "I'd be interested to . . . know more about [Doris Grumbach], so next time you have an occasion to write to me perhaps you'd satisfy my curiosity. How old is she?"

Alas, Doris Grumbach would never have the pleasure of becoming a model for a Barbara Pym character. On the 13th of January 1979, Barbara Pym wrote me:

Dear Mr. De Angelis,

Thank you so much for various letters and for sending me Roger Angel's [*sic*] Christmas Greetings Poem. I'm very touched and flattered to be in such company (at least I *hope* I should be flattered, not being able to identify quite all the people mentioned!). I think as a matter of fact my name goes quite well in such things. Is 'Seymour Krim' a real person?

. . . I have certainly enjoyed the reviews, and it leads me to wonder whether American reviewers are more generous than ours, or is it just kindness to an elderly female novelist?

In your letter of 18th December you asked whether I was a confirmed non-traveller. Not exactly that, though I don't go abroad as much as I used it [*sic*], but I don't really like publicity or parties or having to talk about myself or my books! But this doesn't mean that I wouldn't very much like to meet *you* if you ever came to London. I have also had one or two of the nicest imaginable letters from Americans who have read my books. It is only people en masse that scare me and I also feel that I shouldn't give value, for money in that way (if you helped me with my expenses!)

Anyway at this moment I am not likely to be able to stir very far as I am in hospital in Oxford, awaiting some tests. Hence this handwritten letter which I hope you can decipher. At least the enforced inactivity gives me the chance to catch up on letter writing and even to gather fictional material. I got quite a lot for *Quartet in Autumn* from my hospital experiences in 1974!

With all good wishes

Yours sincerely,
Barbara Pym

Five days earlier she had written in her diary:

Went to Dr S to consult him about my increasing bulk, which seems unnatural. He did tests and told me several things it might be. Naturally I seized on the most gloomy (if it would be gloomy to die at 66 or 67?). He gave me a letter to Mr Webster, a consultant surgeon in Oxford. I went to 23 Banbury Rd where the consultants live. Mr Webster thinks it is fluid in my abdomen (dropsy, but he had a grander name for it) and thinks I should go into the Churchill, perhaps next week. Great relief at getting all this over, even euphoric, though no doubt unjustified.[2]

And on the same day as the handwritten letter to me, in her diary again:

In the Churchill. Lunchtime—purple jelly with a dab of synthetic cream and 'All right dear?' . . .

The analysis of the fluid from my abdomen shows that there is something (malignant) though the X-rays didn't indicate what. It could be something in the ovaries or secondaries from the breast cancer—which could be treated either by an operation or drugs or radiotherapy.

Immoderate laughter of the evening visitors. . . .

In hospital one has to fight very hard to keep one's independence and most of the time it isn't worth it.

How did people die in the old days (not the 19th century but really old days like the 17th century). What did they do about cancer? If I'd been born in 1613 I would have died in 1671 (of breast cancer). I'd certainly have been dead in 1674. (322–23)

A week later:

Mr Webster said it is probably 'an ovarian problem.' He says the drug will work—it is a poison and may make me feel sick. It is a long-drawn-out treatment, may last months—injections every three weeks. (323)

And two weeks after that:

Home again. Went to see Dr S. Very kind and practical. Asked me to consider now how I wanted my end to be, whether at home, in hospital or hospice, or private nursing home. (323)

And ten days later:

My first visit to the radiotherapy clinic at the Churchill for my second injection. . . . If you think wouldn't it be better if I were just left to die you remember the fluid and how impossible it made things.

In the afternoon I finished my novel in its first, very imperfect draft. May I be spared to retype and revise it, loading every rift with ore! (323)

Less than a month later her diary entry reads:

Today the vet came and helped Nana [Minerva] out of this life. He took the body away. All very quick—a powerful injection and it was all over in a second. She was slumped in the green metal box he had brought, a little limp bag of bones. She would have been 18 in June. (324)

That same day she wrote me the following note:

5th March 1979

Dear Mr. De Angelis,

I'm sure I owe you a letter and also one to Elisabeth Choi [Mr. De Angelis's assistant] for sending me more reviews and her kind enquiries about my 'hospitalisation'. I'm glad to say that I'm better now, and even the weather has improved.

Many thanks for sending the cover of the *SDD*—a very interesting design. But I wonder how the book will be liked on your side of the Atlantic? The Kirkus review rather gave the impression that the central character (Leonora) is the kind of woman that perhaps couldn't exist in America! I shall be interested to see what people think. The book was very well received here, perhaps even better than *Q. in A.*, which some readers thought depressing. . . .

With all good wishes

Yours sincerely,
Barbara Pym

16th March 1979

Dear Mr. De Angelis,

Thank you so much for several things—first the *New Yorker* review by John Updike which I was of course amazed and delighted to see. . . . I'm afraid I hadn't heard of the writer whose name goes so neatly with mine—Mr. Lem—I must repair the omission!

And thank you for the advance copy of the *SDD*—very pretty and spring like with its greenery-yallery jacket. I wish the sight of it could make some improvement in the weather here—heavy snow again today, but it looks rather wet and perhaps won't 'lie'. I *hope* readers and critics will like it, but perhaps some will find the characters unsympathetic.

Yes, I think we had better consider any travel plans for me moribund at the moment. I am certainly much better in health but my aversion to having to talk about myself and my novels still stands and I suppose will never alter. I do appreciate [the offer of a flat], and also some of the nice letters I have had from American readers, though I have not yet answered one from a lady wanting to know my views on sex and violence in the novel!

. . . What James Wright tells you about my next novel is true, except that the touches aren't all that finishing yet, but I am working on it and hope to improve it. At least the first draft is finished and gives me something to work on and cross out.

With all good wishes,

Yours sincerely,
Barbara Pym

The day before, she had written to Philip Larkin:

I have had some super American reviews for *E. W.* and *Quartet in Autumn* including a long one in the *New Yorker* from John Updike. . . . *The Sweet Dove* comes out there this month. The advance copy has a springlike or greenery yallery cover with a design of doves (Miss Pym, the ornithologist). I daresay the Americans won't like that book. . . .

But I have finished the draft of another novel, pretty poor so far and it is so strange to have 'my publisher' asking for it and saying he's longing to see it. I fear he will be disappointed, and anyway I can't suddenly turn into the sort of writer who can produce something quickly. Don't you think one gets slower as one gets older—'stands to reason' as Norman might say! (324–25)

On Easter she wrote in her diary: "A fine Easter, sunshine and things burgeoning. I live still!" (327).
On May Day she wrote to Philip Larkin:

Dear Philip,

Just a brief letter to tell you that four lovely kittens were born on 11th April—all Toms! . . . They are a great pleasure and interest and we have quite a stream of visitors, especially children, wanting to see them. As a result of the birth, watching them with their mother when they were feeding while still very young, I thought of a splendid title for a novel, *Blind Mouths at the Nipple*. (327)

And in her diary of May 26th:

> In the early morning I woke having dreamed of finding a splendid title for
> a novel (the one about the two women, starting off with their Oxford
> days) which has been simmering in my mind. The Keats poem:
>
> > In a drear-nighted December
> > Too happy, happy tree
> > Thy branches ne'er remember
> > Their green felicity[.] (328)

On June 2nd, her birthday: "I am now in my 67th year—shall I make
70?" (328). A month later she wrote to me,

> 5th July 1979
>
> Dear Mr. De Angelis,
>   Many thanks for your letter of 19th June, only just received. . . .
>   Summer is really here today but we had a miserable June, cold and dull.
> *But* I *have* been struggling on with a new novel and am now doing the
> final version (I hope). The trouble is that I seem to find so much to im-
> prove as I go along, so my progress is no quicker than when I could only
> write part-time! And now I don't even know whether it will be liked—a
> country setting with not much plot. So if people enquire—and how kind
> and flattering it is to know that they do—please give them an edited ver-
> sion of what I have told you.
>   Yes, I am delighted to know that my story in the *New Yorker* is appear-
> ing so soon.[3] I am not much of a story writer but this one came to me and
> proved acceptable. To be published in the *New Yorker* gives one tremen-
> dous kudos here!
>   . . . I see, from one of the letters you sent on to me, that I have been
> unanimously elected A Daughter of Mark Twain!
>   All good wishes,
>
> > Yours ever,
> > Barbara Pym

Exactly a month later she dressed up to get her picture taken:

> Mark Gerson came to photograph me—a nice, easy to get on with person.
> Luckily it took my mind off my poor physical state. Very blown out and
> feeling disinclined to eat and rather sick. I wore my loose black cotton
> dress and a red scarf. (331)

The next day:

I feel awful on waking but a bit better now sitting in the sun writing this, also trying to finish off my novel. Shall I write more in this notebook?

Perhaps what one fears about dying won't be the actual moment—one hopes—but what you have to go through beforehand—in my case this uncomfortable swollen body and feeling sick and no interest in food or drink. (331)

A few days later: "9 August. Woke up in the Churchill, Ward 7 (Radiotherapy) this time, having had the fluid removed yesterday and so feeling better" (331).

The end of August:

I went to the clinic and they have decided to take me off the thiotepa . . . Has it worked? I asked the doctor but he gave me a somewhat non-committal answer. . . . They have lots of other things they can try, he said. (331)

On the first of October, in her diary:

As I am not feeling well at the moment (more fluid) I find myself reflecting on the mystery of life and death and the way we all pass through this world in a kind of procession. The whole business as inexplicable and mysterious as the John Le Carré serial, *Tinker, Tailor, Soldier, Spy,* which we are all finding so baffling. (331)

A week or so later, she wrote me the last letter I ever received from her:

9th October 1979

Dear Mr. De Angelis,

Many thanks for your letter of 1st October. Of course I'm delighted to be in Harper & Row paperbacks, even if the offer isn't quite as substantial a one as you would have wished. (If anyone questions it, I shall just murmur 'Solzhenitsyn' and that ought to impress!)

You ask about my latest novel—I have finished the first draft and am now attempting to go over it and improve it, assisted by the comments and criticisms of a friend who always reads my works in the early stages. I'm not very pleased with it—perhaps you won't even like it when you do see it—but it may be liked by the people who didn't like *The Sweet Dove Died,* as it is a rural novel, more like my first one. But such speculations get one nowhere—I'd better stop writing this letter and get on with the 'improvements.' (Yes, it does give me a good feeling when people actually want to know about my new novel!)

All good wishes.

Yours sincerely,
Barbara Pym

On October 31st, in her diary: "In the Churchill hoping for relief from my fluid" (333).

On November 21st:

> Churchill. Ward 7. A cold, raw, typical November day . . . The curious mixed or unisex ward is surely Donne's
>
>> Difference of sex no more we know
>> Than our guardian angels do. (333)

In a Christmas card to Philip Larkin she mentioned another, brief visit to the hospital for January 2nd.
Barbara Pym died on January 11, 1980.

~

And yet, we know, there is an afterlife for great writers. After Barbara Pym's death was to come the mourning, then the rebirth in the minds and hearts of thousands of readers. The 1980s were to be the years of the great Barbara Pym boom, the days when even in America one of her books—perhaps, particularly appropriately, her autobiography—would appear on the *New York Times* best-seller list.

Did Barbara Pym have a presentiment of this growing notoriety? I do not think it's coincidental that her last novel, *A Few Green Leaves,* begins, if not on Easter Day itself, then a week later: "On the Sunday after Easter—low Sunday, Emma believed it was called—the villagers were permitted to walk in the park and woods surrounding the manor."[4] Here again is an example of Barbara Pym's methodical "shrinking" of expectations or aspirations: if *she* is to have a resurrection, then surely it will be a *low* Resurrection. Grandeur, pomp, empire . . . are topics suitable only for fantasy, and the long lost past.

I also don't think it's coincidental that most of the characters in *A Few Green Leaves* spend a large part of their time wandering in the woods, bumping into death at every corner, but always all of them—or almost all of them—somehow slip past. Having just reread *Quartet*, I found I had to reread the "more hopeful" final book as well. The heroine, Emma Howick, is almost a symbol of drabness, barrenness, and sterility: "Emma glanced at the flowers in the distance. She was becoming rather tired of daffodils. Their Wordsworthian exuberance had been overdone. . . . She would have liked to see the woods bare in winter . . ." (4). People in *A Few Green Leaves* are always speculating about other people "dropping down dead." At the novel's start it's the young geriatrist Dr. Martin Shrubsole speculating guiltily about his mother-in-law Magdalen Raven going to an early grave; at the end of the novel it's old Dr. Gellibrand, during the talk he gives about "Death in the Olden Days" recommending that ladies take up the practice of jogging, "but under medical supervision of course. We couldn't have ladies dropping down dead, could we?" (243).

At other points it's the cleaning lady Mrs. Dyer gossiping about the elderly gentleman who, during a neighboring village's bus excursion, was inconsiderate enough to expire in his seat on the tour coach.

Or it's Emma's would-be paramour Professor Graham Pettifer, using the announcement of the death of Esther Clovis ("Esther Clovis, with her tweed suits and dog-like hair, was no more" [147]) as an opportunity for a long-postponed roll in the hay. Or it's Emma herself speculating about the death of the rector's wife: "What had she died of? What *did* people die of nowadays? Not consumption or a Victorian illness like typhoid or scarlet fever—but cancer, and various kinds of heart disease were always with us, so probably it was one of those." (195) Or the rector in turn, reading the obituaries on the back page of the *Daily Telegraph*: "So many people dying, he read, and none of them buried in woolen!" (213–14). And looming over the village in summer and winter are the mausoleum; the church graveyard; the automobile cemetery, located directly opposite the graveyard; the decrepit, stink-ridden old chicken house in the woods once run by Mrs. Dyer's son Jason, the one who wears a crucifix in his ear and who shoves his business card under Emma Howick's door "bearing the ghoulish information 'Deceased Effects Cleared'" (40).

For a few pages we are quite convinced that the character who will drop dead will be the much-discussed Miss Vereker, one-time caretaker of the mausoleum and last governess to the children of the de Tankervilles, former lords of the manor, who develops a sudden pain as she walks through the woods on a surprise return visit to her former village home. We are caught off guard when the one who actually dies—ambiguously, a possible suicide, and during Miss Vereker's stay, by strange coincidence—is Miss Lickerish, known for her attachment to hedgehogs and all other nonhuman life. She was the eccentric old lady who in the first pages of the novel complained of fleas to Dr. Shrubsole: "It's these fleas . . . and that stops me sleeping. I'd like some of those sleeping pills" (14).

As if, after the disappointments and rejections of *An Unsuitable Attachment*, the distant detachment of *The Sweet Dove Died*, and the self-immolating sacrifices of *Quartet in Autumn*, Barbara Pym has decided to cast off the Marcia and Miss Lickerish within her and instead go wandering into the woods. There, dodging her own death, she comes to life yet again through her heroine, the fortyish spinster Emma. As the last lines of the book tell us, "*She* could write a novel and even, as she was beginning to realise, embark on a love affair which need not necessarily be an unhappy one" (249–50).

NOTES

Letters from Barbara Pym to Paul De Angelis are used by permission of Mr. De Angelis.

1. Barbara Pym, *Quartet in Autumn* (New York: E.P. Dutton, 1978), 18.

2. Pym, *A Very Private Eye: An Autobiography in Diaries and Letters*, ed. Hazel Holt and Hilary Pym (New York: E.P. Dutton, 1984), 322.

3. The story, "Across a Crowded Room," appeared in the *New Yorker* in 1979 and is republished in Pym, *Civil to Strangers and Other Writings* (New York: E. P. Dutton, 1987), 367–80.

4. Pym, *A Few Green Leaves* (New York: E.P. Dutton, 1980), 1.

Barbara Pym as Comforter

JOHN BAYLEY

CAN WE DEFINE THE COMFORT FACTOR IN A WORK OF ART? OR DIStinguish it from the other forms of pleasure or inspiration that art may bring us? When Matthew Arnold stated that Great Art calms and satisfies us as nothing else can, his judgment raised a certain number of eyebrows among Victorian *bien pensants*. Cardinal Manning is said to have observed that art should not be spoken of, even figuratively, as if it were laudanum or alcohol. For him, art, like religion, concerned the spiritual side of humanity. The moral side, too. Matthew Arnold would not have disagreed with that view; in fact, he would have warmly endorsed it. As bringers of sweetness and light, art and morals—and the Great Ideas that went with both—had, at least for Arnold, replaced the role of religion in the life of nineteenth-century man, and it was the business of education to see that they continued increasingly to do so.

The word "comfort," easily definable in itself, might seem to have little to do with all of this. We associate it normally, and quite justly, with hot-water bottles and flannel underwear. Barbara Pym herself speaks of the comfort and importance of the properly boiled and filled hot-water bottle, one that will not have grown tepid if the solitary sleeper awakes in the early hours of the morning. But here, married couples, even those as civilized and enlightened as the clergyman Nicholas Cleveland and his wife Jane of *Jane and Prudence*, can be guilty of insensitivity. They fail in sympathy by not imagining themselves in the position of their unmarried guest, Prudence Bates. The point leads us naturally to other matters even more absorbing than pastoral shortcomings in such wholly domestic matters, even among the most civilized members of the clergy. How do the married and unmarried feel about each other? Has each group found itself envying the state of the other, particularly in relation to beds? Pym will tell us in her novels, but what were her own feelings on the subject? It is here, perhaps surprisingly, that our word "comfort" comes again unobtrusively into the picture. Specifically, it is a comfort to imagine a state other than one's own—to be invisibly stimulated in the art of doing so by a writer who quite naturally and even voluntarily exercised that art.

There is no aggression in Pym's wish to "make you see," as Conrad the novelist put it. She does not say to us, "I am going to make you feel like a spinster, a homosexual, a retired woman with anorexia whose only point of pride is to have had 'major surgery,' whose only joy is to have fallen in love with her surgeon."[1] As readers, we are more accustomed than we know to writers who are intent, perhaps honorably intent, on doing just that to us: making us feel, making us realize. Pym is totally innocent of this almost ubiquitous literary instinct—one that is as common in great writers like Dickens or Zola as it is in a host of inferior ones who want to give us their all in the form of themselves or their chosen characters.

Pym provides the comfort of total non-insistence. If anything could persuade me to be a practicing member of the Church of England rather than a tepid well-wisher who belongs to, but seldom enters, the club, it would be the way Pym writes about that institution, its ministers and congregations, its ceremonies and customs. She does not question or satirize it; she does not even tease it as a spiritual institution. Its role in her novels, and in her life, is like that of a cozy and happy family group, with its own jokes and procedures, its own unconscious mutual support. Questions of doctrine and belief occur as forms of aesthetic variation, in the same way that one member of a family has different tastes, hobbies, and eccentricities that mark him or her out from the others and are fondly accepted by them. In *A Glass of Blessings,* for example, the South India question is referred to and discussed not in the spirit of a family problem, but as something that has the entertainment value, for its various members, of a family gathering.[2]

Although both are equally reassuring, church is different from family in one respect: the church has a sexual role to play in the lives of those Pym characters who are involved in it. The role of the curate in Pym is too obvious and too well known to require comment. More important is the sexual authority conferred on such a figure as Archdeacon Hoccleve of *Some Tame Gazelle* by his style in the pulpit—particularly his grasp of our lesser-known metaphysical poets and divines. Literature, particularly works by obscure poets and witty quotations, has a powerful sexual charm in Pym's world, a charm that excites and even titillates, but is never threatening or disturbing. While she would appreciate a decently prepared hot-water bottle, the spinster in Pym does not even slightly envy the married clergy and what goes on in their beds, or have much interest in the subject. It is

for us the happy reader to imagine as we read about a state that seems
so mysteriously other than our own, even though we are perfectly
aware that what goes on or does not go on in the novel is just as humdrum and commonplace as what occurs in ordinary life. Pym, like all
great novelists of this kind, confers the gift of enchanted strangeness
on how we see the world in her novels. This, once again, is the comfort of being in a place other than one's own, of being in a world that
can exist only in art, but that nonetheless belongs there as if it possessed a positive and total domestic presence.

Artistically speaking, the magic of that world can be threatened, the
charm broken, when Pym seems to become too aware of her respon-
sibilities toward the novel. An "interesting subject" can be a fatal, or
very nearly fatal, disturber of the Pym comfort factor. Enchantment
can give way to something very much like banality. In my experience,
one infallible way of separating a Pym reader who is, as it were, comfortably domesticated in the Pym world from one who merely appreciates and is intrigued by it, is the response he or she gives to *The
Sweet Dove Died*.

With this novel, Pym was, of course, writing outside herself. In her
unhappy exile from publishers and publication, she was deliberately
seeking a mode of writing in which she should speak to the change in
novel-reading taste that had taken place, or that she at least seems to
have accepted as having taken place. My second category of admirer—
those who think Pym a good and interesting novelist, a writer whose
development is worth examining—naturally regard *The Sweet Dove
Died* as one of her most unusual but rewarding achievements. The
first category of readers enjoy it too, but at the same time fully realize
that what they are experiencing is, in Pym terms, wholly inauthentic.
And about this inauthenticity there is the sadness, even the bathos,
that goes with banality. It is as if an artist like Vermeer has been imi-
tated in paintings (as was actually done, and for a time done successfully, by the modern Dutch painter Van Meegeren) whose
effectiveness as forgeries lies not only in their remarkable likeness to
the style of the original artist but also in their seeming to increase that
artist's range and enterprise.

The Sweet Dove Died is a fascinating variant, and one of the more
subtle factors that makes it misleading stems from Pym's attempt to
imagine with precision a state other than her own. This kind of imagining should be left to the reader, and in the real Pym novels it is.
Leonora Eyre has the unreality of a good forgery. The Pym attributes
are there in a challengingly different way, but instead of a real "state
other than one's own," we have a new and, for the first category of
Pym fans, depressing awareness of this novel's primary unreality. It

is the kind of unreality that sharply reminds us of just how totally authentic the Pym world usually is.

Comfort is missing too. This is appropriate, it might be said, but such an answer will hardly do. The sadness that fills the book instead of comfort comes from the absence of authenticity. Pym here makes some attempt, in keeping with what she understood to be the tastes and preferences of the time, to explain the sexes to each other, instead of leaving them in their wonderfully hopeless and comfortable situation of difference and noncomprehension. "Male and female created he them"—there is no more to be said. Yet *The Sweet Dove Died* makes the rash attempt to say a good deal more. James's relations with Leonora; Humphrey's relations with Leonora; James's relations with Ned, the American homosexual; even James's with Phoebe, the aptly named feeble but amiable girl (a "modern" girl, one suspects, at least by the author's half-hearted intention)—they are all gone into. But they are disastrously gone into because Pym's effort is equally half-hearted, bringing home to the reader how entirely confident in her depiction of the two so-different sexes she usually is. Her sense of them, and their relations with each other, is almost always as amused and unerring as it is uninsistent.

But in *The Sweet Dove Died,* this depiction has become tentative and apologetic. We blush at our author's determination to get James and Phoebe into bed together, in accordance with the clichés of the up-to-date novel. Phoebe seems quite a promising person, in the Pym style, when "after some time," she sits up in bed and "with rather a distressing lack of purpose," says, "I suppose we ought to have something to eat."[3] This prompts James at once to recall Leonora's ability to knock up a delicious little something at a moment's notice. But after a look at the kitchen in Phoebe's cottage, he begins to feel that he is not hungry. Phoebe's inertia is well done, but too tentatively. It is as though Pym is only too aware that the happy confidence and alertness she generates in her reader have been disturbed by the new anxiety, leading her to try to do things in a new way. For Pym to be tentative in this way is fatal: it dissipates the comforting and secure sense she gives us of a world quite other than our own—a world in which, for example, Miss Grimes of *An Unsuitable Attachment* is found to have quietly gotten married to a Pole she met in the pub. And, of course, the attachment Miss Grimes has formed parallels and contrasts with the one in which Ianthe Broome, who like Leonora is in love with a man who is several years her junior, is herself involved. Part of Pym's true (and comical) confidence about the sexes comes from her sense of the arbitrary, almost ruthless, way they join up—or, in Pym's own case, don't.

This comforting robustness of Pym's did not survive the trauma of rejection by so many publishers, leading to the new uncertainty that is so visible in *The Sweet Dove Died*. I have suggested that Pym gives us a world quite other than our own, but this important point requires a clearer definition. Many novels, it can be said, introduce us to a different world, the world of coal miners or stockbrokers or down-and-outs, and this constitutes a major part of their effect. Pym's world is not in the least like that. It is totally familiar, or seems so, and yet, like a Vermeer canvass, it can exist only inside the absolute confines of art—a world of art on its own, like the one in which Wilmet and Piers and Keith and Wilmet's accommodating husband live so naturally and comprehensively in *A Glass of Blessings*. Ultimately, the comfort of Barbara Pym depends on the completeness of this osmotic absorption of her characters' humdrum personalities by the mysteriousness of her artistic being.

There is none of this peculiar completeness in *The Sweet Dove Died*, even though we are given tantalizing glimpses of it, as in the brief appearance of Rose Culver, whose enigmatic comment so startles Leonora: "The odd thing about men is that one never really knows," said Miss Culver. "Just when you think they're close they suddenly go off" (118). This is characteristic of Pym's old Vermeerlike "completeness." So, too, is the picture we're given the next moment of Leonora carrying a bunch of parsley from Rose's herb garden "with such elegance that it looked like an exotic accessory to her outfit" (118–19). It is remarkable how the simple and perfect totality of such pictures can actually remind us of the greatest examples of pictorial art. Keith's photograph in the knitting catalogue, showing off with weary dignity the points of a shawl-collared sweater, complements the picture of Wilmet in the park, going to meet Piers among the spring tulips and wearing a garnet-colored dress that shows off her discreet jewelry in *A Glass of Blessings*. Pym's memory, the memories that Pym leaves with us as an enduring legacy, is full of such pictures, equally vivid in their sharpness of definition and their warmth of comfort.

Nor is painting the only nonliterary art of which Pym can suddenly and satisfyingly remind us. According to Sir Thomas Beecham, the great conductor, good music gives us a sense of "both wonder and contentment." That is just what Pym, at her most Pym-like, can do and does. On the one hand, she is reserved; on the other, totally straightforward and forthcoming. Each side of the paradox displays the other. Does Prudence go to bed with Fabian? Jane longs to know, as any of us might like to do in real life. And yet Jane is also pleased that she will never know. The uncertainty is at the root of her feeling for the entertainment and the richness of life.

Pym does not know or want to know such things herself. She finds people fascinating, and loves to try to find out about them, as her character Dulcie does in *No Fond Return of Love*. She longs to know more of them, but she knows that in another sense they are quite ordinary. This is never more true than when they are in bed, and her imagination does not concern itself with the anticlimax of what happens there. Like her admired friend, the poet Philip Larkin, Pym wanted in her art the exact truth of what she felt and thought, no matter how trivial such thoughts and feelings might be. Her art, like his, can confer on such thoughts and feelings its own sort of magic. Larkin's personality, she noted in her diary, was just like his poetry, and the same is true of Pym and her novels.

Yet she is never defined by those novels, even though what is most aesthetically humorous and delightful in her work is what most directly reflects her own temperament. And—final paradox—how can we distinguish between that temperament and those of her characters, even when they seem wholly different from herself? Her accord with them is instant and unsentimental, as it is with the dying Marcia in *Quartet in Autumn*, who has just had a last glimpse of her surgeon, Mr. Strong, wearing his green tie

> with a small, close design on it. . . . That beautiful neat scar. . . . Marcia remembered what her mother used to say, how she would never let the surgeon's knife touch her body. How ridiculous that seemed when one considered Mr. Strong. . . . Marcia smiled and the frown left his face and he seemed to be smiling back at her. (181)

Pym the comforter? Well, no one with any literary sense has ever wanted to call her a sentimental writer. She herself once remarked that some readers, chiefly men, found her novels depressing, even painful. Perhaps in keeping with her unquenchably amused sense of the difference between women and men, she went on to say that, "Women don't, particularly." The question does lead to a notoriously tricky area: what cheers us up in literature, and what doesn't? Tragedy? It can be very heartening. The harrowing novel, well furnished with horrifying detail? These come two-a-penny nowadays and give their readers a sense of facing up to what life is really all about. They are "powerful." And they are fashionable. Not for nothing has a distinguished South African novelist who certainly has told us naught for our comfort won the Booker Prize and the Nobel Prize for Literature.[4]

Fashions are always significant, yet there is always something crude about them. Pym suffered from a change in fashion, and even made efforts to adjust her way of writing to it. But deep down, she was well aware how irrelevant fashion was for her and for that part of the public who appreciated and enjoyed her novels. It is probably a mistake to think of a good novel as either disturbing or comforting. Only writers who wish or need to conform to what they see or feel as the fashion will deliberately seek either to harrow their readers or to compel them to face "reality"—still less to give them what Trollope, with the fashion of his own time in mind, wearily described as "a feast of sugarplums."Good novelists write their stories without any such deliberate intentions. Nonetheless, a good novel does have its effect on the reader's state of mind, one way or another.

The novel is, ultimately, a very personal form, so I will conclude on a personal note. My wife, the novelist Iris Murdoch, suffered in the last years of her life from Alzheimer's disease. When she had been well and writing her own novels, I would sometimes read her bits of Pym that had amused or delighted me. I continued to do this when she was ill, and she always smiled, at me or at the writer, even if she did not understand. After I had put her to bed, I came down for my own drink and supper, during which I usually and avidly read a Pym. The novels not only sustained but calmed and satisfied me during those days, as nothing else could. Matthew Arnold's words about what Great Art does were true for me then. I wonder what he would have thought of the writer who had brought this about? I think he would have enjoyed her.

NOTES

1. Spinsters appear in all of Pym's novels, a homosexual in *The Sweet Dove Died* (New York: E. P. Dutton, 1979), and the retired woman in *Quartet in Autumn* (New York: E. P. Dutton, 1978).

2. Barbara Pym, *A Glass of Blessings* (New York: E. P. Dutton, 1980), 7–8, 142–43.

3. Pym, *The Sweet Dove Died* (New York: E. P. Dutton, 1979), 63.

4. South African novelist Nadine Gordimer won the Booker Prize in 1974 for *The Conservationist* (London: Jonathan Cape) and the Nobel Prize for Literature in 1991.

Philip Larkin: Barbara Pym's Ideal Reader

JANICE ROSSEN

"I AM ALL THE THINGS YOU SUSPECT," WROTE PHILIP LARKIN TO Barbara Pym in 1961, early in their acquaintance, adding, "not that they add up to much. My early ambition was to write novels, but I never got very far."[1] This was a characteristically modest description of himself. Philip Larkin was, at this time, the University Librarian at Hull and had indeed published two novels while still in his twenties, *Jill* (1946) and *A Girl in Winter* (1947), in addition to an early volume of poetry, *The North Ship* (1945) and a more recent one, *The Less Deceived* (1955). Despite the lyrical, passionate desire expressed in his youth to be a great artist, the early 1960s may well have seemed to urge him to damp down this aspiration and accept a limited literary role. *The Less Deceived* was gaining a steady and admiring readership by the time he first wrote to Pym, but it may well have been difficult to imagine the honors and accolades that were to follow.

Larkin's literary reputation grew enormously until his death in 1985, by which time he had been awarded the Queen's Medal for Poetry, received an honorary doctorate from Oxford (that caused him to muse on the theme of *nunc dimittis*), and was invited to become Poet Laureate (he refused). He was clearly one of the preeminent poets of his generation, indeed of the century, although his own chronic difficulties in writing and publishing gave him a fund of heartfelt sympathy for Barbara Pym, particularly in her years of literary eclipse. In the midst of stunning success, late in his life, Larkin still complained of dearth: "You must realize I didn't want to write poems at all," he told an interviewer from the *Observer* severely: "I wanted to write novels."[2]

Happily for Pym, the beginning of a very trying situation—her seventh novel being refused for publication—coincided with the unexpected appearance of Larkin's first letter through the post. He first wrote to her on January 16, 1961:

Dear Miss Pym,
 I wonder if you are preparing to publish another novel soon? I ask because, if you are, I should like to give further consideration to an idea I

had of a general essay on your books, which I might persuade *The Specta-tor* to publish in the form of a review of the next. (*SL*, 323)

In Larkin's own view, Pym was the novelist who was successful where he (in this regard) was not. But his admiration for her works—indeed, his deep and abiding affection for them—was the true link between the two authors. Larkin's essay, "The World of Barbara Pym,"[3] showed a keen critical appreciation of her books. Yet his main tribute to her work was simply that he read the novels again and again, talked of them repeatedly to friends, and wrote to her with warm admiration. He was, in his sheer intelligence and delight, her ideal reader.

He treated Pym as a fellow writer whose craft might be judiciously assessed on technical points. The second exchange of their letters touches on the use of recurring characters in subsequent novels. While acceding to Pym's right to choose her own mode of novel-writing, Larkin cautioned her: "my feeling is that Angela Thirkell, for instance, vitiated her later books by mentioning everyone in every one, and I think it's a device needing very sharp control if this danger is to be avoided" (*SL*, 326). Larkin approached this element of artistic camaraderie in their correspondence with a scrupulous honesty. He offered considered and thoughtful responses to the manuscripts Pym sent to him in hopes of helping her to find her way into print again. Voicing his reaction to an early version of *An Unsuitable Attachment,* for instance, he wrote on October 27, 1963, "I found myself not car-ing very greatly for Ianthe," and went on to observe that there was a "certain familiarity" about several characters in the novel (*SL*, 360). At the same time, these musings were clearly intended to point the way toward improving the novel, and in fact to discover why it might have been refused.

In addition to attempting to advise her—or, at the least, to provide an objective reading of her manuscript—Larkin made repeated offers of practical help in finding a new publisher. His encouragement was steady and warm: "I am glad to hear *An Unsuitable Attachment* is coming on," he wrote to Pym two years later (*SL*, 370). He ap-proached editor Charles Monteith with Pym's manuscript, and its re-fusal by Faber and Faber was still a cause of indignation several years later when Pym's novels were being republished.

Larkin shied away from offering Pym advice about subject matter. Urging his inadequacy to impart any significant insights about Pym's intention to write on "redbrick academic life," he explained in a letter of July 18, 1971, that "I should love to offer to stand as technical ad-viser, but in fact even after 25 years I really know little about provincial university life" (*SL*, 442). Yet he made clear his predilection for Pym's earlier style, and tried to steer her away from attempting to adopt a new tone in her writing (which aim had in part motivated Pym to choose the redbrick university subject). "It seems fearful that you should be trying not to be 'cosy,'" he wrote with some apprehension, urging her not to betray her innate gifts: "really it is what one comes to you *for*, it's what people want . . ." (*SL*, 420).

Still, he was courteous and straightforward in offering his reaction to Pym's later novels in progress, notably *The Sweet Dove Died* and *Quartet in Autumn*, despite Pym's obvious intent in these books to write differently than she had before—to be less "cosy"—and it was precisely this quality that Larkin valued in her work. Of his first impressions of *The Sweet Dove Died* (first titled *An Unfortunate Attachment*), he wrote on October 17, 1968, "I found it a curious mixture of successful & unsuccessful: the characters all strong and credible, & Leonora wins one's sympathy (I wonder if she's supposed to?), but their destinies aren't clear, and they move briefly and jerkily, & without any sense of inevitability" (*SL*, 405–6). He undercut his own criticism by adding, "I expect I am being irritating by trying to tell you how to write your book," and assuring Pym that "Your writing always moves me one way or another, even when it's this tiresome way of rewriting it for you, without any of the hard work, of course." His reactions to *Quartet in Autumn* were similarly mixed, though he joked about this when returning the manuscript: "[I]t w[oul]d be wrong to say I *enjoyed* it in the simple sense of the word, because I found it strongly depressing, but I seem to recall that some Greek explained how we can enjoy things that make us miserable" (*SL*, 547).

Hazel Holt has seen Philip Larkin's friendship with Pym as having sprung primarily from their naturally reserved temperaments: "Although neither of them had any wish to be part of The Literary World, both were absorbed by Literature," she observes.[4] Indeed, Pym's distance from London literary circles could hardly have been greater, and this made Larkin's respect and support for her work particularly valuable. Larkin was crucial to Pym's artistic development because he was virtually the only fellow writer with whom she discussed her work in progress. As Oxford scholar Barbara Everett has observed, Pym's publishing difficulties were immense: "*not* getting published was almost more intrinsic to her career than its opposite."[5] And although she kept on writing in spite of repeated manuscript rejections, it would have been difficult for her to continue to feel that she was a professional writer, especially without Larkin's tacit support. The extreme politeness that they exhibited toward each other precluded any very radical comments on the part of either regarding the other's work. Still, the fact that Pym could send her manuscripts in progress to a sympathetic and knowledgeable reader (who was also a fellow craftsman) must have been heartening in itself.

If Larkin's particular suggestions for revising her novel manuscripts tended to be guarded, they exhibited a common sense and practicality that must have been useful in encouraging her to tackle further revisions. He suggested that she make an early version of *Quartet in Autumn* a bit longer, which did not particularly affect its final state. His direct influence on the writing of *The Sweet Dove Died* was perhaps greater, though this advice too was of a cautiously general nature. Anne M. Wyatt-Brown notes that when the manuscript was rejected by both Cape and Chatto and Windus, Pym sought Larkin's counsel: "He advised her to cut out everything that diverted attention from Leonora's story. Three days later, Pym welcomed his editorial guidance. Despite feeling inadequate to the task, Pym quickly and skillfully followed Larkin's advice."[6] Yet Larkin showed himself to be Pym's ideal reader not in specific suggestions about her later writing but in his constant reassurances that her work was of extraordinary value. Paying her the highest tribute possible, he *reread* her books frequently, and he repeatedly told her so. "In fact I have been re-reading *your* novels in one fell swoop," he wrote to her in July 1964. "Once again I have marvelled at the richness of detail and variety of mood and setting" (*SL*, 368). Five years later he described his devotion to her works in terms of a regular cycle: "I've reached the point when I read all your books: it happens every 18 months or so. How *good* they are! How much what one wants after a hard, or even a soft, day's work! How vivacious and funny and observant! And feeling, of course" (*SL*, 420).

It must have been particularly gratifying for Larkin at last to have been able to affect Pym's literary fortunes in a concrete way, after having championed her work in public and private for over a decade. Although it took several years longer than either of them might have imagined, Larkin (along with Lord David Cecil) did eventually come to the rescue of Pym's literary reputation. When offered a chance to comment with several other writers on the most overrated and underrated writers of the century by the *Times Literary Supplement* in 1977, Larkin and Cecil promptly and independently chose Pym's novels for the latter honor. This had all the force of genuine conviction behind it, as Larkin *had* been reading her novels for years. Moreover, his description of them reveals a profound insight into their essential character; in "The World of Barbara Pym," he shrewdly ob-

serves that "Amusement is constantly foiling more pretentious emotion. But emotion is there all the same" (*RW,* 241).

This shared sense of understatement in human relations formed a
significant strand of the relationship between the two writers. Yet another mutual benefit of Larkin's correspondence with Pym was the
wit that it allowed each to exercise for the delight of the other. This
was enhanced, perhaps, by the fact that they remained formal rather
than close friends; living in different parts of the country, they met
relatively few times. Larkin also expressed some of his melancholy to
Pym, in the way that is possible only when one's confidante is detached from one's daily life. Worrying about the prospect of retirement, Larkin wrote admiringly of Pym's enjoyment of this state: "We
have talked before of the dangers of self-indulgence, and to them I
expect (for me) would be added the dangers of depression. Already I
find it incredible to be over 50 and 'nothing done', as I feel" (*SL,* 520).

The repeated expression of Larkin's esteem for Pym's work was
reinforced by his recounting of shared enthusiasm with other readers.
He wrote to Pym on December 29, 1975, about one such occasion:

> Last July I was at a little dinner party in London, and was speaking in a
> rather hostile way of J. Cape, the publishers; my neighbour asked why, so
> I said they had dropped from their list one of my favourite novelists.
> 'Who's that?' 'Barbara Pym.' '*Barbara Pym!!!*' I had discovered a fellow-
> enthusiast. . . . (*SL,* 535)

The affection that Larkin felt for Pym, intricately bound up with the
pleasure he received from her novels, was given free rein when the
efforts of many years at last came to fruition. "Super news!" he wrote
on February 22, 1977, on hearing that *Quartet in Autumn* had been
accepted by Macmillan (*SL,* 57). He regarded her belated acclaim as
no more than her due, and rejoiced in the republication of her earlier
books.

Larkin can only be said to have directly affected three or at most
four of Pym's books, since he first wrote to her after her first six novels had been published. And yet we probably would not have Pym's
final works in their present form had he not warmly supported her
ongoing efforts during the several years she remained unpublished.
His crucial role in Pym's rediscovery and republication had the practical result of creating a wider audience for her books. And Larkin
remained not only a faithful reader, but a discerning one, willing to
help Pym to find her way out of writing difficulties.

Above all, he was her ideal reader not only because his own eminence as a literary person must have made his praise flattering to her,

but because his admiration was sincere. As a self-proclaimed "failed novelist" himself, Larkin profoundly understood the difficulties Pym had had to overcome in creating her books. In valuing her unique gifts, he also exercised his own on Pym's behalf.

NOTES

1. Philip Larkin, *Selected Letters of Philip Larkin, 1940–1985*, ed. Anthony Thwaite (New York: Farrar, Straus & Giroux, 1992), 334; hereafter cited in text as *SL*.

2. Larkin, *Required Writing: Miscellaneous Pieces, 1955–1982* (London: Faber & Faber, 1983), 49; hereafter cited in text as *RW*.

3. Larkin, "The World of Barbara Pym," *Times Literary Supplement*, 11 March 1977, 260.

4. Hazel Holt, "Philip Larkin and Barbara Pym: Two Quiet People," in *Philip Larkin: The Man and His Work*, ed. Dale Salwak (London: Macmillan, 1989), 62.

5. Barbara Everett, "The Pleasures of Poverty," in *Independent Women: The Function of Gender in the Novels of Barbara Pym*, ed. Janice Rossen (New York: St. Martin's Press, 1988), 11.

6. Anne M. Wyatt-Brown, *Barbara Pym: A Critical Biography* (Columbia: University of Missouri Press, 1992), 118.

Reading Charlotte M. Yonge into the Novels of Barbara Pym

BARBARA J. DUNLAP

R EADING CHARLOTTE MARY YONGE'S *THE DAISY CHAIN* IN 1943, BAR-
bara Pym characterized the novel as "so well written . . . and very
sad."[1] Nearly thirty years later, another reading prompted the response that it was "enjoyable and very readable" (*VPE*, 260).[2] These
remarks supplement several specific references to Charlotte Yonge in
Pym's own novels. But above and beyond these, the Victorian novelist's work infuses Pym's, and the two writers might be said to gloss
each other. Pym's fiction is steeped in the work of Yonge, and knowledge of Yonge's novels adds another layer of enjoyment to our reading of Pym. Both novelists' most sympathetic protagonists are
immersed in English literature and the Anglican Church; these characters devalue worldly success and are endowed with a spiritual humility, though this does not preclude them from making acute
observations of the life around them. This essay will look at certain
elements in Yonge's novels and explore their refraction in the work of
that enthusiastic reader, Barbara Pym.

In 1989, the Victorian scholar John Sutherland characterized Charlotte Yonge as "the best of the Tractarian (or 'Oxford Movement')
writers and a formidable woman of letters."[3] From the publication of
her first novel, *Scenes and Characters* (1847), with its overtones of
Sense and Sensibility, to her posthumous tract, *Why I Am a Catholic
and Not a Roman Catholic* (1901),[4] Charlotte Yonge wrote or edited
some two hundred books. These include historical novels and histor-
ies, biographies, children's stories, tales of village life, and volumes on
religious instruction, geography, and onomastics. For nearly fifty
years she edited a magazine, *The Monthly Packet; or, Evening Readings for Members of the Church of England*. Pym especially appreciated her domestic novels, a genre Yonge enriched but did not
originate.[5] In these novels, Pym found complex stories of family life,
superb character drawings, and skillful use of dialogue and discourse.
As Alethea Hayter points out, Yonge's "build-up of plot and charac-

terization depends . . . on the accretion of her characters' reactions to
the small rituals and disturbances of life in a large family. . . ."[6]

Yonge lived all her life (1823–1901) in the village of her birth, Otterbourne, near Winchester. Her father guided her studies in mathe-
matics, Latin, Italian, and French, and she was steeped in English
literature and history. Except for annual visits to "the bliss of that
cousinland" in Devonshire where her father's people lived, her childhood was lonely;[7] however, she compensated for her lack of play-
mates by inventing a family of ten brothers and eleven sisters who
lived in the summerhouse of the Otterbourne garden.[8] Before she
reached her teens she was using her father's visits to Devonshire and
to his friends to prepare for her career as a novelist, paying careful
attention to the conversations during the day and writing them down
accurately at night.

Pym also recorded actual conversations and events in her own distinctive world of Anglican parish life, anthropologists, and spinsters.
In Pym's world, the Church of England survives as a rich cultural
property as much as it is a guide to salvation, but both novelists valo-
rize the Tractarian ethos, which militates against easy emotionalism in
religious expression. It may have been as early as the mid-1930s that
Barbara Pym began her "Anglo-Catholic Diary," which she maintained into the 1970s. The "diary" is actually a chronology of events
connected with the development of the Oxford Movement and its influence. An early entry reads, "1833. John Keble's Assize Sermon on
National Apostasy preached at St. Mary's Oxford (July 14)."[9]

Barbara Pym shared with Charlotte Yonge not only her interest in
the church, but also her zeal for writing. In 1938, Pym wrote to Elsie
Harvey: "I honestly don't believe I can be happy unless I am writing"
(*VPE*, 86). Likewise, when asked what she would have done if her
family had forbidden her to publish on the grounds that it was un-
seemly for a gentlewoman to put herself forward, Yonge replied that
she would have delayed publication, but "I *must* have written."[10] For-
tunately for her vast nineteenth-century public, the Yonge family was
won over by Keble's perception that her story-making facility, excel-
lence with dialogue, and ability to create character could be used to
advance Tractarian aims through fiction. Her domestic novels have
appealed to many readers who have no interest in these aims and at
best an amused tolerance for her exaggerated exaltation of parental
authority and unwavering belief in the natural inferiority of women.
Clearly, her association with these attitudes has not helped her reputation with modern audiences.

In the years of Pym's girlhood, Yonge's novels might still linger on
the shelves of middle-class English homes, and Hilary Pym Walton

recalls that the family in Oswestry owned a copy of *The Heir of Red-clyffe* (1853). Barbara Pym apparently started to read Yonge's novels in the 1930s on the advice of her Oxford friend, Robert Liddell. She continued to read them after the war, and understood, as Hazel Holt notes, that "Yonge with her brilliant gift for narrative" promoted the Oxford Movement in her novels.[11] At her death, Pym's library held *The Heir of Redclyffe, The Daisy Chain* (1856) and its sequel, *The Trial* (1864), *Dynevor Terrace* (1857), *Hopes and Fears* (1860), *The Pillars of the House* (1873), and *Nuttie's Father* (1886).[12]

Despite this evidence of Pym's interest in Yonge, Janice Rossen, in her otherwise perceptive study of Barbara Pym, prompts the reader to wonder why Yonge's novels would have had any appeal to Pym by describing them as "patently sentimental."[13] Similarly, Anne Wyatt-Brown does not view Pym's affinity for Charlotte Yonge in a positive light. On the basis of her examination of the novels and Pym's unpublished materials in the Bodleian, she concludes that "Pym never outgrew her youthful obsession with both Jane Eyre and the vicarage novels of Charlotte Yonge."[14] Having first analyzed Pym's father as "gentle but ineffectual," Wyatt-Brown contrasts the tolerance of Pym's mother with "the repressive older relatives in Charlotte Yonge's novels . . . who are determined that their female relations shall exhibit all the feminine graces."[15] By the time of the publication of *Excellent Women*, Wyatt-Brown suggests, Pym's social attitudes had become "too old-fashioned for the mood of the times," with the real difficulty being "Pym's nostalgia for the world of Charlotte Yonge's novels." She finds it odd, almost disturbing, that Pym enjoyed reading this fiction, with its "repressive" social attitudes.[16]

However, Yonge's novels are not merely "vicarage novels"; rather, her domestic fiction most often deals with young people emerging into adulthood. As they chart their paths in the family or in the world, they contend with the death of a parent or sibling, schoolboy bullying and drunkenness, academic success and failure, serious illness, and occasionally exile and prison. Generally, the families belong to the gentry and professional classes, and one of Yonge's great talents is her ability to differentiate the many characters who share the same class and family background with such skill that the reader does not mistake one speaker for another. The lives of the most admirable characters are shaped by the discipline of their religious life, yet the Tractarian ethos precludes much discussion of theological issues and inner religious experience, in contrast to evangelical fiction.

With *The Daisy Chain*, Charlotte Yonge created Dr. Richard May, a man who must learn to be both father and mother to his eleven children, aged six weeks to twenty-one years. Knowing his careless driv-

ing has caused his wife's death and the crippling of one daughter, he
wishes the younger children to defer to the eldest daughter Margaret's
judgment in household matters. But, at eighteen, she is naturally
shown to be imperfect in judgment and engages in much self-examination. The most outstanding member of the family is fifteen-year-
old Ethel, who has a terrible time maintaining the appearance required of a young Victorian lady. Her hair and skirts are never orderly, and she is always rushing through her tasks, both domestic and
intellectual. When she undertakes to open a school for the neglected
children of quarrymen in a nearby hamlet and to build a church, the
addition of these activities to her regular lessons and home duties
keeps her in a perpetual state of hurry. Margaret advises Ethel to give
up the Greek studies she loves so she can slow down and cultivate the
graces that "dear Mamma" wanted her to have: a smooth appearance,
good French, and passable needlework.

Wyatt-Brown declares that this "painful scene" left a mark on
Pym: "It taught her that women have no defense against social pressure, a lesson which helps explain why so many of Pym's later heroines seem passive by contemporary standards."[17] This assumption
seems to ignore the fact that Margaret's concern is not with the study
of Greek, of which she approves, but with the all-consuming competition of writing correct Greek verses: " 'The work is getting harder,
and,' said Margaret kindly, 'we all know that men have more power
than women, and I suppose the time has come for Norman to pass
beyond you. He would not be cleverer than anyone if he could not
do more than a girl at home.' "[18] Margaret urges Ethel to abandon the
competition and fix a period in the day for *reading* Greek. Dr. May
is not present during this scene, nor is his name ever invoked. Margaret's "we all know that men have more power than women," is almost
undercut by "[Norman] would not be cleverer than anyone if he
could not do more than a girl at home."

We may regret that the England of 1847 did not offer women the
opportunity to attend Oxford and that Ethel has to curb her "aspirations" for the sake of the family and her charitable work. Yet it is difficult to see how the active Ethel is responsible for Pym's "passive"
heroines—if women with such intense mental lives can indeed be
called passive;[19] in the Anglo-Catholic Diary, Pym wrote, "Ethel is
the real heroine of the book. . . ."[20] *The Heir of Redclyffe,* like *The
Daisy Chain*, does not preach Tractarian ideals. It simply dramatizes
them within the context of a vivid family drama: regular churchgoing,
reliance on the sacraments, and self-examination. For the basic impulse of *The Heir,* Yonge credited a friend who had said, "There were
two characters she wished to see brought out in a story, namely the

essentially contrite and the essentially self-satisfied."[21] Ethel May is one of the "essentially contrite," and stands in contrast to her sister Flora, who for much of the novel qualifies as "essentially self-satisfied."

In emulation of Yonge, Pym juxtaposes "contrite" characters such as Belinda Bede, Mildred Lathbury, and Dulcie Mainwaring with the "essentially self-satisfied" Harriet Bede, Helena Napier, and Viola Dace. Their contrition has nothing to do with glumness, but everything to do with Christian humility. In *Jane and Prudence,* Jane Cleveland uses her memory of Yonge's novels as a distorting prism. She reflects that she has not played the part she had imagined as a clergyman's wife, having had little success with parish affairs. After several months in their new parish, Jane observes, "I was going to be such a splendid clergyman's wife when I married you, but somehow it hasn't turned out like *The Daisy Chain* and *The Last Chronicle of Barset.*"[22] Also, because she has only one child, she is again "conscious of failure, for her picture of herself as a clergyman's wife had included a large Victorian family like those in the novels of Miss Charlotte M. Yonge" (8). Jane's delightful confusion takes the form of an untidy appearance reminiscent of the young Ethel May, and her use of quotations is sometimes wide of the mark. Her remark to her husband Nicholas—"I feel that a crowd of our new parishioners ought to be coming up the drive to welcome us"—receives an "indulgent" reply: "That only happens in the works of your favorite novelist" (15). If this novelist is Charlotte Yonge, there are no such scenes. Has she created her own idealized Yonge world of "splendid" clergy families?

Although Pym did not own *Beechcroft at Rockstone* (1889), she creates in Jane Cleveland a character who is an inversion of that tireless parish worker, Miss Jane Mohun. Yonge's Jane is introduced as a pertinacious little girl in *Scenes and Characters,* the first of what would become Yonge's "linked novels." She remains among the "lifelong friends" of Yonge's imagination and reappears forty years later in *Beechcroft at Rockstone*—less shrill and bossy, but still recognizably the personality from *Scenes.* Jane Mohun's work takes place in a Devonshire resort town and reflects the organization and professionalization of the church's social role since the period of *The Daisy Chain.* Had this Jane been a clergyman's wife, she would never have committed the blunder of missing the Mother's Institute tea during her husband's first year in the parish. Jane Cleveland rationalizes her decision to skip the event in part by saying, "I don't really feel so much of a mother, having only *one* child" (*JP,* 66). The spinster Charlotte Yonge was for ten years editor of the Mother's Institute journal,

Mothers in Council. Jane Cleveland's daughter Flora, domestically and socially competent and clever with her dress, has her counterpart in Flora May of *The Daisy Chain.* At the end of *Beechcroft at Rockstone*, Jane Mohun tours Italy with her teenage niece: "They had not been afraid of being British spinsters with guide-books in their hands."[23]

A definite reference to Yonge's work appears in Pym's *A Few Green Leaves*, where we meet Beatrix Howick. A teacher of the Victorian novel, she has bookshelves "filled with novels by Charlotte M. Yonge and other lesser Victorians." She has a desk placed in the window of her cottage where she can look out over the village street. Beatrix likes to sit here, "hoping to witness the kind of events that might have taken place a hundred years ago";[24] more often than not, she is disappointed. Here is a clear allusion to the homes of the May and Underwood families in *The Daisy Chain* and *The Pillars of the House*, respectively. Situated in country towns rather than villages, these houses on the "High Streets" are central in their communities. When the Underwoods move into quarters above a bookshop, "the amusement of looking out of the window into the High Street was alone a perpetual feast to the little ones."[25] Beatrix also looks back on her husband's death at Dunkirk a few months after their marriage, noting that her situation as the mother of a young child and "her work, the Victorian fiction" explain her lack of subsequent relationships. But then she recalls that "Charlotte M. Yonge's novels contained more than one attractive widow" (*FGL*, 100). Could Beatrix/Pym have been thinking of the young widows in *The Trial* and *The Pillars of the House*, who exploit their good looks with expensive mourning costumes as a showcase for their "interesting" grief, and attract second husbands?

Letty of *Quartet in Autumn* reflects, "the position of an unmarried, unattached, ageing woman is of no interest whatever to the writer of modern fiction."[26] Nor was it of great interest to writers of Victorian novels (Mrs. Gaskell's *Cranford* is an outstanding exception). Courtship plots were central to much Victorian fiction, and Yonge was rather unusual in drawing detailed portraits of older unmarried women as well as of marriageable girls. As the narrator remarks in *Hopes and Fears*, "Youth is but a fraction of human experience."[27]

Ethel in Yonge's *The Trial* chooses spinsterhood, but she has no confidante of her own. As her brothers and sisters become adults, her relations with them become complex and, in some cases, more distant: "the pain at her heart made her guard her tongue; but she had begun to feel middle-aged and strangely lonely."[28] Pym placed Mildred Lathbury of *Excellent Women* in the same position. Ethel could be imagined as preparing herself to be the Pym protagonist described by

Judy Little as "a well-educated single woman in her thirties, unmistakably a 'lady,' living in London or nearby and making a life for herself without the aid of husband, love or family."[29]

For much of the 1850s, Yonge was contemplating a novel (*Hopes and Fears*) that would foreground an unmarried woman's life over a period of thirty-five years. In her twenties, Pym projected a reasonably contented future for herself thirty years later in *Some Tame Gazelle*; in her thirties, Yonge took Honor Charlecote from an idealistic seventeen-year-old to a disappointed woman of fifty-five. Yonge consciously guarded against elevating Keble or her own father to the status of, as she would put it, a domestic "pope." Yonge understood the danger of idolizing a man to the point where one's own judgment is blinded. When dying of tuberculosis, Owen Sandbrook appeals to Honor's former feelings for him and to her misty idealism, insinuating that his deceased wife's family is too "worldly" for his tastes, though for the last several years he has been a popular London preacher to the wealthy. Although she realizes the shallowness of his character, Honor pounces on these gazelles and embarks on an unrewarding course of pseudo-parenthood, soon elevating the younger Owen Sandbrook into her idol. She feeds him a steady diet of chivalric romances and idealized missionary stories, which he sweetly reflects back to her while keeping his real life hidden. By the end of the novel, Honor has learned to accept a chastened Owen as he really is, and cedes the agricultural management of her estate to a younger cousin. This novel and *The Trial* reinforce the lesson Ethel May has learned at the end of *The Daisy Chain*—that the single woman cannot expect to remain "first" with anyone. The novels explore loneliness: not just the loneliness occasioned by siblings or children leaving home, but the deeper loneliness of the single woman who realizes that the younger people have grown beyond the tastes and ideals that used to unite them all.

A feature of Pym's early fiction is the dominating older spinster who wants to control the young. Charlotte Yonge knew the type. In *The Pillars of the House* she sketches the "Misses Hepburn," four unmarried sisters in their fifties who live encased in the social attitudes of their parents' generation. Around 1867, the Underwood family regains its estate, Vale Leston. The ladies in the parish are appalled that Robina Underwood plans to retain her delightful governess post. One of them tells her, "There is no reason why [you] should not remain at home, which is the only proper place for young women." When Robina replies that she would rather maintain herself than be a burden on the encumbered estate, Miss Isabella counters:

'Ah! my dear, that is a dangerous because plausible spirit of pride and independence. As those who have tried can tell you, very little suffices single women, who have long ago broken with the world.' This beautiful sentiment was received with an assenting breath by the other three, while Miss Isabella triumphantly added, 'And that your brother is bound to provide.'(276)

Miss Isabella is a prototype for Miss Doggett and other aging women in Pym who attempt to control others. Yet the Hepburn sisters' genteel poverty also connects them with the gentlewomen of slender means who people the margins of Pym's novels. By the time of *Quartet in Autumn,* the State has replaced the older brother. At the retirement of Letty and Marcia, the narrative voice rationalizes that "the State would provide for their basic needs which could not be all that great. Elderly women did not need much to eat. . . ." (101). Of all her novels, *A Glass of Blessings* most thoroughly glosses the "richness" Pym found in Yonge and particularly in *The Pillars of the House.* Piers Longridge finds Wilmet Forsyth's Christian name "sad . . . [because] it seems to be neither one thing nor the other."[30] Yonge's pioneering work on onomastics, *A History of Christian Names* (1863), defines "Wilmet" as "helmet of resolution."[31] Along with her brother Felix, Wilmet Underwood is one of the earthly "pillars" whose resolve upholds the house of Underwood after the death of their parents. She is constantly occupied, either in teaching school, managing the household, sewing, or supplying motherly affection to the younger children. She is thrifty and totally disinclined to believe that any man could ever fall in love with her. Even her beauty is a burden in the nasty little town of Bexley, where suspicious mothers think she is out to snare their sons. In all these points she is the mirror opposite to Pym's extravagant and idle Wilmet Forsyth.

In *Womankind* (1876), her guide for the Anglo-Catholic gentlewoman from youth to old age, Yonge warned young women against "idle busyness . . . the curse of the English gentlewoman."[32] Eighty years later, Wilmet Forsyth labors under this same curse. At one point in her ambiguous relationship with Piers Longridge, Wilmet, lacking a more serious occupation, indulges in a rescue fantasy: "I gave myself up to a happy dream in which I went to look after Piers when he was ill or depressed or just had a hangover. . . . I felt that Piers really needed me as few people did" (*GB*, 163).

Neither this vision nor her daring scheme to see Piers's lodgings secretly is realized to Wilmet's satisfaction. When the chance does arrive to see his lodgings, she feels compelled to tell her mother-in-law about it. Soon thereafter she humiliatingly discovers that the person he has "needed" to improve his life is the comic and common Keith. Pym has Wilmet Forsyth's story invert that of Wilmet Underwood, who can scarcely believe that John Harewood has fallen in love with her. Two years later he is terribly scalded in a train accident in Egypt and the normally cautious Wilmet gives up her job and, accompanied only by Harewood's father, goes out to nurse him. She is very skillful at changing his dressings, even in the most sensitive part of his body, and "the pleasure and comfort" she gives him serve "to bear him through" (144). When Canon Harewood is forced to return to England, he doubts that Wilmet can remain alone with his son John and his servant although almost all of Wilmet's properties have vanished. The recovered John Harewood becomes Wilmet's attentive husband, valuing his wife's domestic capabilities, but urging her to dress well and helping her overcome her anxieties about money. Wilmet Underwood lives the experiences Wilmet Forsyth can only imagine.

In the Anglo-Catholic Diary, Pym asked the following question of *A Chaplet for Charlotte Yonge*, a collection of essays published in 1965: "Why did nobody write an essay about her churchmanship?"[33] Both novelists wove their concerns as churchwomen into their novels. The Oxford Movement promoted the reintroduction of sisterhoods to the Church of England, the establishment of inner-city missions with clergy houses, and the ideal of celibacy for Church of England priests.[34] Though most priests did marry, the celibate ideal remained, especially for priests attached to missions, and is reflected more than a hundred years later in Mary Beamish's query to Wilmet Forsyth, "Do you think it wrong for a priest to marry?" (*GB*, 228).

Although the early Oxford Movement had little interest in ritual, the ongoing effort to recover common Catholic traditions for the Church of England led to the reintroduction of such practices as the observance of lesser saints' days and such outward gestures as making the sign of the cross during certain portions of the church services. Many members of the "Low" and "Broad Church" wings of the Church of England looked on these developments as undesirable "Romish" practices.[35] In *Excellent Women*, Mildred Lathbury reflects that her parents would have disapproved of her attending a "high" church: "I could imagine my mother, her lips pursed, shaking her head and breathing in a frightened whisper, 'Incense.'"[36]

The Heir of Redclyffe alludes to the "home missions" that the leading Tractarian Edward Bouverie Pusey was advocating. Guy Morville is persecuted by his self-satisfied cousin Philip, who interprets Guy's mysterious request to his guardian for a thousand pounds as evidence that he has been gambling, but discovers too late that he desired the money to help endow a nursing sisterhood. Such Anglican sister-

hoods developed as small communities of women in London in the
1840s and became objects of suspicion to many within the Church of
England. One hundred years later, Gerald Beamish looks with suspicion on "this nunnery business" when his sister Mary plans to pursue
a vocation in a sisterhood (*GB*, 126–27).

Robert Fulmort of *Hopes and Fears* determines to use his fortune
to counteract the terrible conditions in "Whittingtonia" (the East
End of London) that his family's "gin palaces" and breweries have
helped create. Ordained as a priest, he builds St. Matthew's, a church
with a small community of celibate priests and choristers who hold
daily services, and a mission that helps the poor and educates or-
phans. St. Matthew's may have been based on the activities of St. Barnabas's, a mission founded in 1846 by W. J. E. Bennett in the poorer
part of Pimlico, which had a "Clergy House and college of four
priests, schools for the children, and a sisterhood to visit and nurse
the sick."[37] In *The Pillars of the House*, St. Matthew's welcomes
Clement Underwood as a chorister. Barbara Pym first glossed this
rich material in *Excellent Women*, showing how Tractarian ideals live
on even in a shabby corner of postwar London. Julian Malory is a
devoted priest in the "tough" district of Pimlico, with a bent to celibacy that is only temporarily interrupted by the machinations of Allegra Gray.

Pym's next novel, *Jane and Prudence*, makes passing reference to a
Mollie Holmes, who has "the settlement and her dogs" (10), and by
the time of *A Glass of Blessings* Mary Beamish and Sybil Forsyth are
active there. The renewal of the church of England inspired many
"well-born" clergy to take up posts in industrial towns or in poor
districts of London. In doing up a parcel of clothes for a needy clergyman, Sybil alludes to this tradition: "Canon Adrian Reresby-Ham-
ilton . . . St Anselm's Vicarage, E.1. . . . Such a good name and such a
poor address! You see there is still that ideal of service among the
nobly born as there was in Victorian days" (24).

When Rodney and Wilmet Forsyth visit the clergy house at St.
Luke's, she notes the contrast between the richly furnished rooms of
Father Thames and that of Father Bode, which is "quite disconcertingly bare," with personal touches being "of the simplest and cheapest"
(*GB*, 110). Rodney speculates that the room is like this because Father
Bode lacks Father Thames's private income; however, the room also
recalls the simple, cheap furnishings the wealthy Robert Fulmort
chooses for his room at St. Matthew's because he does not want to be
distracted by possessions.

Earlier in *A Glass of Blessings*, Wilmet refuses Father Thames's
half-articulated offer that she become the clergy housekeeper. It is a

task for which she is certainly unsuited, but in *The Pillars of the House* Charlotte Yonge creates a role that Wilmet might well have liked to fill. At the end of that novel, Robert Fulmort leaves St. Matthew's to become a bishop in Australia and offers the post of director to Clement Underwood, the parish priest at the family estate, Vale Leston. Underwood is celibate, but also the only "home" companion to his sister Geraldine, a witty, successful artist. Fulmort explains that she can live next to the mission in a beautiful old house: "Her quickness, ready judgment, and especially her sense of the absurd, are just what would be valuable. Mind, I don't think of her as a worker, only as an Egeria to the clergy-house" (550). Egeria, a wise nymph, was the counselor of Numa, the legendary king whom the Romans believed was the creator of their ancient religion. At the end of *A Glass of Blessings*, Wilmet and Rodney move into their new flat, "a good hundred yards nearer the clergy house" than before (247). As that house has now presumably passed to the care of Father Bode, it is uncertain whether Wilmet will fill the role of Egeria.

This novel glosses other concerns sympathetic to Yonge. Mary Beamish in *A Glass of Blessings* is a Tractarian figure with her extreme submission to her mother and very disciplined religious life. She experiments with life as a nun in a sisterhood. Like Charlotte Yonge, Barbara Pym displays a realistic attitude toward the clergy of the Church of England, neither idealizing nor disparaging them. Mary understands that their status as priests in the apostolic tradition means that it is the office and not the man that must always be held in respect. The services at St. Luke's, with their elaborate music and decoration, reflect the ritualistic wing of the Oxford Movement. In her novel *The Three Brides* (1876), Charlotte Yonge mocked excessive ritualism, though gently; she does so much more openly in a late novel, *Beechcroft at Rockstone* (1889). Here, the ritualist Augustine Flight presides over a church "oppressed with ornament" and observes days such as the Feast of St. Remigius, where a short discourse is given after the Lesson "on the conversion of Clovis, not forgetting the sacred ampulla" (20, 46).

In *Less than Angels*, Rhoda Wellcome and Mabel Swan, under the influence of their ritualist priest, Father Tulliver, compete to see who can be more observant of such feasts and fasts. In *A Glass of Blessings*, Wilmet Forsyth and Marius Ransome reflect ironically on this sort of competitive churchmanship. When Wilmet observes that "All these abstinences and fastings are rather difficult for lay people to remember," Marius advises her to "write to your favorite church newspaper. 'Is there liturgical objection to eating hot cross buns on Maundy Thursday?'" (146–47).

Hot cross buns lead us to thoughts of tea as a suitable accompaniment. "[T]he tea ritual [in Pym] celebrates reality and the continuity of daily life assured by an immanent deity," Judy McInnis notes. "Neither crises in the romantic lives of the characters, nor the exigencies of work, nor the obligation of religious devotion, disrupt the sanctity of the tea ritual."[38] While tea does provide comfort, the context of the tea drinking can be serious or comic, an ordinary occasion or a special one, but it is always integrated into the story. Robert Emmet Long observes that "When Pym's characters have tea at the vicarage, Charlotte M. Yonge's *The Pillars of the House* or Mrs. Gaskell's *Cranford* might well come to mind."[39] Aside from making the prevalent assumption about the ubiquity of vicarages, Long seems to suggest that the tea scenes function merely as decoration. Yet both Yonge and Pym use such scenes to advance their stories. Twelve-year-old Lancelot Underwood prepares an impromptu tea with mismatched china for his older sister Geraldine in the harum-scarum home of his friend Bill Harewood. The scene dramatizes Lance's thoughtfulness and humor, but also advances the story as Lance provides information about the Harewood family, who will be so important to the Underwoods.

This comic tea is counterpointed by an important tea scene in *The Heir of Redclyffe,* when Guy Morville's widow and her invalid brother Charlie journey to Redclyffe out of concern for their cousin Philip. Earlier in the novel, Philip's stubbornness led to his contacting the fever that caused Guy's death. Though physically recovered, Philip is now disabled by remorse. When the brother and sister arrive at the estate on the wild coast of Cumberland, they find its new owner lying on the sofa with a bad headache. Amabel soon takes matters in hand, and says, "we only want a little tea" (40). At this communal meal the reconciliation of the characters is completed, with "Amabel making tea and waiting on her two companions; both she and Charles pleasing each other by enjoying the meal, and Philip giving his cup to be filled again and again and wondering why one person's tea should taste so unlike another's" (500).

From a tea of reconciliation to a tea of comedy, Charlotte Yonge uses the occasional tea scenes in her novels to strategic effect, as Barbara Pym would a century later. The tea Mildred is co-opted into providing for Rocky and Julian in *Excellent Women* brings her relationship with the two men into sharp focus. At the tea served under the chestnut trees in *Jane and Prudence,* Jessie Morrow uses tea as a physical weapon to discomfort Prudence Bates, but this same event introduces Prudence to Edward Lyall. Tea is preeminently a secular sacrament dispensed by women; even marginalized women such as

Miss Prideaux in *A Glass of Blessings* can offer this simple hospitality. At its best, this secular rite, performed by Amabel and Ethel, Mildred and Belinda, provides moments of community and comfort.

Judy Little has commented with sensitivity on the relationship between Charlotte Yonge and Barbara Pym. She remarks on "the discourse of contemplative dailiness that Pym found in Anglo-Catholic hymns and in Charlotte Yonge's fiction," and notes that "her qualified acknowledgment of Keble and her enthusiasm for Yonge gave her a double dose of Christianity as a domesticated discourse of sacramental attentiveness to the trivial."[41] Barbara Pym found the atmosphere of Charlotte Yonge's fiction congenial to her own temper and interests. She wove into her novels many concerns central to her Victorian predecessor and dramatized them from her own unique perspective.

NOTES

1. Barbara Pym, *A Very Private Eye: An Autobiography in Diaries and Letters*, ed. Hazel Holt and Hilary Pym (New York: E. P. Dutton, 1984), 117.

2. The diary passages also indicate that the novel has foreshadowings of Ivy Compton-Burnett and suggest how she might have developed the situation. The young Compton-Burnett and her sisters knew *The Daisy Chain* well; see Hilary Spurling, *The Life of Ivy Compton-Burnett* (New York: Knopf, 1984), 54.

3. John Sutherland, *The Stanford Companion to Victorian Fiction* (Stanford, Calif.: Stanford University Press, 1989), 685.

4. On arriving in Rome, Mark Ainger of Pym's *An Unsuitable Attachment* (New York: E. P. Dutton, 1982) reflects that a sermon entitled "Why I am not a Roman Catholic" might be salutary for his congregation (144).

5. A good introduction to this genre remains Vineta Colby, *Yesterday's Women* (Princeton: Princeton University Press, 1974). Also of great interest is Nancy Armstrong, *Desire and Domestic Fiction: A Political History of the Novel* (New York: Oxford University Press, 1987). For a discussion of Charlotte Yonge's popularity in her own day, see Alethea Hayter, *Charlotte Yonge*, Writers and Their Works (Plymouth, Eng.: Northcote House in Association with the British Council, 1996).

6. Hayter, *Charlotte Yonge*, 6.

7. Christabel Coleridge, *Charlotte Mary Yonge: Her Life and Letters* (London: Macmillan, 1903), 63.

8. Yonge, "Lifelong Friends," *Monthly Packet*, November 1894; reprinted in *A Chaplet for Charlotte Yonge*, ed. Georgina Battiscombe and Margharita Laski (London: Cresset Press, 1965), 181.

9. MS Pym 89, fol. 2, Bodleian Library, Oxford. In this sermon, Keble, author of the highly successful book of poems, *The Christian Year* (1827), noted that governmental power was encroaching on affairs of the established church to the degree that many people were regarding her as merely a "polite adjunct to social life." In the following months a number of churchmen began meeting to discuss the need for a movement which would bring the Church of England back to her Catholic heritage. As several were attached to Oxford University, and the group soon began to issue a

series entitled "Tracts for the Times," this impulse to renewal became known as the Oxford Movement or Tractarianism. In 1836, Keble left Oxford to become the vicar of Hursley, near Otterbourne, where he and his wife became close friends of the Yonge family. In August 1838 Charlotte became, in her own words, "Mr. Keble's catechumen," quoted in Yonge, *Musings Over "The Christian Year" and "Lyra Inno-centium," Together with a Few Gleanings of Recollections of The Reverend John Keble* (London: John Parker, 1872), iii.

10. Yonge, quoted in Georgina Battiscombe, *Charlotte Mary Yonge: The Story of an Uneventful Life* (London: Constable, 1943), 62.

11. Hazel Holt, *A Lot to Ask: A Life of Barbara Pym* (New York: E. P. Dutton, 1991), 152.

12. For the role of Robert Liddell in directing Pym to these novels, see Anne Wyatt-Brown, *Barbara Pym: A Critical Biography* (Columbia: University of Missouri Press, 1992), 39. The list of Yonge's novels was supplied by Hilary Pym Walton in a letter to the author (31 July 1991).

13. Janice Rossen, *The World of Barbara Pym* (New York: St. Martin's Press, 1987), 8.

14. Wyatt-Brown, *Barbara Pym*, 6.

15. Ibid., 15.

16. Ibid., 73, 39.

17. Ibid., 39.

18. Yonge, *The Daisy Chain; or, Aspirations: A Family Chronicle*, vol. 1 (London: John Parker, 1856), 179.

19. Hayter notes that "Miss Yonge wanted women to be capable, even intellectual, so long as they did not assert their independence and self-sufficiency aggressively"; see *Charlotte Yonge*, 64.

20. MS Pym 89, fol. 19.

21. Yonge, *Musings*, xxix.

22. Pym, *Jane and Prudence* (New York: E. P. Dutton, 1981), 212.

23. Charlotte Mary Yonge, *Beechcroft at Rockstone* (London: Macmillan, 1893), 289.

24. Pym, *A Few Green Leaves* (New York: E. P. Dutton, 1980), 90.

25. Yonge, *The Pillars of the House; or, Under Wode and Under Rode*, vol. 1 (London: Macmillan, 1873), 173.

26. Pym, *Quartet in Autumn* (New York: E. P. Dutton, 1978), 3.

27. Yonge, *Hopes and Fears; or, Scenes from the Life of a Spinster* (London: Macmillan, 1889), 59.

28. Yonge, *The Trial: More Links in the Daisy Chain* (London: Macmillan, 1884), 276.

29. Judy Little, *The Experimental Self: Dialogic Subjectivity in Woolf, Pym, and Brooke-Rose* (Carbondale: Southern Illinois University Press, 1996), 87.

30. Pym, *A Glass of Blessings* (New York: E. P. Dutton, 1980), 72.

31. Yonge, *A History of Christian Names*, rev. ed., vol. 2 (London: Macmillan, 1884), 556.

32. Yonge, *Womankind* (London: Smith & Mozley, 1876), 81.

33. MS Pym 89, fol. 38.

34. Barbara Dennis, *Charlotte Yonge (1823–1901): Novelists of the Oxford Movement* (Lewiston, N.Y.: Edwin Mellen Press, 1992), 60–61.

35. Ibid., 119.

36. Pym, *Excellent Women* (New York: E. P. Dutton, 1978), 11.

37. Dennis, *Charlotte Yonge*, 108.

38. Judy McInnis, "Communal Rites: Tea, Wine, and Milton in Barbara Pym's Novels," *Renascence* 48 (1996): 285, 282.

39. Robert Emmet Long, *Barbara Pym* (New York: Ungar, 1986), 213.

40. Yonge, *The Heir of Redclyffe*, 9th ed. (London: John Parker, 1855), 499.

41. Little, *The Experimental Self*, 75.

Reading Barbara Pym with College Students

JAN FERGUS

In the post-television, post-internet, postmodern world, teaching any literature is a challenge—even at universities. Students here seem increasingly to resent the time that reading takes and to deny its pleasures. In fact, most freshmen, even in my advanced classes, say that they never read for pleasure; after all, a film takes only two hours, while a book takes a day even if they skim. Curiously, however, such students—who have all taken advanced placement courses in high school—are often willing to read and even to admire "classic" writers, particularly Shakespeare. The reasons to enjoy Shakespeare are, of course, legion, but I would argue that among the most important for students is that he wrote tragedies. In my experience, tragedy is much easier to teach than comedy, and most instructors, given a choice, will assign *Hamlet* rather than *Twelfth Night*. Students seem almost instinctively to accept Aristotle's notion of hierarchy in genres: tragedy is high art, comedy low. Perhaps, though death is unreal to most of them, they can accept that it is important; laughter seems trivial unless it is obviously satiric. As a result, most of us have to work very hard (often in vain) to convince students that social comedy has any significance or value.

The problems of teaching Barbara Pym to college students might, therefore, seem almost insuperable, and I admit I would never try teaching her with freshmen. When I teach Jane Austen, for instance, I have the advantage of working with a writer whose name most of them have heard and whose comedy is often obviously satiric. But even so, I come immediately upon the conversation-stopper, "It's just soap opera"; some students never advance beyond that notion. Pym's comedy presents American students with all the problems of Austen's: a mysterious class system, opaque manners, and above all meaning that is conveyed between the lines rather than on the surface. That is, the deepest pleasures of a Pym text come from rereading, as with Austen. Though Pym does not alienate moderns as regularly as Austen does by reliance on the marriage plot, she sins by presenting

194

women who do not work or, when they do, find their jobs tedious or marginal. She does have one great advantage, however: Pym's brilliantly observed comedy focuses on details of physical description and behavior in ways that Austen's deliberately does not, and these details can come home to students. When I taught Pym's novels for the first time in 1997, I found that she could both teach and inspire college students, primarily due to such details of comic observation.

The class succeeded partly because it was small and an "extra" for all of us. The English Department and the College of Arts and Sciences at Lehigh University had recently adopted a system wherein students generally took four courses of four credits each semester, rather than five of three credits. As a result, we offered fewer courses, students had fewer choices, and English professors generally stuck to (or were stuck with) their specialties and writing courses. I decided to vary my own schedule—the Eighteenth Century and Practical Writing—by overloading and offering a one-credit course on Pym, purely for enjoyment. Students could not fulfill any requirements with a one-credit course, so for them, too, it had to be just for fun. A short course was practical, too, for although now all of Pym's works have been reprinted, at that time only two were in print, and I chose one of them to start with. The one-hour class met Monday, Wednesday, and Friday for about six weeks: fifteen class meetings and a one-hour final examination. I wondered, among other things, if Pym could appeal to modern American college students, especially privileged students at an expensive private university. Would anyone sign up? Seven did. What would students make of her? Would they understand and enjoy her writing? They did—so much so that the course was one of the most successful I have ever taught.

I recently managed to get in touch with all seven students to ask their permission to include them in this essay; all agreed. Talking to them about their lives after college and what they recalled of the class was a great pleasure. I have never tried to get in touch with former students before, and I now heartily recommend the effort to all teachers who have, like me, left it to students to take the initiative. What the students remembered chiefly is what I remember: relaxed, friendly, open discussions in which everyone always took part. Certainly some of our enjoyment arose also because the class was so short and so focused. We read *Quartet in Autumn* closely, as well as parts of *Some Tame Gazelle*, comparing those parts with their original versions in the much longer typescript that Pym had actually started to write while at Oxford University. (I had photocopied this manuscript while reading at the New Bodleian years earlier.) These were good choices, as it turned out, but equally important was the good fortune that the class was very small yet nicely varied in gender, race, majors, even class in the academic sense—from a sophomore to seniors. There were two men and five women, six counting me. The students were Michelle Fisher, a graduating senior majoring in biology; Shareef Rashid, a junior studying psychology; Becky Russell, a junior English major; Sarah Stewart, a graduating senior majoring in International Relations; Ron Voloshin, graduating with a degree in English; Barbara Worchick, another senior graduating with a biology major; and Danielle Collins, a sophomore business student.[1] (Two of the seniors, Sarah and Barbara, took the course for two credits, staying on to read more Pym after the six weeks were over.)

In a class like this, much depends on the first real meeting, which took place a few weeks into the semester. I decided to have the students read closely the remarkable opening paragraph of *Quartet in Autumn*. We all took sentences successively, reading each one aloud. Each of us would talk about what details helped to make Edwin, Letty, Marcia, and Norman come alive, and I suggested that we all focus special attention on details of hairstyle. Others would add what they also saw in the sentence before we went on. This process worked so well that we used it at some point in nearly every other class, with the important difference that we would all suggest passages to review in this way.

That first paragraph of *Quartet in Autumn* is particularly brilliant and the opening three sentences worth quoting in full:

> That day the four of them went to the library, though at different times. The library assistant, if he had noticed them at all, would have seen them as people who belonged together in some way. They each in turn noticed him; with his shoulder-length golden hair. Their disparaging comments on its length, its luxuriance, its general unsuitability—given the job and the circumstances—were no doubt reflections on the shortcomings of their own hair.[2]

The first sentence wonderfully encapsulates the relations among the "four of them": they are united by some of the choices they have made in their lives (here they all go to the library), but they are isolated by something in their natures (they go "at different times"). The second sentence deepens this perception: an outsider, the library assistant, would see them as "people who belonged together in some way"—but he would probably not notice them "at all," for they tended toward not just isolation but invisibility. The third sentence takes us for the first time into their points of view, here united: all four notice the librarian because all four are observers. They unite too in "disparaging" the librarian's hair. Their impotent grumpiness toward youthful styles and their respect for choices suitable to jobs and circumstances are both poignant and comical, given the "short-comings of their own hair." But we find, in the rest of the paragraph, that although not one expresses youthful rebellion through hairstyle, all reveal quite a bit of themselves in that manner. Edwin's preten-sions to gentility and his anxious adherence to convention allow his sparse hair to extend into a "bob," an "easy" and "not unbecoming" style, Edwin feels, for what his barber calls "older gentlemen." Nor-man's "difficult" hair is precisely himself, "coarse, bristly, and now iron-grey," cropped in something like a "crew-cut." The men's regu-larly tended styles contrast with the neglected hair of Letty and Mar-cia. Letty has "faded light brown hair, worn rather too long," "soft and wispy," that she does not treat with a "brightening 'rinse'," while of course Marcia's "short, stiff, lifeless hair was uncompromisingly dyed a harsh dark brown" (1–2). Almost every word tells.

Speaking as a teacher, I can remember very few actual classes I have taught: they blur. Even this first Pym class does, too, for I can't recall any actual statements except vaguely. What I do recall is my own ex-citement as I heard students get so much out of the lines. I had thought that understanding of, let alone sympathy for, four charac-ters on the verge of retirement would be a stretch for people aged nineteen through twenty-two. But focusing on how carefully Pym delineates them at first, how much she reveals in how few details, seemed to short-circuit that problem. We saw the characters as odd and comic initially, then with increasing depth and poignancy—as Pym presents them, I believe, though they remain comic too. What struck us most at the beginning was the tension between how much each character needed others and their simultaneous repulsion of help, sympathy, human contact—a tension present in the first para-graph. What moved most of us later was the way the book insists that however narrow your choices, you still have them: that sense of infi-nite possibility in small things that is the hallmark of Pym's work. Not all were satisfied with this sense, however, particularly not Ron Voloshin, who expresses (I think) an important combination of resis-tance to and acceptance of Pym's vision when he now says,

> I cannot forget her vivid descriptions of a drab life—the kitchen, espe-cially, remains a stark image of dusty cans. I don't know if I remember her exact point, but I know that I am often frustrated by what appears to be a vividly lived drab life by so many. And as my frustration kept me from seeing then, it makes it difficult, now, to see how these folk can rightfully find happiness in such grayness.

A drab life that is "vividly" lived—a powerful image, encapsulating Pym's art as well as resisting it.

Though I have neither notes nor memory of other specific passages from *Quartet in Autumn* that the class discussed, I recently read Pym with another college student, Colleen Watts, in an independent study. We considered the notion of a "drab life vividly lived." As this is of course easy to see in Marcia's intensity, Letty's anxiety, even the anger that enlivens Norman, we focused instead on analyzing a passage about Edwin, who had initially seemed to both of us the dimmest and drabbest figure of the quartet—a perfect test case for showing how Pym presents the vividness of the ordinary through telling details. The passage, a paragraph near the end of Chapter 2, takes him from the office at lunchtime for shopping, a snack, and his "church crawl" (24). It reveals that Edwin is not drab but wonderfully balanced in his alternations between the routine and the fresh, between acceptance of and resistance to change.

Overall, Edwin seems to alter least in the novel, perhaps because he organizes his own life around the regular changes of the church year and his own equally regular cycling through a variety of churches. He also produces change, particularly by arranging a new home for Letty. The passage devoted to his lunchtime practices thus alternates between describing small changes in the routine that figure as decay and loss—not just the unpleasantly changed decor in the teashop, itself a substitute for the loss of Gamage's as a regular lunchtime venue, but also changes in the Church—and describing parts of the routine that offer variety and possibility, especially through his regular church crawl.

The paragraph begins with Edwin's point of view, after he has announced his plan to feed Father G. with "one of my specials" in the evening:

> 'baked beans on toast with a poached egg on top.' The women smiled, as they were meant to, but Edwin was known to be a competent cook and it was not as if they had anything much grander for their own evening meals, he thought, as he came out of a teashop that sold bread, carrying a large white loaf wrapped in a paper bag. (24)

This glimpse into Edwin's mind reveals a defensiveness that his self-sufficiency usually conceals: though he provoked the women's smiles at his modest, ordinary hospitality, he assures himself that their meals are no "grander," pointing to the way that food serves to characterize him in the passage much as hair does in the novel's opening. Unlike Marcia with her canned food, Edwin obtains a new loaf to make toast later, its wrapped freshness countering bland, mundane whiteness. Although he is abstemious (he "had had a light lunch, snack really" [24]), the "large" loaf suggests balance here also: no stinting for himself or Father G. At the end of the paragraph, Edwin is making the rounds of churches, studying "notice boards to see what was offered in the way of services and other activities," as if checking a menu. The parallels between the church's offerings and those of restaurants (showing change and sameness both) become wholly clear when Edwin is "attracted" by "an announcement of an austerity luncheon in aid of a well known charity, but rather surprisingly 'with wine'—that might be worth a visit" (24). That the paragraph begins with bread and ends with wine subtly reminds us of what the church offers at a deeper level. But additionally, the comedy of wine being served at an austerity luncheon lights up the end of the paragraph and complements the comedy of Edwin's gourmet-like sampling of church treats; the unexpected, sharply observed detail "with wine" transforms the mundane and opens up variety, possibility, vividness in what might otherwise seem a drab existence.

Ron Voloshin produced this analysis when I asked him and other students what they remembered of Pym more than two years after the class ended. They tended to focus either on character or on something more inclusive—on philosophy, perhaps, like Ron. Marcia's cans loom large for many; they are perhaps Pym's most memorable detail. Michelle Fisher loved the way Pym set up the characters, so that we felt as if we knew them, "as if we'd sat next to them for a month and knew exactly how this person would behave, entirely through descriptions and the details she gave—details like Marcia's hoarding the cans." Sarah Stewart concurred: "The greatest part about reading the books by Barbara Pym was that her characters related to a cross-cultural and cross-generational audience. The idiosyncrasies of hoarding cans of soup (or whatever it was) or finding humor and love in the strangest places can be found in people of all ages."

Shareef Rashid, too, said that he appreciated the "understanding" Pym conveyed of the characters, as if they were "actual people . . . you get into their minds through detail." Becky Russell agreed that the "little details" were important, but responded to the ideas of life that the novels convey, saying, "I had never heard of Barbara Pym, but her work was a window onto ordinary life that makes it not glamorized but comical and cynical at the same time. She answers the question 'what is it all for?' but I can't put the answer into words: it is something like, in seeing other people, I understand myself better." Ron Voloshin's response to the "vividly lived drab life" is perhaps echoed in part by Dani Collins Cushion, who admired Pym's "candor" in portraying Belinda in *Some Tame Gazelle*:

> I remember some members of the class remarking that she was desperate, pitiful, etc. because of her actions—almost approaching a stalking mentality. However, the fact that Pym opened up and wrote about the character's (akin to her own?) feelings was impressive . . . it takes a truly courageous person to delve into the truths which lie within. . . . I suppose, then, what I most remember of Pym—and hope to have applied some to my own life—is to reach inside and express what I really feel, whether it will be laughed at by others or not.

Barbara Worchick wrote in a letter, "I do quite a bit of reading and Barbara Pym's books have been amongst my favorites. Other than what we read in class, I went on to read *Excellent Women*. I have bought a few more of her books at a second-hand bookshop. Her language is so rich—every sentence adds more texture to her literary world. And Pym has a way of recognizing the humor and simple beauty of everyday life."

Though Pym's work clearly deserves most of the credit for pleasure and instruction, probably what made the course most successful as an academic offering was the "creative project" connected to reading *Some Tame Gazelle*—and in fact Michelle Fisher and Shareef Rashid said that for them the project was the best part of the course. The earlier reading of *Quartet* was useful in this project precisely because of its focus on age. I wanted students to think about the whole process of growing older, the simultaneous narrowing and opening out of choices and possibilities. From the beginning, I told the class that Pym had written a novel at university, projecting her friends into their forties in the early version, into their fifties in the later, published one. I had encouraged them all to think about doing the same thing for their final paper in this course, rather than a usual literary analysis. If they chose this "creative project," they would copy the first draft of their paper for the class to read and discuss and would lead the discussion, indicating similarities or differences between their work and what Pym did. In preparation for this assignment, we read the parts of *A Very Private Eye* that refer to Pym's college life and her writing of the novel; the first three chapters of *Some Tame Gazelle* (on library reserve, since it was then out of print); and the corresponding parts of the original version in manuscript in the Bodleian, which I had photocopied on an earlier research trip.

Although as a class we had a good time with the literary analysis of Pym's works, closely reading passages, sometimes tracking allusions, and so forth, I was delighted that all the students chose to attempt the creative project instead of a traditional paper. All wrote substantial stories; all were discussed at length in class and revised based on discussion (sometimes not much revised); and one of them won the school's Williams Prize for Seniors in Creative Writing. I copied their drafts for the final class discussions, and still have six of them. Some of the details show a sense of having consciously drawn from Pym's work. For instance, Barbara Worchick imagined four college friends uniting after twenty years or so in Florida, where the heroine Anne works with dolphins. Avoiding some rather tense pre-meal moments,

> Anne retreated into the kitchen, hoping to find solace in the garlic bread. . . . Dinner was comfortable, but Jellica and Michael had begun to pick at each other about the merits of hanging mugs versus stacking them in a limited space. It was time to move. Although each had arrived at Anne's place separately (Michael had been in the area for a teaching conference, Jellica to get a break from her job had flown in from Boston, Michelle who came in just for fun also flying in from Boston), they decided that it was best to take only one car to Anne's center. Since no one knew the way, there were no arguments as to the most direct route.

Michelle Fisher liked the opportunity to make up her own story of her future, and tried to put herself in Pym's frame of mind to write it. She wrote of an unmarried older woman, Michael, with a matchmaking younger sister Marja:

> Marja hated when her sister dated 'no brainers,' as Marja would call them. They were the men who had no kind of conversational skills or wit; they were just there occupying useful space. The two boys came downstairs to kiss their parents and their aunty Michael goodnight. Finally the dreadful night was over, what's-his-name had taken Michael home—no doubt her sister would have a boring night. 'Oh, no . . . I forgot to tell Michael about Shawn,' Marja exclaimed as she handed the dishes to her husband David. David and Marja had met each other in junior high and had been together ever since. She was one of the lucky ones, for none of her friends nor her sisters had ever married. But it was never too late for all that to change, and Marja was determined to get both her sisters married, especially Michael. Her goal was a double wedding for both by the end of the year. She would have to start taking action very soon since the end of the year was only three and a half months away.

Sharif Rashid imagined his older brother taking the subway home on his fortieth birthday:

> Mr. Rashid loved taking the train. . . . The intense heat the subway produced in the summer was ironically comfortable to him. Not physically,

but mentally; when it's your birthday you start to think about the past because at that age your present is your future. The heat reminded him of the summer he met his girlfriend in the train station. It was more his wife's memory than his, but he enjoyed her description of him as a 'sweaty, little, skinny boy all dressed up, looking like he was ready to pass out.' . . . A sloppily dressed homeless man apparently in his mid 70s started singing a 1960 R&B classic. 'Like the tears of a clown,' the homeless man sang off tune, with a painful look of joy on his face as he shook his cup full of loose change. 'Smokey Robinson, right?' Mr. Rashid asked as he searched in his pocket for a couple of dollars. 'That's right, man, how you know that? Smokey was way before your time, young blood.' 'Yeah, but my father played those tunes all the time when I was growing up.'

Sarah Stewart began her story with a cast list, made up of classified ads—an amusing variation on the opening of *Quartet*:

Lisa: Investment Banker in Manhattan. Single, wealthy, and magnificently put together. Seeking single corporate man from the Upper East Side. Must enjoy throwing parties, eating hot dogs, and drinking Stoli.

Jess: Restaurant owner/partner New Jersey suburb. Sports fan, Star Wars expert, and tennis player, I am seeking a middle-aged housekeeper to help with daily cleaning and childcare. Accepting applications now, will pay in cash.

Joy: Executive consultant for an exclusive private firm in New York. Seeking young and energetic nanny to help with carpools for three children to sports practice, music lessons, student council, volunteer work, Boy Scouts, Girl Scouts, tutors, and dancing classes. Ready to hire immediately.

Stacy: Iranian terrorist expert and Middle Eastern diplomat. Seeking professional secretary, preferably female, to help organize files, tend to paperwork, answer phones, and keep track of appointments. Must be tolerant of cigarette smoke.

Becky Russell described three people who lived in different places and were not in touch with each other, but all received a holiday card at the same time from their old friend Rachel. One was Laura:

Laura has always been alone, or at least never married. But she spent her fair share of time with miserable husbands of the world. The one place mat never bothered her. The mini-coffee machine was just right and best of all, there was never any debate of any kind in her home. It was a place of silence and rest. Some people probably thought she was a little stuck up, maybe she thought her long legs were too good for anybody. That, however, wasn't the case. She was alone, happy, successful, but never, ever, lonely.

Jacoba also received a card. As Jacoba lay in bed, John doted on her.

First a fresh cup of coffee, then a bagel with her favorite vegetable cream cheese. It was rare they they ever got to eat breakfast together, spend time in the morning together and simply relax into the mood of a freshly started day. After breakfast, John walked over to the bed with a card from yesterday's mail.

'You missed this yesterday in your typical lobbyist frenzy,' he said as Jacoba gave him that disapproving look that came whenever her name was associated with any adjective implying obsessive compulsive behavior. She gingerly opened the letter; one must not tear a letter. She slid out the card with a cartoon of 'Hannukah Harry' on the front. She chuckled and knew just who it was from. John looked on intently as if the cure for the common cold were on the inside.

Ron Voloshin won the Williams Prize with a very complex story, beginning on December 25, 2025, with an exchange of letters between Niv, who is operating a restaurant in the Israeli desert, and Pauly, a Federal judge with a strange case to report. A mad religion professor who says he knows both of them is appealing his conviction in a complex cloning, murder, and conspiracy case; Pauly wants Niv and others to reunite at their old college campus for fun just before all this blows up, when Pauly imagines he will have to "escape to Israel with my family. . . ." He includes airplane tickets and a copy of the bizarre poem the madman has sent him, with lines like "green is not green against a sky of red." Then the story switches from such non-Pym-like elements to the early spring reunion of four men, on a hill above their former campus where they "gathered as if to replay younger days" and accordingly get stoned. The event ends with a very ordinary crisis:

'Hey, seen my keys?' asked Bob, in that nonchalant voice that is simply the vocal manifestation of internal hope.

'Nah, man. Where d'you leave 'em?' Niv replied as his eyes began to dart along the grass that was beginning to take a shadier perspective in response to the bluing sky.

'I know I left them here,' confirmed Bob, 'keys don't just move themselves.' What an absurd, arrogant notion that was.

'So, we look. Ain't got nowhere that's any more gorgeous than here,' muttered Niv before hollering out to Pauly and Dudan, while basking in the neon purple glow of five o'clock.

The moral here is simple. The four men searched, each in his own pattern, guided by a logic peculiar to each, and ultimately unconnected with the circumstance. . . . To an outsider these four men may have initially looked like they were each pondering a common problem, which, in fact, they were. Only it looked more like that four of them had taken a brainstorming break atop a hill. Could the marketing scheme be found in a sunset? Could the accidental transformation of a sheep into a human ear be reversed? To an outsider, it would least resemble a search for lost keys.

That is, until they were on their knees: as Niv, with his white dress pants, squatting Bedouin-style, taking crab-like steps with his hands purging the top inch or so of soil. Or, as Bob, roaming efficiently in the style of an Atat-walker. Or as Dudan jumping about, occasionally spurting out, 'We'll never find them,' but failing to continue in that logic and asking, 'Where is the nearest copy?' or something to that effect. Or finally like Pauly, pacing off quadrants military style, kicking about but lost in other thought.

The four, thus characterized by their different search modes, are unsuccessful until Niv gets the idea to place his keys on the grass to see what they look like, Pauly drives those keys into the ground so they can see what lost keys really look like, and finally Niv's hands fell on two sides of a ring that was mildly exposed but brought to sight by the frame his hands created. Vision, to be accurate, must be in one way or another limited, that is, defined. He pulled on the ring, not yet fully aware that three keys were responsible for anchoring it to the ground. . . . The four men walked down the hill chattering about persistence, when in actuality they were simply alluding to vision.

The quiet ending of Ron Voloshin's story after the dramatic start was a surprise. Other endings sometimes tended to be more romantic or melodramatic than Pym usually permitted: Barbara Worchick's tale closed with two former lovers reunited, Michelle Fisher's in tragedy, with the heroine struck by a car trying to avoid her former lover's old girlfriend. But on the whole, despite such wide departures, I was fascinated by how far, in different ways, the stories were inspired by Pym—a sure sign of her power. Hazel Holt has quoted Pym's "surprise and gratification" at learning that she was "being taught in an American university!"[3] In fact, in 1997, she was clearly teaching at one.

NOTES

1. By the fall of 1999, all seven students had taken up professional jobs or training. Danielle Collins Cushion received her degree in business, married in June 1999, and now works for ISL United States, a sports marketing firm. Michelle Fisher teaches biology in an alternative high school in New York City and loves the students, ages 17–21. Shareef Rashid has been teaching works like William Golding's *Lord of the Flies* in a juvenile detention center in the Bronx, New York.

Becky Russell has served as an administrator at a family services agency on the east coast, but is in the process of moving to San Francisco; she plans to pursue a graduate degree in this profession. Sarah Stewart started attending law school in August 1999, reporting that she was "thrilled to get back to school! I was doing sales in Manhattan for the past two years—Yuck!" Ron Voloshin is in his job-finding year of law school at the University of Michigan. Having completed majors in biology and political science, Barbara Worchick has decided to apply to medical school after volunteering on an ambulance and working for some months in a nonprofit organization.

2. Barbara Pym, *Quartet in Autumn* (New York: E. P. Dutton, 1978), 1.

3. Pym, *A Very Private Eye: An Autobiography in Diaries and Letters,* ed. Hazel Holt and Hilary Pym (New York: E. P. Dutton, 1984), 291.

A Critic's Confession

JANE NARDIN

SOMETIME DURING THE SPRING OF 1980, I WENT TO HAVE TEA AT MY friend Joe Guerinot's apartment. Although Joe and I shared a number of literary tastes, a common passion for Jane Austen was the main bond between us. Our birthdays fell within a few days of one another and every year Joe would cook us a festive dinner of sweetbread and asparagus, to commemorate the delicate fricassee which Mr. Woodhouse sent back to the kitchen because he feared that the asparagus might not be sufficiently boiled. On this occasion, I had no sooner seated myself on Joe's rather uncomfortable Regency sofa than he put a paperback novel into my hand and said, "I think you're going to like this." It was a copy of *Excellent Women*.

I did indeed like it, and I quickly read all the Pym novels then in print, from *Some Tame Gazelle* to *A Few Green Leaves*. I liked them too, a lot—but here's the rub. As an associate professor of English, it just wasn't in me to accept Pym as the simple gift of God, a writer to be enjoyed without an ulterior thought. No, I couldn't help seeing her novels as an incredible professional windfall that had landed squarely in my undeserving lap. I had discovered a novelist so wonderful that she could be called the "twentieth-century Jane Austen" without irony, but almost no literary criticism had yet been written on her considerable body of work! I hadn't written much criticism myself for several years, but my daughters were growing up, and I finally had a bit of free time at my disposal. Clearly Pym was my chance to get back into the game. I wrote a modest book proposal and in due course got a contract.

In 1982 I traveled to the Bodleian Library to read Pym's letters and diaries. I felt rather uneasy when I came across a joking reference to "the young man from the University of Texas" who would someday become a specialist in her work, because I saw it as a reference to myself. Though not male, I certainly was a youngish American on the faculty of a mediocre state university—a phenomenon that, as Pym's comment implied, the *Zeitgeist* was certain to spawn. When I read those words, I had already seen that Pym's novels do not present literary criticism in a particularly flattering manner, though perhaps— being much inclined to self-doubt and self-laceration—I exaggerated their hostility toward critics simply because I was a critic myself. In any case, I sensed Pym's spirit regarding me with wry disapproval as I sat there in "the *Library*" taking notes and occasionally using the toilets that had been so memorably discussed in *Some Tame Gazelle*.[1]

Pym's novels are full of characters who read, or at some time in the past have read, canonical English literature. They read in different ways and for different reasons. One of my favorite scenes in *The Sweet Dove Died* contrasts two types of readers. The novel's aging heroine, Leonora Eyre, has gone to visit Keats's house in Hampstead with her young friend, James, and his lover, Ned, an American academic who is writing a doctoral dissertation on Keats's minor poems. Though Ned claims that the visit means a lot to him, he actually spends only a few moments looking around the house. Instead of devoting his mind to Keats, he uses the occasion to flaunt his intimacy with James in a highly successful attempt to arouse Leonora's jealousy. But another visitor to the house reacts very differently to its literary associations. This "middle-aged woman wearing a mackintosh pixie hood and transparent rainboots," is carrying "a shopping bag full of books, on top of which [lies] the brightly coloured packet of a frozen 'dinner for one.'" Catching "a glimpse" of the woman's "face, plain but radiant, as she look[s] up from one of the glass cases that held the touching relics [of Keats and Fanny Brawne]," Leonora notices "tears on her cheeks."[2]

All the evidence in *The Sweet Dove Died* goes to prove that Ned doesn't care much about poetry. But he uses it professionally and personally, just as he uses the visit to Hampstead for purposes that have nothing to do with Keats. What Ned revealingly calls "my wretched thesis" is no labor of love, but simply a practical chore (*SDD*, 145). It goes without saying that he chose Keats's minor poems as his subject simply because they had not yet been "done" by anyone else. Literature is more than a job for Ned, however; it is also part of an elaborate, multidimensional game of self-presentation in which he is deeply invested. Religion also plays a role in this game: "Catholic services are very much *me*," Ned says, to explain his motives for renting a flat near Brompton Oratory (157). And so it makes sense that "the pleasure of flinging quotations back and forth" with people he wants to impress should be the only literary pleasure Ned is capable of experiencing (169). In this respect, he is the polar opposite of the woman in the pixie hood, whose intense emotional response to Keats has no connection with her (unglamorous) appearance and earns her no admiration from anyone, since there is no one with whom she can share it. Unlike Ned, this woman gets nothing more from her reading than the intrinsic pleasure it provides.

No opposition quite this stark appears in Pym's other novels, but, in milder terms, they often contrast readers who enjoy literature privately with those who display their knowledge. Pym's own literary tastes blossomed while she was an undergraduate at Oxford. And so it is not surprising that her novels should present academic study as a good way of learning to enjoy English literature or that several of her reader-heroines should possess university degrees in this field. But she dislikes the impulse to use expertise acquired in school for self-aggrandizing purposes. In its least attractive forms, such an impulse is characteristic of many, though not all, academics–and it also characterizes *some* students who never become academics.

In *Some Tame Gazelle*, the semi-autobiographical character Belinda Bede still retains a "smattering of the culture acquired in her college days" (7), though she has reached her fifties. "Even now a light would shine in her mild greenish eyes, so decorously hidden behind horn-rimmed spectacles, at the mention of Young's *Night Thoughts* or the dear Earl of Rochester's *Poems on Several Occasions*," the narrator remarks (7). But Belinda's favorite lines are more likely to be mentioned by someone else than by Belinda herself. Though passages from our greater English poets constantly pop into her mind, and often delight her, Belinda rarely quotes aloud, restrained by a sense of personal modesty and strict propriety at once pathological and deeply lovable. When a young man remarks that a woman friend of his is "not exactly *beautiful* . . . but very nice and so kind," Belinda remembers the lines, "Ah, had she been more beauteous and less kind, / She might have found me of another mind" (91). But she decides not to quote them, presumably because they refer too openly to sexual matters and, even worse, do so in a cynical tone. Though the lines are amusingly relevant to the occasion, Belinda will not risk upsetting others by making her amusement public.

Belinda's old college friend Archdeacon Henry Hoccleve, however, "could never resist a literary allusion and was delighted, in the way that children and scholars sometimes are, if it was one that the majority of his parishioners did not understand" (12). Henry's strident attempts to impress all and sundry with his literary attainments are very different from Belinda's moments of quiet enjoyment. They also backfire constantly and comically. A showy, quotation-laden sermon, in which Henry cannot resist comparing "his congregation to such as *'call aloud for ev'ry bauble drivel'd o'er by sense,'*" gives great offense, so that at its conclusion some of his listeners "even let the [collection] plate pass them, waving it on with an angry gesture" (112). When a man insists that literature must serve him, instead of serving her, she sometimes takes her revenge.

The pompous Henry finds the role of literary scholar an attractive one, though he has chosen to enter the church rather than the academy. He is ever ready with a prefabricated critical judgment or "a short dissertation" on such matters as "the Beast Fable in the Middle Ages" (152) and "the history of the rare word *dingle*" (42). In addition, he is "always threatening" to start a literary society in the village (130). Belinda considers and then, predictably, rejects the idea that she might present a paper to this society. She plans an essay in which she would argue that, contrary to popular belief, English poets often wrote "about unhappy lovers *not* dying of grief." But when she imagines the "audience of clergy and female church workers, most of them unmarried" who would come to hear her paper, she decides that "it would hardly be suitable" (130–31).

True lovers of literature like Belinda have a hard time functioning simultaneously as professional scholars or critics, even if they have received academic training. For in Pym's novels, there is a tension between the impulse to read and the impulse to contextualize or interpret. The quintessential reader, who is often female, submits passively to the power of literature. She lets phrases and the ideas those phrases evoke flow through her mind and take her whither they will. Such a reader must be prepared to arrive at the quirkiest and most "unsuitable" destinations, and precisely for that reason, she must often arrive there alone. The quintessential scholar or critic, however, who is usually male, approaches literature in a more self-assertive way. Though he should ideally be responsive to the patterns adumbrated in literary works, he must ultimately assume control, deciding which patterns are important enough to discuss and devising meta-patterns of his own. And the destination he hopes to reach—a publishable book or article—is predetermined in form and partly predetermined in content.

It therefore makes sense that the pleasures of passive reading should prove more attractive than those of active criticism to several of Pym's more intelligent characters. The eponymous heroines of *Jane and Prudence*, who both studied English literature at Oxford, return for a Reunion of Old Students, where they meet their ex-tutor, Miss Birkenshaw. This "ageless, immaculate" woman has been admired by many generations of students, despite the fact that her "great work on the seventeenth-century metaphysical poets [is] still unfinished, would perhaps never be finished."[3] Although her pedagogical achievements suggest that Miss Birkenshaw was right to give teaching precedence over research, she still places a high value upon

literary scholarship and is unwilling to admit that her great work will
never be written. But Jane Cleveland is more imaginative than her old
tutor, who thinks conventionally and likes things "to be clearly la-
belled" (10). Like Barbara Pym herself, the skeptical Jane questions
the value of every achievement that the world admires and rewards,
including scholarship. At the reunion, Jane remarks loudly to Miss
Birkenshaw that none of the old pupils "gathered round [her]" has
"fulfilled her early promise" (11). Her cheerful, almost congratula-
tory, tone implies that this is by no means a matter of regret.

Unlike her teacher, Jane understands that failure as a literary critic
or scholar is not an end but a beginning: for a well-educated woman
it opens the door to the freedom and pleasure that only the most dis-
interested readers can enjoy. Though there is "a moment" when Jane,
influenced by the atmosphere of Oxford, "almost regret[s] her own
stillborn 'research'—'the influence of something upon somebody'
hadn't Virginia Woolf called it?—to which her early marriage had put
an end" (11), she doesn't really regret it at all, as the pleasantly disparaging quotation from *To the Lighthouse* implies. In fact, Jane can
"hardly remember now what the subject of [her research] was to have
been—Donne, was it, and his influence on some later, obscurer poet?"
(11). Though she once published a scholarly study, and though she
still loves literature, Jane does not seriously consider producing any
more literary criticism. She toys with the idea only in moments of
depression.

At the meeting of a literary society, a fellow member asks Jane what
she has written. "A book of essays on seventeenth-century poets,"
Jane answers, "The kind of book you might put in the bathroom if
you have books there—with Aubrey's *Brief Lives* and *Wild Wales*—
really, I wonder why, now! It would be an interesting study, that!"
(119). In fact, the principles according to which bathroom reading is
selected are more interesting to the mature Jane than the academic
study of literature. Shortly after delivering this pronouncement on
the value of her own work, Jane takes her final revenge on literary
scholarship by "stepping backwards into a critic and causing him to
upset his coffee over himself." As she herself remarks, "Things like
that aren't as trivial as you might think" (120).

I don't want to describe the tension between reading and criticism
in Pym's novels as if it were a binary opposition. It isn't. For the novels not only suggest that, as I noted earlier, a little learning can pro-
mote appreciation, they also depict several scholars and critics who
manage, personally, to resolve the tension, continuing both to love
literature disinterestedly *and* to write about it professionally. Thus
the literary scholar Beatrix Howick in *A Few Green Leaves* regrets

that her daughter Emma is not "better read in English Literature," because she understands, from her own experience, how much "comfort it can give."[4] Yet it seems significant that Beatrix's relation to literature is ultimately less satisfactory than Emma's. Though she read anthropology, not English, in college, Emma remembers a lot more than the "few sad Hardy poems" with which Beatrix credits her (165). In fact, a far greater range of literary allusions pops into the daughter's mind than into the mother's. When *A Few Green Leaves* ends, the observant, ironic Emma is thinking about writing a novel— and she might well write a good one. Beatrix's research, on the other hand, seems to have blunted her perception of the world she lives in. At her desk overlooking the main street of a small village, Beatrix hopes "to witness the kind of events that might have taken place a hundred years ago," in the Victorian fiction she studies, "but more often than not" is disappointed (90).

Barbara Pym's novels thus construct a rough hierarchy of readers that unsettles our usual judgments: the undisciplined reader is in some important sense a better reader than the disciplined literary critic. If we heed Pym's own opinions about criticism, we may well think twice before becoming critics of her work. How naughty of her to put us all in such an untenable position!

At a dinner party in *No Fond Return of Love*, the scholar and editor Aylwin Forbes announces to the assembled company, "in a full, satisfied tone," that his book on the minor poet Edmund Lydden has just been accepted by Oxford University Press. His hostess, Dulcie Mainwaring, somewhat surprised by his choice of topic, asks if Lydden really left "enough poetry for it to be worth writing about him . . . there surely can't be very much?" "That may be," Aylwin answers defensively, "but what remarkable stuff it is! The 'Winter' sonnets— unfinished, admittedly—and the three Epithalamia, not to mention the fragments."[5] After reading this scene, one feels distinctly unenthusiastic about setting to work in order to put oneself in a position to announce, someday, that one's own study of Barbara Pym has been accepted by a prestigious publisher. Or so it seemed to me as I wrote my little book. Clearly, since I felt that way, the only thing to do was to take the pledge against writing any more literary criticism, at least about Pym herself. And I did—from that day to this I have not published a word on the subject of Barbara Pym, though I must confess that I have continued to write about other subjects. But I did not believe that Pym would have objected to my teaching her novels in several courses. And I was sure she wouldn't have minded my keeping a few favorites on my bedside table.

I often think about Pym as I perform my share of "the trivial

round, the common task." Doing my laundry, I recall Mildred
Lathbury's remark about *hers*: "Just the kind of underclothes a person like me might wear . . . so there is no need to describe them."[6]
Introducing myself with the words, "I am Jane Nardin," I remember
how the declaration, "I am Leonora Eyre," gave the speaker "courage
and a feeling of security" (*SDD*, 114). Waking in the night, I think,
like Letty Crowe, about "the strangeness of life, slipping away like
this."[7] Sometimes a couple of lines pop into my mind for no particular
reason: "But he's a celibate, of course. . . . Anyone can see that. It sticks
out a mile" (*NFRL*, 149). But I don't say them aloud if they seem, as
they often do, to be utterly unsuitable for public consumption.

And so, for over fifteen years, I have tried to read Pym as I thought
Pym wanted to be read. Of course, I succumbed to temptation when
I agreed to write this essay and perhaps it makes matters worse that
I've quoted so many of my favorite lines, in the style of Archdeacon
Hoccleve. In the end, I just wasn't able to shake off my callow *Dop-
pelgänger*, the young man from the University of Texas.

NOTES

1. Barbara Pym, *Some Tame Gazelle* (New York: E.P. Dutton, 1983), 94, 102.
2. Pym, *The Sweet Dove Died* (New York: E.P. Dutton, 1979), 155.
3. Pym, *Jane and Prudence* (New York: E.P. Dutton, 1981), 11.
4. Pym, *A Few Green Leaves* (New York: E.P. Dutton, 1980), 165.
5. Pym, *No Fond Return of Love* (New York: E.P. Dutton, 1982), 121–22.
6. Pym, *Excellent Women* (New York: E.P. Dutton, 1978), 85.
7. Pym, *Quartet in Autumn* (New York: E.P. Dutton, 1978), 27.

A Last Literary Collaboration

RONALD BLYTHE

THERE IS A LUXURY ATTACHED TO ANTHOLOGY-MAKING IN THAT one can include all one's favorites. Just twenty years ago I was invited to make an anthology called *Places* to raise funds for Oxfam, the well-known charity in Great Britain. A wonderfully distinguished list of contributors gave their work, among them Barbara Pym, a writer I much admired. On July 5, 1979 she wrote, "I shall be pleased to contribute to the book you are editing . . . I hope I may be able to produce something acceptable . . . Of course I accept all the conditions!"

The "something acceptable" arrived on August 28, 1979:

> I'm afraid it may not be at all the sort of thing you want, but when I came to do it (having been so pleased to be asked) I found that I seem to have no talent for descriptive writing, so that although I have a deep affection for this part of the country I am incapable of conveying it! So I've done a sort of diary of life here in the hope that it may give some kind of impression that may perhaps be a little different. But if you don't want it, I shan't take umbrage—and do feel free to edit the piece, if you do put it in.

> If John Piper is going to illustrate it, the book will indeed be something special. . . . I must apologize for my poor typing—which I hope is decipherable—and also the sudden change of typewriter ribbon!

> I'm so glad you liked the hymns—one doesn't often find people who take much interest in them or their authors. (But I must not forget John Betjeman). We don't seem to have any hymn writers now— certainly not those great Victorian women!

> Let me know if there's anything more I can do for you.[1]

Shortly after this, to my distress, there arrived postcards from the hospital. She was dying. We had never met, but like most of her readers I felt close to her witty vision of life. As a Reader in the Church of England whose duty it is to minister to three small country parishes, I never have a week when I do not encounter characters who are "pure Pym," and situations that would have no difficulty at all in finding a place in those peerless novels. She remains an original.

213

"A Year in West Oxfordshire"[2]
Barbara Pym

About twelve miles west of Oxford, in the Wychwood Forest area on the edge of the Cotswolds, is a cluster of remote villages off the main tourist track.[2] Few of these villages would win a prize for tidiness and elegance, and some of them even now have an air of romantic decay, dating from the depressed Thirties (when my own village, Finstock, was described by one visitor as "a tattered hamlet," and by another as being imbued with an evil emanation from the forest). Today there is an interesting mixture of carefully restored cottages and bright new bungalows with broken dry-stone walls, corrugated iron, and nettles, and even the occasional deserted or ruined homestead.

Every writer probably keeps some kind of diary or notebook, and my own (mercifully less personal and introspective as the years go on) has provided these few observations on the weather and natural surroundings, history and literary associations of the area.

January. Cold, snow, and blizzard and from my window I can watch cars failing to get up the hill to Wilcote. Later in the month a visit to Swinbrook, a pretty, well-kept village. In the church the Fettiplaces lie on their stone shelves—the mansion where they lived was demolished early in the last century and the family has now died out. But Swinbrook still has its Mitford associations—a tablet to Tom Mitford in the church, and the graves of Nancy and Unity in the churchyard. Go to Asthall nearby and stand in the churchyard to took at the manor where the Mitfords lived as children.

February. Sometimes a mild, false spring. The month for gathering firewood in the forest (and once finding half of a deer's antler).

March. (Roses should be pruned by the end of this month.). On the 21st, the first day of official "summer" with its bleak, cold-light evening. A good walk from Finstock, up the hill to Wilcote (with greystone Wilcote House, not all quite as old as it looks, and the apricot-washed manor), past the little romantic-looking church, then down to Ramsden, a more beautiful village than Finstock. Meanly trying to find examples of "direness" (ugly bungalows, corrugated iron, nettles and general squalor), but it is less in evidence here than in other villages in these parts. The main street is pretty and orderly, but you seldom see people walking about.

April. Four kittens born in time for a fine warm Easter. On Low Sunday "reviving" the Easter decorations in the church. Some of the daffodils have survived in the chilly atmosphere (no central heating). Finstock Church is neither ancient nor particularly beautiful, but it has the distinction of being the place where T. S. Eliot was received into the Church of England on 29 June 1927. A bronze plaque to commemorate this has been put up in the church and was dedicated by the Bishop of Oxford on 23 June 1974. There is an account of Eliot's baptism in *T. S. Eliot: A Memoir:*

> William (Force Stead) was living some fifteen miles distant from Oxford in a fine, seventeenth-century gabled house at Finstock on the borders of Wychwood Forest. He arranged that Tom should come and stay with him there and meet two friends who were to be his godfathers (B. H. Streeter and Vere Somerset). On the afternoon of 29th June 1927, St. Peter's Day, William met with his three guests and locked the doors of the little church at Finstock before pouring the water of regeneration over the head of one who in future years was to be as much the leading layman in the Church of England as Lord Halifax was at that time.[3]

William Force Stead, I believe, was a chaplain at one of the Oxford colleges. There are some lines in *Little Gidding* which are said to refer to this event. Only which ones, I wonder? Perhaps these:

> Thus, love of a country
> Begins as attachment to our own field of action
> And comes to find that action of little importance
> Though never indifferent. History may be servitude,
> History may be freedom. See, now they vanish,
> The faces and places, with the self which, as it could,
> loved them,
> To become renewed, transfigured, in another pattern.

May. In a good year this is the best month in this part of the country. Buttercups, cow parsley, and sun. And, of course, the cuckoo (A. E. Housman's poem, "The cuckoo shouts all day at nothing / In leafy dells alone. . ."). And, if it isn't too hot, a walk up to Wilcote and a beautiful "sepia" portrait of sheep grazing in the churchyard round the tombstones. Another walk in Patch Riding, on the edge of the forest going into Cornbury Park (though you can't go into the Park). The bluebells will be out and towards the end of the month you can sometimes see bluebells and wild garlic out together.

June. The most variable month of the year—hottest, coldest, wettest. The eleventh is St. Barnabas's (Hymn 222 in the English Hymnal, by Mrs. Maude Coote—"The Son of Consolation! / Of Levi's priestly line . . ." A walk up to the church for evensong (poorly attended these days). The Collect for St. Barnabas, who came from Cyprus and who introduced St. Paul to the new church at Jerusalem, says that he was endued with "singular gifts" and asks God not to leave us "destitute of thy manifold gifts." Barnabas was with the disciples at Antioch, the place where the word "Christians" was first used.

July. This year (1979) summer at last! Garden full of honeysuckle, syringa, roses (June is hardly ever the month of roses in this garden). Later in this month the almost overwhelming scent of elder-flowers. Sitting in front of the cottage in the early evening, looking at the light on a creamy-grey stone barn opposite, seeing down the hill from Wilcote a hay cart (motorized now, of course!) approaching—huge rolls of hay are the fashion now—said to be easier, more convenient, for the cows to eat. As the hot weather goes on, especially with this year's wet spring and early summer, the countryside becomes "luxuriant"— luscious grass and uncut hedgerows with the scabious coming out, and many weeds in the garden, almost a plague of self-seeded violets. Excursion to Rousham, a Jacobean house, redecorated mid-eighteenth century by William Kent who also designed the landscape and the gardens—temples, follies, terraces, grottoes, and sculptures, and a view down the river. On a summer Saturday you might be the only people there, with the pigeons (Norwich Croppers) in the seventeenth-century dovecote, and bantams with feathered legs.

August. This month Ditchley Park is open to the public. The poet John Wilmot, Earl of Rochester, was born here in 1647. His poems are hymns—to girls.

> My light thou art—without thy glorious sight
> My eyes are darken'd with eternal night.
> My Love, thou art my way, my life, my light.
>
> Thou art my way; I wander if thou fly.
> Thou art my light; if hid, how blind am I!
> Thou art my life; if thou withdraw'st, I die.

According to John Evelyn, it was in Rochester's day "a low timber house with a pretty bowling green," but now it is larger and more imposing, turned into a conference centre. Churchill used to stay here during the war when it was owned by the late Ronald Tree. He was an American who bought the house from Lord Dillon in 1933. Tree described his first view of it in his book, *When the Moon Was High:*

> I remember the hedges on either side of the road being full of wild roses and honeysuckle, and the smell of the new-mown hay. A few minutes later we came out of the lane and before us was the great double avenue of beech trees leading up the lodge gate. I remember that first sight of it: we marvelled at it. Once through the gates we found ourselves in a heavily

wooded park where the deer, many of them white, were grazing or lying in the bracken, their little heads turning enquiringly towards the car as we passed. Ahead, another avenue of elm trees, and then the house itself appeared, stark grey against the blue sky, its two lead statues of Loyalty and Fame looking far out over the trees towards the Churchill Palace at Blenheim, its neighbour to the east.[4]

The poet Rochester and his family are buried in the vaults of Spelsbury church, but there is no tablet to record his memory. The beautiful monument you will see in this church is to the third Earl of Lichfield (1776) who also lived at Ditchley. In the churchyard outside is the large square-oblong tomb where the Cary family are said to be buried, but the top is broken and there is a scattering of bones (can they be human bones?), dry and grey-white. The grass in the churchyard bleached creamy-white and a distant view of what look like downs (though they can't be).

September. This is the month of plums and jam-making, beans and the last courgettes and tomatoes ripening in the garden. (A London friend doesn't appreciate the courgettes, so carefully nurtured and proudly tended, thinks them "tasteless"—and may well criticize the tomatoes of which one is equally proud.) And of course September is the great blackberry month and the lanes round here are full of them.

October. This is still a good blackberry month and they are often at their best, but after a certain date (I can't remember exactly which) they are said to belong to the Devil, or even (in some parts) the Devil is thought to be in them! This is usually the month for Harvest Festival, though the harvest is gathered in earlier—much fruit and flowers in the church, of course, but one year it was noted that vegetables were "not given sufficient prominence in the decorations." (What is Harvest Festival without at least one enormous marrow?) For a change you could go to South Leigh church (St. James's) where a nineteenth-century vicar (Gerard Moultrie) made the translation from the Greek of the magnificent Communion hymn which is No. 318 in the English Hymnal. It is called the Liturgy of St. James.

> Let all mortal flesh keep silence
>   And with fear and trembling stand;
> Ponder nothing earthly-minded,
>   For with blessing in his hand
> Christ our God to earth descendeth,
>   Our full homage to demand.

A nostalgic visit to the Trout Inn at Wolvercote for a memory of Oxford days in the Thirties. Guinness and sandwiches outside—eight peacocks but no trace of the wisteria of forty years ago. Now red creeper and what looks like a vine. A man and a girl embracing by the river, so nothing changes all that much. Huge car park.

November. Still a few roses in the garden and even on the altar in the church. The first iris stylosa may begin to come out so that you have the remains of summer and (perhaps) spring, though there's probably a lot of winter to be got through before then.

December. Hyacinths coming out in the house. Gathering and sawing wood for the fire is good exercise. A grey-white sky and a bleak landscape—plenty of bare trees but the death of the elms has left many gaps. Christmas seems suddenly mild and green, and as the days gradually lighten you begin to look forward to starting the year in West Oxfordshire all over again.

NOTES

1. Letters from Barbara Pym to Ronald Blythe are reprinted by permission of Mr. Blythe.

2. This piece originally appeared in *Places: An Anthology of Britain*, ed. Ronald Blythe (Oxford: Oxford University Press, 1981). It is reprinted by permission of Mr. Blythe.

3. Robert Sencourt, *T. S. Eliot: A Memoir*, ed. Donald Adamson (London: Garnstone Press, 1971), 109.

4. Ronald Tree, *When the Moon Was High* (London: Macmillan, 1975), 37.

Epilogue: The Literary Reputation
of Barbara Pym

DALE SALWAK

"No REPUTATION IS MORE THAN SNOWFALL. IT VANISHES."[1] TRUE
for some writers, perhaps, but Barbara Pym is an exception. Twenty
years since her death, her literary reputation is secure; indeed, her
novels continue to attract an ever-widening audience, and few readers
react to her work with indifference. A survey of over five decades of
review and critical commentary reveals a full range of appraisals, from
condemnation to high praise, from dismissal as "trivial" to admiration for a novelist of considerable originality and force.

To her many admirers, she is a writer of distinctive qualities who,
having suffered discouragement and neglect for sixteen years, was for-
tuitously rediscovered toward the end of her life. Her impeccably
constructed novels—which are often compared favorably with Jane
Austen's (and, more recently, with those of Elizabeth Taylor, Penelope Mortimer, and Anita Brookner, among others)—are essentially
the product of a private, solitary writer who employs precise social
observation, wry understatement, and gentle irony in an oblique approach to such universal themes as the underlying loneliness and frustrations of life, culture as a force for corruption, love thwarted or
satisfied, and the power of the ordinary to sustain and protect men
and women who shelter themselves within it. Her novels are both
period pieces and absolutely contemporary even in the twenty-first
century.

Although hers is a closed world—what Robert Smith called "an enchanted world of small felicities and small mishaps"[2]—it is also real
and varied in theme and setting, with its own laws of human conduct
and values, its peculiar humor and pathos, and its sometimes quirky
cast of middle-aged or elderly ladies, middle-aged or elderly gentlemen, civil servants, clergymen, anthropologists and other academics.

To her detractors, the narrowness of Pym's own life inevitably imposed limitations on her work, making it, they say, too "cozy," too
"clever," too "sad," too focused on the "ordinary" to appeal to mod-

ern and postmodern readers. Bernard Levin, for instance, wrote in
The Sunday Times (London): "I cannot for the life of me understand
what all the fuss is about; *A Few Green Leaves* seems to me thin, dull
and very nearly pointless."[3] But those sharing such a perspective are
in the minority, as readers everywhere continue to find that beneath
the calm surface of her novels, the events of Pym's fictive day *do* make
an imprint. Central characters from one novel appear in passing or are
mentioned in another; delightful minor ones turn up in unexpected
places. Pym relies on neither the violent nor the bizarre. Nothing outwardly momentous happens, but frustrations emerge clearly and poignantly. She makes us *care* for her characters, and that, no doubt, is
one of the many reasons for her sustaining power.

   In the quiet comfort of *No Fond Return of Love*, for example, a new
face is an occasion for speculation, and the pleasantness and security
of everyday life dominates. Only small crises—such as a fainting literary editor or a vicar missing during Easter services—form the coun-
terpoint to comfort. Marriage is a central issue, and so is professional
advancement or stagnation, as the case may be. Most pertinent of all,
perhaps, the reader sees in this novel (as in all of her fiction) the ways
in which people relate or fail to relate to one another, and why. Although Dulcie Mainwaring here is preoccupied with order, stability,
and routine, her *raison d'être* is found in the lives and crises of those
around her. This "involvement" is of central importance to her, providing compensation for the frequent dreariness of her own existence
and, as in the case of Dulcie and Viola, creating one of the fragile
bonds of relationship with others. "In minute, breathtaking ways,"
noted Lisa Schwarzbaum, "[Pym] sizes up the harms, the conventions, the pleasures, and the perversities of small lives and bestows
upon them the rare beauty and clarity of her genius."[4]

   Commentators are correct when they say that Barbara Pym's critical reception can be divided into "two distinct phases"—before and
after 1977 (the year of her literary revival), or between what Philip
Larkin identified as the "high-spirited comedies" written before the
rejection of *An Unsuitable Attachment* and the subsequent, more
somber novels.[5] Indeed, her first six books established her style, were
politely reviewed, and enjoyed a following among a small but steady
readership. F. Seymour Smith called *Some Tame Gazelle* "a quiet,
charming novel [and] a comedy of distinction."[6] Anne Duchene
would later call *Excellent Women* the "most felicitous" of Pym's novels;[7] and Philip Larkin would regard *A Glass of Blessings* as the sub-
tlest of all her books.[8] When *No Fond Return of Love* appeared, the
Times Literary Supplement reviewer thought this "subtle and penetrating book" confirmed Pym's place as "a witty chronicler of the shy

and delicate.''[9] In America, one reviewer praised her grace and "rare mastery of dialogue" in *Less than Angels*, calling it "a quietly and consistently funny book."[10]

After both Larkin and Lord David Cecil named Pym as the most underrated novelist of the century, her literary fortunes turned measurably upward. Anne Duchene found "the ties of consanguinity" between *Quartet in Autumn* (published early in 1977 and later that year short-listed for the Booker Prize) and its predecessors to be very strong.[11]

When *The Sweet Dove Died* was published a year later (followed by E. P. Dutton's adding her books to its list for American readers), the reviewers recognized its brilliance and its modernity. Writing in *Newsweek*, Walter Clemons said, *"The Sweet Dove Died* is lethally funny and subtly, very pronouncedly sensual to a degree new in Pym's work. . . . This is a brilliant, perfect piece of work."[12] Susannah Clapp, writing in the *Times Literary Supplement,* noted the "modernity" of sexual themes, "a suddenly lustful lunge by Humphrey . . . and versatile dalliance by James, who tangles first with a perky and eager girl, afterwards with a manipulative homosexual."[13] Philip Howard called the book "deceptively simple" and added that it was "sharp, funny and sad in its bitchy observations of these people living and partly living their lives of quiet desperation."[14]

The posthumously published *A Few Green Leaves* (1980) was praised on both sides of the Atlantic as "charming and funny," "beguilingly comic," "magical," and "one of her best."[15] The appearance of *An Unsuitable Attachment* (1982), *A Very Private Eye: An Autobiography in Diaries and Letters* (1983), *Crampton Hodnet* (1985), *An Academic Question* (1986), and *Civil to Strangers and Other Writings* (1987) was followed by Hazel Holt's much-anticipated biography, *A Lot to Ask: A Life of Barbara Pym* (1991). All of this additional work, together with the illuminatingly large collection of notebooks, diaries, and manuscripts now held at the Bodleian Library, ensures exploratory work for many decades to come.

One of the best indications of the steady pace of academic interest in Pym's work is the appearance since 1985 of twenty full-length book studies or anthologies, with more soon to arrive. The early treatments—Charles Burkhart's *The Pleasure of Miss Pym* (1987), for example, or Michael Cotsell's *Barbara Pym* (1989)—offer thoughtful analyses of the novels in chronological order, searching along the way for sources and connections between the author's works and her life, between her subjects and the historical context. In one chapter of her elegant book *One Little Room an Everywhere: Barbara Pym's Novels* (1987), Lotus Snow examines in meticulous detail the literary allusions in the novels. In *The Subversion of Romance in the Novels of Barbara Pym* (1998), Ellen M. Tsagaris explores how Pym subverts the discourse of the romance novel through her use of food, clothes, characterization, and marriage customs. Judy Little compares the "dialogic subjectivity" of Virginia Woolf, Christine Brooke-Rose and Pym in *The Experimental Self* (1996), while Mason Cooley examines her comedy (*The Comic Art of Barbara Pym*, 1990). Mary H. Myers's listings of secondary sources in the 1991 and 1992 issues of *Bulletin of Bibliography* supplement my *Barbara Pym, A Reference Guide: 1950–1991*, and in due course there is bound to appear another supplement. The recent reprinting by the American publisher Moyer Bell of almost all the novels, ensuring that there will be copies available for future students and general readers, is yet another key development toward preserving the reputation of and opportunities for research on this writer.

With increasing frequency, Pym's name is also appearing in graduate studies. From 1984 through 1998, there were thirty-three dissertations on Pym, and she is frequently referred to in other graduate writing about her contemporaries. Dissertation, thesis, and article topics range from a focus on the Anglican clergy to gender and alienation, from the language of food to the discourse of clothes. Early source studies and exegesis by young scholars in the United States, Canada, Great Britain, Africa, and Italy have progressed to investigating Pym's themes, philosophy, symbolism, and language. These treat her interpretation and representation of reality, her use of narrative, the paradox of loss and spiritual gain, her satire and caustic sarcasm, her interest in food, and her sympathy—or lack of same—for the small catastrophes of ordinary people.

But there is another reason for Barbara Pym's staying power in the evolving readership of the twenty-first century. In a world that devalues those who make time to listen to the inner self, in a society that tends to equate a need for introspection and solitude with laziness, inactivity, and nonproductiveness, many people have lost possession of what Emily Dickinson called the "appetite for silence."[16] In school and at home, among friends and at play, there seem to be ever-lessening opportunities for quiet time. And as people grow older and their lives become steadily more hectic and fragmented, they find themselves caught up in a race against time, with no time to be alone—and silent.

Barbara Pym's novels invite us to slow down, retire within ourselves, remove ourselves from peripheral concerns, from the pressures of a madly active world, and return to the center where life is sacred—a humble miracle and mystery. It is this ideal reader, I believe, that Joseph Epstein had in mind when he wrote of those who "seek in fiction news of the inner life, who seek solace, who seek the pleasures of a superior imagination at work on the materials of everyday life."[17] Barbara Pym's novels meet that need.

I have heard of numerous instances in which people grieving the loss of a loved one (or of their own health) have found consolation in Pym's novels during the blackest hours. Perhaps this mysterious affinity comes in part because her plots and moral clarities remind readers of the importance of staying connected with others and, ultimately, with hope, with a simple faith in the durability of the human spirit. Her novels, wrote Robert Liddell, "often seem to come to us like gifts of nature, like the air we breathe or the water we drink (but purer and more wholesome)."[18] All this denotes a gentle and genteel sensibility desperately needed in our age, when violence, brutality, and cynicism are all too prevalent.

"Quiet, paradoxical, funny and sad," Eudora Welty wrote in 1982, Barbara Pym's novels "have the iron in them of permanence too."[19]

I cannot improve upon that judgment.

NOTES

1. Delmore Schwartz, quoted in Lance Morrow, "We Need More Writers We'd Miss," *Time*, 26 July 1982, 64.

2. Robert Smith, "How Pleasant to Know Miss Pym," *Ariel* 2, no. 4 (1971), 63–68.

3. Bernard Levin, "Middle Marches . . . ," review of *A Few Green Leaves*, by Barbara Pym, *Sunday Times* (London), 27 July 1980, 40.

4. Lisa Schwarzbaum, "A Cup of Pym," review of *No Fond Return of Love*, by Barbara Pym, *The Real Paper*, 14 June 1980, 16.

5. Philip Larkin, foreword to *An Unsuitable Attachment*, by Barbara Pym (London: Macmillan, 1982), 7.

6. F. Seymour Smith, "Novels," review of *Some Tame Gazelle*, by Barbara Pym, in *What Shall I Read Next?* (Cambridge: Cambridge University Press, 1953), 98.

7. Anne Duchene, "Brave Are the Lonely," review of *Excellent Women*, by Barbara Pym, *Times Literary Supplement*, 30 September 1977, 1096.

8. Larkin, "The World of Barbara Pym," *Times Literary Supplement*, 11 March 1977, 260.

9. See "The Milieu of Love," review of *No Fond Return of Love*, by Barbara Pym, *Times Literary Supplement*, 17 February 1961, 108.

10. P. C., "Fiction," review of *Less than Angels*, by Barbara Pym, *San Francisco Chronicle*, 28 April 1957, 23.

11. Duchene, "Brave Are the Lonely," 1096.

12. Walter Clemons, "The Pleasures of Miss Pym," review of *The Sweet Dove Died*, by Barbara Pym, *Newsweek*, 16 April 1979, 90–91.

13. Susannah Clapp, "Genteel Reminders," review of *The Sweet Dove Died*, by Barbara Pym, *Times Literary Supplement*, 7 July 1978, 757.

14. Philip Howard, "Fiction," review of *The Sweet Dove Died*, by Barbara Pym, *Times* (London), 6 July 1978, 14.

15. See "The Top Shelf," review of *A Few Green Leaves*, by Barbara Pym, *Chicago Tribune Book Review*, 3 August 1980, 5; Paul Bailey, "The Art of the Ordinary," review of *A Few Green Leaves*, by Barbara Pym, *Observer* (London), 27 July 1980, 29; and Walter Clemons, "An Unnoticed World," review of *A Few Green Leaves*, by Barbara Pym, *Newsweek*, 14 April 1980, 96, 99.

16. Emily Dickinson quoted in John Evangelist Walsh, *The Hidden Side of Emily Dickinson* (New York: Simon and Schuster, 1971), 218.

17. Joseph Epstein, "What's Left to Shock When Anything Goes?" *New York Times Book Review*, 5 February 1984, 14.

18. Robert Liddell, *A Mind at Ease: Barbara Pym and Her Novels* (London: Peter Owen, 1989), 8.

19. Eudora Welty, quoted in "Symposium: Books That Gave Me Pleasure," *New York Times Book Review*, 5 December 1982, 61.

Selected Bibliography

THE EDITORS LIST HERE ONLY THE WRITINGS THAT HAVE BEEN OF USE in the making of this book. This bibliography is by no means a complete listing of all the works and sources our contributors and we have consulted. It indicates the substance and range of reading upon which they and we have formed our ideas. We intend it to serve as a convenience for those who wish to pursue the study of the life and oeuvre of Barbara Pym and the theory, psychology, and history of reading as it pertains to her works.

BARBARA PYM, HER WORKS AND LIFE

Holt, Hazel. *A Lot to Ask: A Life of Barbara Pym.* New York: E. P. Dutton, 1991.

Pym, Barbara. "Anglo-Catholic Diary." MS Pym 89. Bodleian Library, Oxford University.

———. *An Academic Question.* New York: E. P. Dutton, 1986.

———. *Civil to Strangers and Other Writings.* Ed. Hazel Holt. New York: E. P. Dutton, 1987.

———. *Crampton Hodnet.* New York: E. P. Dutton, 1985.

———. *Excellent Women.* New York: E. P. Dutton, 1978.

———. *A Few Green Leaves.* New York: E. P. Dutton, 1980.

———. *A Glass of Blessings.* New York: E. P. Dutton, 1980.

———. *Jane and Prudence.* New York: E. P. Dutton, 1981.

———. *Less than Angels.* New York: E. P. Dutton, 1980.

———. *No Fond Return of Love.* New York: E. P. Dutton, 1982.

———. *Quartet in Autumn.* New York: E. P. Dutton, 1978.

———. *Some Tame Gazelle.* New York: E. P. Dutton, 1983.

———. *The Sweet Dove Died.* New York: E. P. Dutton, 1979.

———. *An Unsuitable Attachment.* New York: E. P. Dutton, 1982.

———. *A Very Private Eye: An Autobiography in Diaries and Letters.* Ed. Hazel Holt and Hilary Pym. New York: E. P. Dutton, 1984.

———. "Young Men in Fancy Dress." MS Pym 1, fol. 263. Bodleian Library, Oxford University.

SECONDARY LITERATURE ON BARBARA PYM: HER READERS, HER READING, HER WRITING AND LITERARY INFLUENCES

Ackley, Katherine Anne. *The Novels of Barbara Pym*. New York: Garland, 1989.

Allen, Orphia Jane. *Barbara Pym: Writing a Life*. Metuchen, N.J.: Scarecrow Press, 1994.

Arnold, Matthew. *Essays in Criticism, First Series*. London: Macmillan, 1883.

Auerbach, Nina. *Woman and the Demon: The Life of a Victorian Myth*. Cambridge: Harvard University Press, 1982.

Battiscombe, Georgina. *Charlotte Mary Yonge: The Story of an Uneventful Life*. London: Constable, 1943.

Benet, Diana. *Something to Love: Barbara Pym's Novels*. Columbia: University of Missouri Press, 1986.

Bowman, Barbara. "Barbara Pym's Subversive Subtext: Private Irony and Shared Detachment." In *Independent Women: The Function of Gender in Barbara Pym*, ed. Janice Rossen, 82–94. New York: St. Martin's Press, 1988.

Brookner, Anita. *The Bay of Angels*. New York: Random House, 2001.

———. *The Debut*. New York: Random House, 1982.

———. *Hotel du Lac*. New York: Random House, 1984.

Burkhart, Charles. *The Pleasure of Miss Pym*. Austin: University of Texas Press, 1987.

Byatt, A. S. "Barbara Pym." In *Passions of the Mind*, 241–44. New York: Turtle Bay, 1992.

Chapman, Raymond. *Faith and Revolt: Studies in the Literary Influence of the Oxford Movement*. London: Weidenfield and Nicholson, 1970.

Coleridge, Christabel. *Charlotte Mary Yonge: Her Life and Letters*. London: Macmillan, 1903.

Cooley, Mason. *The Comic Art of Barbara Pym*. New York: AMS, 1990.

Cotsell, Michael. *Barbara Pym*. London: Macmillan, 1989.

Dennis, Barbara. *Charlotte Yonge (1823–1901): Novelists of the Oxford Movement*. Lewiston, N.Y.: Edwin Mellen Press, 1992.

Eakin, Paul John. *How Our Lives Become Stories: Making Selves*. Ithaca: Cornell University Press, 1999.

Graham, Robert J. "The Narrative Sense of Barbara Pym." In *The Life and Work of Barbara Pym*, ed. Dale Salwak. Iowa City: University of Iowa Press, 1987.

Hayter, Alethea. *Charlotte Yonge*. Writers and Their Work. Plymouth, Eng.: Northcote House in Association with the British Council, 1996.

Holt, Hazel. "Philip Larkin and Barbara Pym: Two Quiet People." In *Philip Larkin: The Man and His Work*, ed. Dale Salwak. London: Macmillan, 1989.

Interdonato, Deborah Ann. "Reading Barbara Pym." Ph.D. diss., City University of New York, 1996.

Kaufman, Anthony. "The Short Fiction of Barbara Pym." *Twentieth Century Literature* 32 (1986): 50–77.

Keble, John. *The Christian Year: Thoughts in Verse for the Sundays and Holidays Throughout the Year*. 1827. 43rd ed. London: John Henry Parker, 1854.

Kennard, Jean. "Barbara Pym and Romantic Love." *Contemporary Literature* 33, no. 1 (1993): 44–61.

Larkin, Philip. Foreword to *An Unsuitable Attachment,* by Barbara Pym. London: Macmillan, 1982.

———. *Required Writing: Miscellaneous Pieces, 1955–1982.* London: Faber & Faber, 1983.

———. *Selected Letters of Philip Larkin, 1940–1985.* Ed. Anthony Thwaite. New York: Farrar, Straus & Giroux, 1992.

———. "The World of Barbara Pym." *Times Literary Supplement,* 11 March 1977, 260.

Lenckos, Frauke Elisabeth. *Knowing the World through Reading: Literature of the British Isles; Barbara Pym's* Excellent Women *and Frank McCourt's* Angela's Ashes; *A Study Guide.* Brookings: South Dakota Humanities Council (National Endowment for the Humanities Program), 2001.

Lewis, C. S. "The Sermon and the Lunch." In *God in the Dock: Essays on Theology and Ethics,* ed. Walter Hooper. Grand Rapids, Mich.: Eerdmans, 1970.

Liddell, Robert. *A Mind at Ease: Barbara Pym and Her Novels.* London: Peter Owen, 1989.

Little, Judy. *The Experimental Self: Dialogic Subjectivity in Woolf, Pym, and Brooke-Rose.* Carbondale: Southern Illinois University Press, 1996.

Long, Robert Emmet. *Barbara Pym.* New York: Ungar, 1986.

McInnis, Judy. "Communal Rites: Tea, Wine, and Milton in Barbara Pym's Novels." *Renascence* 48 (1996): 279–93.

Miller, Ellen J. *Barbara Pym: Out of the Wilderness.* Belmont, Mass.: Greybirch Productions, 1984. Videocassette.

Milton, John. *The Complete Prose Works of John Milton.* Ed. Douglas Bush. 8 vols. New Haven: Yale University Press; London: Oxford University Press, 1959.

Moorhead, Caroline. "How Barbara Pym Was Rediscovered after Sixteen Years Out in the Cold." *Times* (London), 14 September 1977: 11.

Nardin, Jane. *Barbara Pym.* Boston: Twayne, 1985.

Olney, James. "Autobiography and the Cultural Moment: A Thematic, Historical, and Bibliographical Introduction." In *Autobiography: Essays Theoretical and Critical,* ed. Olney, 3–27. Princeton: Princeton University Press, 1980.

———. *Memory and Narrative: The Weave of Life-Writing.* Chicago: University of Chicago Press, 1998.

———. *Metaphors of Self: The Meaning of Autobiography.* Princeton: Princeton University Press, 1972.

Rochester, John Wilmot, Earl of. *The Complete Poems of John Wilmot, Earl of Rochester.* Ed. David Vieth. New Haven: Yale University Press, 1968.

Rossen, Janice. "Love in the Great Libraries: Oxford in the Work of Barbara Pym." *Journal of Modern Literature* 12 (1985): 277–96.

———. *The World of Barbara Pym.* New York: St. Martin's Press, 1987.

———, ed. *Independent Women: The Function of Gender in the Novels of Barbara Pym.* New York: St. Martin's Press, 1988.

Rubenstein, Jill. "Comedy and Consolation in the Novels of Barbara Pym," *Renascence* 42 (1990): 173–83.

Salwak, Dale. *Barbara Pym: A Reference Guide.* Boston: G. K. Hall, 1991.

———, ed. *The Life and Work of Barbara Pym*. Iowa City: University of Iowa Press, 1987.

Schulz, Muriel. "The Novelist as Anthropologist." In *The Life and Work of Barbara Pym*, ed. Dale Salwak. Iowa City: University of Iowa Press, 1987.

Snow, Lotus. "Literary Allusions in the Novels." In *The Life and Work of Barbara Pym*, ed. Dale Salwak. Iowa City: University of Iowa Press, 1987.

———. *One Little Room an Everywhere: Barbara Pym's Novels*. Orono, Maine: Puckerbrush Press, 1987.

Strachey, Lytton. *Eminent Victorians*. London: Chatto & Windus, 1928.

Sutherland, John. *The Stanford Companion to Victorian Fiction*. Stanford, Calif.: Stanford University Press, 1984.

Tsagaris, Ellen Marie. *The Subversion of Romance in the Novels of Barbara Pym*. Bowling Green, OH: Bowling Green University Press, 1998.

Weld, Annette. *Barbara Pym and the Novel of Manners*. New York: St. Martin's Press, 1992.

Wyatt-Brown, Anne M. *Barbara Pym: A Critical Biography*. Columbia: University of Missouri Press, 1992.

Yonge, Charlotte Mary. *Beechcroft at Rockstone*. 1889. London: Macmillan, 1893.

———. *The Daisy Chain; or, Aspirations: A Family Chronicle*. 2 vols. London: John Parker, 1856.

———. *The Heir of Redclyffe*. 1853. 9th ed. London: John Parker, 1855.

———. *A History of Christian Names*. 2 vols. Rev. ed. London: Macmillan, 1884.

———. *Hopes and Fears; or, Scenes from the Life of a Spinster*. 1860. London: Macmillan, 1889

———. *Musings Over "The Christian Year" and "Lyra Innocentium," Together with a Few Gleanings of Recollections of the Reverend John Keble*. London: John Parker, 1872.

———. *The Pillars of the House; or, Under Wode and Under Rode*. 1873. 2 vols. London: Macmillan, 1873.

———. *The Trial: More Links in the Daisy Chain*. 1864. London: Macmillan, 1884.

———. *Womankind*. London: Mozley & Smith, 1876.

Young, Edward. *The Complete Works of Edward Young*. Ed. James Nichols. 2 vols. London: William Tegg, 1854.

THE THEORY, PSYCHOLOGY, AND HISTORY OF READING

Bloom, Harold. *How to Read and Why*. New York: Scribner, 2000.

Booth, Wayne C. *The Company We Keep: An Ethics of Fiction*. Berkeley: University of California Press, 1988.

———. "Why Ethical Criticism Can Never Be Simple." *Style* (Summer 1998): 1–14.

Fetterly, Judith. *The Resisting Reader: A Feminist Approach to American Fiction*. Bloomington: Indiana University Press, 1979.

Rosenblatt, Louise. *The Reader, the Text, and the Poem: The Transactional Theory of the Literary Work*. Carbondale: Southern Illinois University Press, 1978.

Woolf, Virginia. *The Second Common Reader*. Ed. Andrew McNeillie. London: Harcourt Brace, 1986.

Selected Annotated Bibliography
of Barbara Pym Criticism, 1982–1998

Compiled by DALE SALWAK

Ackley, Katherine Anne. *The Novels of Barbara Pym*. New York: Garland, 1989.
Offers a comprehensive survey. "What one notices about all Pym's novels is the way she rarely presents anyone or any issue as purely good or purely bad, purely right or purely wrong." Considers the primary themes, character types, relationships between men and women, neglected females, isolation and loneliness, optimism and affirmation of life, and use of literature as a backdrop for the characters' lives.

Allen, Orphia Jane. *Barbara Pym: Writing a Life*. Metuchen, N.J.: Scarecrow Press, 1994.
Considers Pym, her novels, and the critical response to her work. It is in four parts: "Barbara Pym: Her Life and Work" introduces all thirteen of Pym's published novels and the work collected in *Civil to Strangers and Other Writings*, relating events in her life to topics she writes about. "Writing a Life: Barbara Pym and Her Novels" discusses the ten novels Pym herself prepared for publication, focusing on some of the autobiographical elements in the novels that derive from her concerns about romantic love, the church, and literature. "Critical Approaches to Barbara Pym and Her Novels" summarizes the scholarly literature on the novels. The fourth section is a comprehensive bibliography of primary and secondary sources.

Beard, Jennifer J. "Barbara Pym's Narrative Intersections." Ph.D. diss., University of New Hampshire, 1998.
Places Pym's realism in the context of modernism, antimodernism, and postmodernism in the twentieth-century English novel.

Benet, Diana. *Something to Love: Barbara Pym's Novels*. Columbia: University of Missouri Press, 1986.
Examines the novelist as "a chronicler of universal problems" whose focus—the many guises of love—moves, shapes, or disfigures all of her major characters. When romantic love fails them or is not an option, the characters seek sustenance in the affections of friendship or family ties, in the Christian love of neighbors, in "'child substitutes' human or animal, or in the asexual 'unsentimental tenderness' . . . expressed in small 'gestures of solicitude' that one solitary soul might extend to another."

Berndt, Judy. "Barbara Pym: A Supplementary List of Secondary Sources." *Bulletin of Bibliography* 43 (1986): 76–80.
Supplements Lorna Peterson's bibliography (1984). Lists secondary sources chronologically and is divided into general criticism, reviews, bibliographical articles, obituaries, and miscellany.

Blair, Cairn Fiona. "A Study of the Presentation of Women in the Novels of Barbara Pym." Master's thesis, University of South Africa, 1997.
Evaluates Pym as a feminist writer who successfully illuminates her heroines' "struggles against patriarchy" in the context of a changing British society.

Brothers, Barbara. "Women Victimized by Fiction: Living and Loving in the Novels of Barbara Pym." In *Twentieth Century Women Novelists*, ed. Thomas F. Staley, 61–80. Totowa, N.J.: Barnes & Noble, 1982.
Examines the challenge to the romantic paradigm that echoes in all of Pym's novels. "Though her portrayal of life focuses on its mundaneness and on her characters' self-deceptions and self-pretensions, Pym's is not the pen of a satirist." Her characters seem remote from the modern world, their prospects are dim, but revealed is her sensibility and her deep understanding of human nature.

Burke, Kathleen Michaela. "The Oxford Novel as '*Bildungsroman*': An Analysis of the Works of Six Writers." Ph.D. diss., University of Maryland, 1989.
Finds in Pym's novels a commingling of the German *Bildungsroman* and the Oxford novel. In spite of differences between the two forms, this trend helped to popularize the educational novel in English literature and to improve the literary value of the Oxford novels.

Burkhart, Charles. *The Pleasure of Miss Pym*. Austin: University of Texas Press, 1987.
Discusses Pym's life, autobiographical writings, and fiction through *An Academic Question*. Focuses on her worldview, the unique nature of her comedy, her religion, her place within the history of the novel, and her insights into male-female relationships. Includes photographs.

Byatt, A. S. "Barbara Pym." In *Passions of the Mind*, 241–44. New York: Turtle Bay, 1992.
Offers, from the perspective of a fellow novelist, a unique assessment of Pym's characters, themes, and voice. Pym's attempt to write (in *An Academic Question*) a "sharp," "swinging" novel was a mistake; the result is "thin and unappealing." Byatt wonders why her novels have attracted academic interest.

Bywaters, Barbara Lee. "'Re-reading Jane': Jane Austen's Legacy to Twentieth-Century Women Writers (Pym, Heyer, Gibbons, Brookner)." Ph.D. diss., Bowling Green State University, 1989.
Gives evidence from the novels that Pym is Austen's "literary sister," as Pym draws from her predecessor in treating the theme of sisterhood.

Collu, Gabrielle. "The Language of Food in the Fiction of Barbara Pym." Master's thesis, McGill University (Canada), 1991.
Using social history, structural anthropology, and semiotics, exposes the "language of food" inherent in Pym's novels.

Cooley, Mason. *The Comic Art of Barbara Pym*. New York: AMS, 1990.
Places Pym in the line of the great comic writers from Molière to Beckett. Her comedy ranges from "a witty display of slippage and incongruity of language and behavior (high comedy) to clowning and visual jokes (farce). In mood, it changes over the course of her career from hilarity to gravity." Thus her novels "are not tales of sadness and defeat but of a tenacious will to find sustenance and even enjoyment in the most unpromising circumstances."

Cotsell, Michael. *Barbara Pym*. London: Macmillan, 1989.
Examines all the novels, paying particular attention to thoughts and feelings. Judges the novels to be "unabashedly romantic." Considers her sense of language, unpublished writings, and creative process. Notes ways in which Philip Larkin influenced her work.

Derry, Stephen. "Barbara Pym and Philip Larkin's 'Aubade.'" *Notes & Queries* 44 (1997): 365.

Finds parallels between Larkin and Pym in their concern with the darker side of existence.

Dobie, Ann B. "The World of Barbara Pym: Novelist as Anthropologist." *Arizona Quarterly* 44 (1988): 5–18.
Discusses the influence of anthropology on Pym's writings."Human beings are, in the world of Barbara Pym, poignant in their solitary state, amusing in their pettiness, and admirable in their attempts to transcend their limitations. In her novels they are resilient creatures who quietly battle to realize life's dreams and overcome life's disappointments."

Gordon, Joan. "Cozy Heroines: Quotidian Bravery in Barbara Pym's Novels." *Essays in Literature* 16 (1989): 224–33.
In these charming novels Pym is able to laugh at herself as she pauses for perfect understanding of her characters and the vagaries of their world.

Graham, Robert J. "'Cumbered with Much Serving': Barbara Pym's Excellent Women." *Mosaic* 17 (1984): 141–60.
Accounts for Pym's renewed popularity through a consideration of her subject matter ("the vagaries of heterosexual relationships") in her first ten novels and the changing cultural attitudes toward "the singleness-marriage issue." Sees in Mildred Lathbury the prototypical "excellent woman."

Groner, Marlene San Miguel. "The Novels of Barbara Pym." Ph.D. diss., St. John's University, 1988.
Explores how Pym's characters use their imagination to create a different reality for themselves.

Heberlein, Kate Browder. "Barbara Pym and Anthony Trollope: Communities of Imaginative Participation." *Pacific Coast Philology* 19 (1984): 95–100.
Notes that Pym and Trollope share an interest in the clergy, a comic vision, and a celebration of the ordinary: "we can join their communities of imaginative participation and perhaps, like Pym's novelists *manquées*, create our own."

Hoffman, Karen Marie. "Pym's Peripheral Lives: The Novels, 1952–1963." Master's thesis, University of Victoria (Canada), 1992.
Concentrates on Pym's interest in characters that are "adjuncts" to the male world.

Holberg, Jennifer Louise. "Searching for Mary Garth: The Figure of the Writing Woman in Charlotte Brontë, Elizabeth Barrett Browning, E. M. Delafield, Barbara Pym, and Anita Brookner." Ph.D. diss., University of Washington, 1997.
Challenges "dominant paradigms" whereby woman writers are perceived as "depressed and embittered, raging and rebellious" by exploring their relationship with more "conventional" writers.

Holland, Barbara Windham. "'A Curious Kind of Consolation': Barbara Pym's Ironic Reduction." Ph.D. diss., University of Alabama, 1993.
Pym's reductive approach allows her to manipulate and control her fictional world.

Interdonato, Deborah Ann. "Reading Barbara Pym." Ph.D. diss., City University of New York, 1996.
Pym is important because of the "sensuous/simple" quality of her prose. It is on the level of her style that she excels.

Jacobs, Bruce Richard. "Elements of Satire in the Novels of Barbara Pym." Ph.D. diss., Fordham University, 1988.
Pym's novels are entertaining because they mock a "cold, absurd outer world" and because they change our social attitudes by inviting us into a "warm, imaginative world" of excellent women.

Johnson, R. Neill. "Mainstream and Margins in the Postwar British Comic Novel." Ph.D. diss., Pennsylvania State University, 1998.
Explores Pym's humor in the context of social changes in England. Finds evidence of the subversive.

Jones, Michelle Lynne. "Laughing Hags: The Comic Vision as Feminist." Ph.D. diss., University of Alabama, 1992.
Pym's texts mock societal norms (the academy, the church, and the self) through "comic inversion" and Virginia Woolf's principle of "derision."

Kapp, Isa. "Out of the Swim with Barbara Pym." American Scholar 52 (1983): 237–42.
Appreciates Pym's novels as a "sanctuary from the enormous liberties and vast territory" often found in modern fiction. Considers her settings ("comfortably confining"); heroines ("dignified anachronisms" and superior to men); humor (sometimes tongue in cheek); precise observation of speech, manner, and mentality ("awesome"); plots ("startlingly narrow"); voice (calm but contributing to suspense); allusions to poetry; and universal appeal. Concludes that beneath Pym's extraordinary forbearance and compassion there is "a layer of sheer spinal firmness and imperturbable detachment that puts her into the rank of first-rate novelists." Along with that detachment Pym finds an "ability to see several things at the same time."

Kaufman, Anthony. "The Short Fiction of Barbara Pym." Twentieth Century Literature 32 (1986): 50–77.
Demonstrates how Pym's "preoccupation with kinds of failure" can be seen in her short fiction; often she creates a protagonist "who in one way or another must settle for something less than what is satisfactory or even necessary." Notes that the stories contain "repetitive patterns" that go beyond what is understood to be "very Barbara Pym." Concludes that Pym fulfilled her desire to create a fictional world expressed in her own style.

Keener, Frederick M. "Barbara Pym Herself and Jane Austen." Twentieth Century Literature 31 (1985): 89–110.
Considers the first ten novels and tests the usefulness of comparing Pym to Jane Austen. Keeps the question of Pym's indebtedness to Austen in perspective, for the ten novels are "not by any means the whole story." Includes biographical details.

Kennard, Jean E. "Barbara Pym and Romantic Love." Contemporary Literature 33 (1993): 44–61.
Shows that Pym's understanding, compassion, and precise language make her novels about relationships between the sexes compelling.

Knochel, Mary Jeanne. "Observing the Boundaries: Theme and Technique in the Novels of Barbara Pym." Ph.D. diss., Purdue University, 1994.
Focuses on Pym's voice, themes, and use of language, and on the "voyeuristic content" of her writing.

Lee, Sun-Hee. "Love, Marriage, and Irony in Barbara Pym's Novels." Ph.D. diss., University of North Texas, 1991.
Examines how Pym creates an original voice through irony of dilemma and irony of situation. Beneath this is hidden a romantic point of view.

Levin, Amy Karen. "The Suppressed Sister: A Relationship in the Novel." Ph.D. diss., City University of New York, 1989.
Shows how Pym rejects rules governing female behavior and questions the expectation that women must relate well to one another.

Liddell, Robert. A Mind at Ease: Barbara Pym and Her Novels. London: Peter Owen, 1989.

Draws on his fifty years of friendship with Pym to write a critical survey of those works "which were prepared by herself for publication." Considers the attention she gave to her characters' domestic and emotional lives, examines the reasons for her revival, and guides the reader through her novels, explaining which ones are successful, which are not, and why. Also corrects errors by critics and corrects the common misconception that Pym is a modern-day Jane Austen.

———. "Two Friends: Barbara Pym and Ivy Compton-Burnett." *London Magazine*, August/September 1984: 59–69.
Reminisces about his friendship with Pym, which lasted from 1933 until her death in 1980. Came to appreciate not only her "original and quaint sense of humour," her passion for English literature, and her amusement at "the vagaries of clergy," but also her deeper qualities, including her unselfishness, patience, and endurance. Includes biographical details.

Long, Robert Emmet. *Barbara Pym*. New York: Ungar, 1986.
Studies Pym's life and career. Treats the first eleven novels, paying particular attention to the recurrence of certain themes and character types, to her modes of social comedy and satire, and to her pervasive concern with "unrealized" love and solitude. Concludes by noting the way in which Jane Austen's dynamic English provincial world has reached a point of breakdown in Pym.

McDonald, Margaret Anne. "Alone Together: Gender and Alienation." Ph.D. diss., University of Saskatchewan (Canada), 1991.
Shows how gender roles affect all activity in the novels. Pym envisions a society that respects these differences but that honors community as the only hope for survival.

Myers, Mary H. "Barbara Pym: A Further List of Secondary Sources." *Bulletin of Bibliography* 48 (1991): 25–26.

———. "Barbara Pym: A Supplement to a Further List of Secondary Sources." *Bulletin of Bibliography* 49 (1992): 81–82.
Bibliographical listing of critical works about the author.

Nardin, Jane. *Barbara Pym*. Boston: Twayne, 1985.
Introductory study of Pym's life and career, noting the origins and development of themes, character types, and style. Includes chronology and bibliography (both primary and secondary sources).

Naulty, Patricia Mary. "'I Never Talk of Hunger': Self-Starvation as Women's Language of Protest in Novels by Barbara Pym, Margaret Atwood, and Anne Tyler." Ph.D. diss., Ohio State University, 1988.
Explores, among other topics, Marcia Ivory's self-starvation in *Quartet in Autumn* as a way of rejecting dominant patriarchal ideology. Compares Pym to more famous authors.

Paryas, Phyllis Margaret. "Making a Life from the Margins: The Oblique Art of Barbara Pym." Ph.D. diss., University of Ottawa (Canada), 1992.
Uses structuralist, postformalist, and feminist criticism to discern "contradictory forces" in Pym's prose. Concludes that Pym is essentially optimistic but divided as she negotiates "painful compromises" for her heroines within the "formidable constraints" of the culture.

Peterson, Lorna. "Barbara Pym: A Checklist, 1950–1984." *Bulletin of Bibliography* 41 (1984): 201–6.
Lists primary works and secondary sources, arranged chronologically and divided into general criticism, reviews, summaries of works, biographical articles, obituar-

ies, and miscellany. "Despite the quality of Barbara Pym's work and the volumi-
nous praise for her witty novels of manners, [she] has not received the scholarly
attention she deserves."

Rathburn, Frances Margaret. "The Ties That Bind: Breaking the Bonds of Victimization in the Novels of Barbara Pym, Fay Weldon, and Margaret Atwood." Ph.D.
diss., University of North Texas, 1994.
Explores the way in which Pym's heroines break free from victimization by individuals, institutions, and cultural tradition.

Rees, Heidi Ann. "'A Consolidation of Spinsters': Fiction, Food, and Self-Awareness
in the Early Novels of Barbara Pym." Master's thesis. The University of Manitoba
(Canada), 1994.
Explores the characters' inner and outer worlds in the early novels, with particular
attention paid to self-identity.

Rossen, Janice. "Love in the Great Libraries: Oxford in the Work of Barbara Pym."
Journal of Modern Literature 12 (1985): 277–96.
Examines the influence of Oxford on Pym's novels and unpublished works. "In
the sense that she wrote intensely about Oxford feelings, relationships, and attitudes, she did write the Oxford novel she longed to write."

———. *The World of Barbara Pym.* New York: St. Martin's Press, 1987.
Focuses on twentieth-century England as Pym saw, lived, satirized, and enjoyed it.
Defines her significance within the framework of the modern British novel, traces
her artistic development, explores the relationship between her life and fiction, and
addresses broader themes regarding British culture in her work, such as spinsterhood, anthropology, English literature, the Anglican Church, and Oxford University.

———, ed. *Independent Women: The Function of Gender in the Novels of Barbara
Pym.* New York: St. Martin's Press, 1988.
Seeks to test Pym's reputation by considering her craftsmanship, the literary influences on her work, and her special use of language. Includes biographical, historical, and feminist approaches that explore her unique creative process as it
relates to events in her life.

Roth, Laura Kathleen Johnson. "Performance Considerations for the Adaptation of
Selected Barbara Pym Novels for Chamber Theatre Production." Ph.D. diss., Uni-
versity of Texas at Austin, 1989.
Examines use of point of view, character, dialogue and narration, thematic issues,
and plot structure in *Excellent Women*, *An Unsuitable Attachment*, and *Quartet in
Autumn* from the performer's perspective.

Rubenstein, Jill. "'For the Ovaltine Had Loosened Her Tongue': Failures of Speech
in Barbara Pym's *Less than Angels*." *Modern Fiction Studies* 32 (1986): 573–80.
Examines the "failures of interpretation and infelicities of speech acts" in *Less than
Angels*. This problem is the primary source of both comedy and gloom in Pym's
vision of human relations.

Saar, Doreen Alvarez. "Irony from a Female Perspective: A Study of the Early Novels of Barbara Pym." *West Virginia University Philological Papers* 33 (1987): 68–75.
Considers the development of themes, characters, and social views in the first six
novels.

Sadler, Lynn Veach. "The Pathos of Everyday Living in the Novels of Barbara Pym."
West Virginia University Philological Papers 31 (1986): 82–90.
Pym's heroines relate to characters in literature, they live as observers rather than
participants, and they concern themselves with moral issues.

Salwak, Dale. *Barbara Pym: A Reference Guide*. Boston: G. K. Hall, 1991.
Annotated listing of secondary sources from 1950 through 1991.

————, ed. *The Life and Work of Barbara Pym*. Iowa City: University of Iowa Press, 1987.
Nineteen essays examine Pym's life and work. Includes primary and secondary bibliographies.

Sanford, Rhonda Lemke. " 'Dress Optional?': The Discourse of Clothes in the Novels of Barbara Pym." Master's thesis, University of Colorado at Denver, 1993.
What characters wear and what they notice others wear say much about their interior world and about Pym's satiric view of contemporary life.

Schofield, Mary Anne. "Well-Fed or Well-Loved? Patterns of Cooking and Eating in the Novels of Barbara Pym." *University of Windsor Review* 18 (1985): 1–8.
Explores culinary rituals as thematic center in the novels. Notes parallels between a focus on food and eating in the novels and anthropological interests in Levi-Strauss's *The Raw and the Cooked: Introduction to a Science of Mythology*. Concludes that Pym's novels become "almost anthropological studies of the civilizing process of man, his eating habits, and the culturing powers of certain foods." Pym underscores "the isolation and hunger that twentieth-century men and women continually face."

Sherwood, Rhoda I. " 'A Special Kind of Double': Sisters in British and American Fiction." Ph.D. diss., University of Wisconsin, 1987.
Finds in *Some Tame Gazelle* the "more pleasant features" of sisterhood. Pym makes fun of romantic comedy and suggests that "blessed as the wedded woman may be, more blessed still is the spinster who shares with her sister fantasies about romance and quiet and pleasantly predictable routine."

Smith, Robert. " 'Always Sincere, Not Always Serious': Robert Liddell and Barbara Pym." *Twentieth Century Literature* 41 (1995): 367–80.
Explores the fifty-year friendship between Robert Liddell and Barbara Pym in the context of the novels.

Snow, Lotus. *One Little Room an Everywhere: Barbara Pym's Novels*. Orono, Maine: Puckerbrush Press, 1987.
Discusses the abundance of literary allusions and quotations that filter through the minds of the characters. Examines what the allusions reveal about the characters' interior worlds as well as the novels' themes.

Stanley, Isabel Ashe Bonnyman. "The Anglican Clergy in the Novels of Barbara Pym." Ph.D. diss., University of Tennessee, 1990.
Studies the development of clerical characters, explores their connections with similar characters in Austen, Trollope, and the Brontës, and traces the fortunes of the Anglican Church. Although the Church has lost "much vigor," it still serves as a source of cohesion.

Staunton, S. Jane, " 'Dying in Other Words': Discourses of Disease and Cure in the Last Works of Jane Austen and Barbara Pym." Master's thesis, McGill University (Canada), 1997.
Shows how illness figures both literally and metaphorically in the novels of Austen (as "failures in wholeness") and Pym (as "failures in love").

Tsagaris, Ellen Marie. " 'In Small Things Forgotten': The Subversion of the Discourse of Romance in the Novels of Barbara Pym." Ph.D. diss., Southern Illinois University at Carbondale, 1996.
Through her use of food, clothes, marriage, and characterization, Pym subverts the

discourse of the romance novel. To the question, "Can single women of a certain age live a full life?" Pym offers a resounding, "Yes!"

———. *The Subversion of Romance in the Novels of Barbara Pym*. Bowling Green, Ohio: Bowling Green University Press, 1998.
Book based on Tsagaris's dissertation.

Tyler, Natalie Christine Hawthorne. "Communities of Last Resort: Representations of the Elderly in the Contemporary British Novel." Ph.D. diss., Ohio State University, 1993.
Examines how elderly characters struggle for self-identity. Concludes that there is much opportunity for growth in those characters who fight against the "dying of the light."

Weld, Annette. *Barbara Pym and the Novel of Manners*. New York: St. Martin's Press, 1992.
Defines the novel of manners and Pym's place within the genre. Shows how Pym experimented in her early work with several literary poses as she tried to discover her voice. Examines her early novels for their themes and intents, for their shared "lightness of spirit and tone." Weld considers the reasons for Pym's rejection, resurrection, and valediction, and the significant events from her private life that influenced her creative development.

Whitney, Carol Wilkinson. "'Women Are So Terrifying These Days': Fear Between the Sexes in the World of Barbara Pym." *Essays in Literature* 16 (1989): 71–84.
Explores the relationship between the sexes in twelve novels.

Wilcox, Jacqueline F. "Marriage in the Early Works of Barbara Pym." Ph.D. diss., Southern Illinois University at Carbondale, 1992.
Seeks to discover why the marriages of Pym's protagonists do not necessarily end happily. Reads the novels as a critique of society and concludes that the myths inherent in patriarchy work to the detriment of both sexes.

Wyatt-Brown, Anne M. *Barbara Pym: A Critical Biography*. Columbia: University of Missouri Press, 1992.
Explores the influence of Pym's life upon her work. Demonstrates how Pym's "transformation of everyday experiences into art allowed her to triumph over her social and emotional environments." Shows the importance that gender plays in the novels. Includes primary and secondary bibliographies.

———. "Late Style in the Novels of Barbara Pym and Penelope Mortimer." *Gerontologist* 28 (1988): 835–39.
Considers Pym's treatment of the elderly and aging compared to that of Penelope Mortimer.

Contributors

KATHERINE ANNE ACKLEY is professor of English at the University of Wisconsin–Stevens Point. She is author of *The Novels of Barbara Pym* (1989) and editor of *Perspectives on Contemporary Issues: Readings Across the Disciplines* (1997, 2000), *Essays from Contemporary Culture* (1992, 1995, 1998, 2001), *Misogyny in Literature: An Essay Collection* (1992), and *Women and Violence in Literature: An Essay Collection* (1990). Her most recent research interest is the British crime novel.

ORPHIA JANE ALLEN retired in 1999 after more than twenty years on the faculty of the Department of English, New Mexico State University. Her publications include *Barbara Pym: Writing a Life* (1994), *Publications Management: Essays for Professional Communicators* (coeditor, 1994), and articles in *Genre, Modern Fiction Studies, Latin American Literary Review,* and *Doris Lessing Newsletter.*

JOHN BAYLEY, husband of the late Iris Murdoch, has written two highly acclaimed memoirs about his wife and her battle with Alzheimer's disease, *Iris: A Memoir* (1999) and *Iris and Her Friends* (2000). He is also the Warton Professor of English Emeritus at Oxford University and acclaimed author of the novels *The Red Hat* (1998), *The Queer Captain* (1995), *Alice* (1994), and *George's Lair* (1994). His most recent work is *Widower's House: A Study in Bereavement, or How Margot and Mella Forced Me to Flee My Home* (2001).

RONALD BLYTHE, acclaimed British author, short-story writer, essayist, and editor of a number of literary anthologies on a wide variety of subjects, makes his home in Wormingford, near Colchester in Essex, a place he has made famous through his writings. He is the editor of *The Age of Illusion: England in the Twenties and Thirties, 1919–1940* (1964), *Places: An Anthology of Britain* (1981), *Characters and Their Landscapes* (1983), *Divine Landscapes* (1986), *Each Returning Day: The Pleasures of Diaries; Four Centuries of Private Writing* (1988), and *England: The Four Seasons* (1993). He is the author of *A Treasonable Growth* (1960), *Immediate Possession and Other Stories* (1961), *Aken-*

field: Portrait of an English Village (1969), *The Visitors* (1972), *The View in Winter: Reflections on Old Age* (1979), and *Word from Wormingford: A Parish Year* (1997).

PAUL DE ANGELIS introduced American readers to Barbara Pym in 1978, when he published *Quartet in Autumn* as an editor at E. P. Dutton. Dutton subsequently published all the Pym novels. After twelve years with Dutton, he served as editor-in-chief and then editorial director at Kodansha America from 1990 to 1995. During his twenty-eight years in the book publishing business, Mr. De Angelis has worked with such authors as the Delaney sisters, Mike Royko, Eric Kraft, Peter Guralnick, Jorge Luis Borges, Sarah Rossbach and Lin Yun, and Alexander Dubcek. He lives in Cornwall Bridge, Conn., where he works in book development, assisting authors, agents, publishers, and a packager in turning ideas and manuscripts into books. He is also the copublisher of a quarterly community newspaper and is working on a cultural history/biography of Washington Irving and the Hudson River.

BARBARA J. DUNLAP is professor emerita and retired head of Archives and Special Collections at the Library of the City College of the City University of New York. She is a member of the Academy of Certified Archivists (ACA). Professor Dunlap has published work on Charlotte M. Yonge in the *Encyclopedia of the 1890s* and *The Dictionary of Literary Biography* (volume 18, *Victorian Novelists after 1885*), in addition to several articles for publications of the Charlotte Mary Yonge Fellowship. She is also a coauthor of *From the Free Academy to CUNY: Illustrating Public Higher Education in New York, 1847–1997* (2000).

BARBARA EVERETT is senior research fellow at Somerville College, Oxford University. She has held fellowships and lectureships at both Oxford and Cambridge. Dr. Everett has delivered both the Lord Northcliffe Lectures at University College, London, and the Clarks Lectures at Trinity College, Cambridge. She is author of books on a wide variety of subjects, and her Shakespeare editions include the New Penguin *Antony and Cleopatra* and *All's Well That Ends Well*. She has also written *Poets in Their Time: Essays on English Poetry from Donne to Larkin* (1986) and *Young Hamlet: Essays on Shakespeare's Tragedies* (1989). Dr. Everett has been a popular speaker at several meetings of the Barbara Pym Society in both England and the United States.

JAN FERGUS is professor of English at Lehigh University. She is the author of the highly praised literary biography *Jane Austen: A Literary Life* (1991), as well as a number of articles on the eighteenth-century reading public. For the Juvenalia Press, she has edited two texts of the young Austen, *The History of England* (1995) and *Lesley Castle* (1998). She is the editor of *Literature and Society* (1981) and a frequent contributor to *Persuasions*, the journal of the Jane Austen Society of North America. Her article in *Persuasions* on Barbara Pym's *A Glass of Blessings* deals with its relation to Austen's *Emma*.

HAZEL HOLT first met Barbara Pym in 1950, when they both worked at the International African Institute in London, and was a close friend for thirty years. As Barbara Pym's literary executor, she edited the unpublished novels *An Unsuitable Attachment, Crampton Hodnet, An Academic Question, and Civil to Strangers*, and, with Hilary Pym Walton, edited *A Very Private Eye* (1984), a volume of Pym's diaries and letters. She is the author of the acclaimed Pym biography, *A Lot to Ask* (1991). Hazel Holt lives in Somerset, England, where she writes detective novels. Her son is the writer Tom Holt.

ANTHONY KAUFMAN received his doctorate from Yale University and teaches courses in Comedy, Short Fiction, and Restoration and Eighteenth-Century Drama at the University of Illinois at Urbana-Champaign. He has published articles on Barbara Pym, James Thurber, and J. D. Salinger, as well as on comic playwrights such as Wycherley, Southerne, Congreve, and Aphra Behn.

FRAUKE ELISABETH LENCKOS holds a doctorate in Comparative Literature from the University of Michigan. She teaches in the Liberal Education for Adults programs at the University of Chicago and leads seminars at the Newberry Library, Chicago. Dr. Lenckos has published essays and articles on Victorian and modern women's writings, her areas of expertise. She has spoken at various gatherings of the Barbara Pym Society.

ELLEN J. MILLER is the director of publications at Harvard Law School and founder of the School's Media Services Department. She is the author of two books on video for lawyers, and of numerous journal and magazine articles in legal and general publications, and was the longtime editor of a newsletter for lawyers, *Legal Video Review*. Ms. Miller produced *Barbara Pym: Out of the Wilderness*, the first American video on the author, in 1984. In 1998, she founded the Barbara Pym Society of North America and is the organizer of its annual conferences in the United States. She is the producer of a series of oral history videos documenting the town of Carlisle, Mass., where she lives.

JANE NARDIN has taught English at the University of Wisconsin–Milwaukee since 1973. Her specialty is the eighteenth- and nineteenth-century English novel. She is the author of *Those Elegant Decorums: The Concept of Propriety in Jane Austen's Novels* (1973), *Barbara Pym* (1985), *He Knew She Was Right: The Independent Woman in the Novels of Anthony Trollope* (1989), *Trollope and Victorian Moral Philosophy* (1996), and many articles on British prose fiction.

ANNE PILGRIM earned graduate degrees from Harvard and Brown University, but returned to Canada to teach at York University in Toronto, where she is an associate professor in the English Department. Since writing her dissertation on George Gissing's novels of social criticism, she has done research and written on Victorian fiction, with a focus on Thomas Hardy and his practices in revising such texts as *The Well-Beloved*. Since 1983, when she spoke to the Toronto Women's Research Colloquium on "The Three Last Novels of Barbara Pym," she has also been engaged in studying the Pym canon even as it expanded, using the Pym papers in the Bodleian Library and teaching Pym's novels in juxtaposition to those of Jane Austen in a fourth-year honors seminar.

JANICE ROSSEN wrote one of the first scholarly studies of Pym, *The World of Barbara Pym* (1987), and also edited a collection of essays on her work, *Independent Women: The Function of Gender in the Novels of Barbara Pym* (1988). She has published *Philip Larkin: His Life's Work* (1990) and *The University in Modern Fiction: When Power Is Academic* (1993). She is currently at work on a biography of English novelist and critic Philip Toynbee.

DALE SALWAK is professor of English at southern California's Citrus College. In 1985, he was awarded a National Endowment for the Humanities grant. In 1987 Purdue University awarded him its Distinguished Alumni Award. His publications include *A Passion for Books* (1999), *The Literary Biography: Problems and Solutions* (1996), and studies of Kingsley Amis, John Braine, A. J. Cronin, Philip Larkin, Carl Sandburg, Anne Tyler, and John Wain. He is the author of *The Life and Work of Barbara Pym* (1987) and *Faith in the Family: Honor-*

ing and Strengthening Home and Spirit (2001), and is currently completing a literary study of the English Bible.

HELEN CLARE TAYLOR is associate professor of English at Louisiana State University in Shreveport, where she also directs the Master of Liberal Arts program. She was born in London and holds degrees from Durham University (U.K.), Clark University, and the University of Connecticut. She has published articles on both medieval and contemporary women writers and at present is working on a book-length manuscript about contemporary British women writers.

HILARY PYM WALTON, Barbara Pym's younger sister, read classics at Oxford University. From 1939 until 1971, she produced music programs at the BBC. Upon retirement, she moved with Barbara to a cottage in Finstock, Oxfordshire, where she still lives with her cat Janie. In 1984 she edited, with Hazel Holt, *A Very Private Eye,* and in 1995 coauthored, with Honor Wyatt, *A La Pym: The Barbara Pym Cookery Book.* Mrs. Walton is an honorary life member of the Barbara Pym Society.

ELLIE WYMARD is a professor of English at Carlow College, Pittsburgh, Penn., where she developed one of the first interdisciplinary women's studies programs. Her critical essays have been published in *Studies in Short Fiction, Modern Fiction Studies, Southern Studies,* and *Cross Currents,* as well as *Commonweal* and *The Critic.* She is the author of *Conversations with Uncommon Women: Insights from Women Who've Risen Above Life's Challenges to Achieve Extraordinary Success* (1999); *Men on Divorce: Conversations with Ex-Husbands* (1994); *Divorced Women, New Lives* (1990) and "J. F. Powers: His Christian Comic Vision" (1969).

Index